THE USBORNE
BOOK OF
KNOWLEDGE

CONTENTS

First published in 1979.
This expanded edition
first published in 1988
by Usborne Publishing Ltd.
Usborne House
83-85 Saffron Hill
London EC1N 8RT

Printed in Belgium.
UE

The material in this book is also
available as five separate books:
*How Birds Live, How Animals Live,
How Your Body Works, How
Machines Work* and *How Things
Began*, published by Usborne
Publishing Ltd.

PART 1
HOW
BIRDS
LIVE

Quetzal

Harpy Eagle

Keel-billed Toucan

Written by Tony Bremner
Consultant Editor
Peter Olney, B.Sc., Dip.Ed., F.L.S.,
Curator of Birds, London Zoo

Edited by
Sue Jacquemier and Jessica Datta

Designed by
Sally Burrough

Illustrated by
Trevor Boyer, John Francis,
Robert Jefferson, Ken Lilly,
Malcolm McGregor, Robert Morton

Introduction to Part One

We share our world with many other animals, and of these, I find birds the most fascinating.

This part of the book shows you some of the most interesting and unusual birds and explains their amazing behaviour. It covers all the main groups of birds, from Ostriches to Birds of Paradise, and tells you where they live, what they eat, how they bring up their young, and how they escape from their enemies.

Many of the birds shown in this book are now rare, or even on the verge of extinction, because the places in which they live and their food supplies have been destroyed. People clear forests and drain land for farming, build cities and roads, and pollute the sea, often without thought for the wildlife they damage.

Birds need our protection. I hope that you enjoy this book and that it will help to show you the importance of conserving our bird life.

Peter Olney
London Zoo

Hyacinthine
Macaw

Topaz
Hummingbird

Cock of
the Rock

All these birds live in the jungles
of South America.

Contents of Part One

How Birds Live

The First Birds

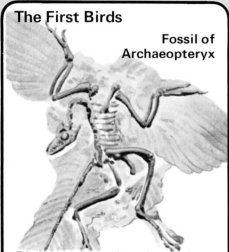

Fossil of Archaeopteryx

Birds are the only animals that have feathers. They have been on earth for millions of years, long before there were any people. Birds are said to have developed from flying reptiles, and the earliest known bird is Archaeopteryx. It was discovered in Germany as a fossil, and we know it was a bird because you can see where the feathers were. It lived about 150 million years ago.

Birds are not the only animals that can fly: bats are flying mammals, and nearly all insects fly at some time in their lives.

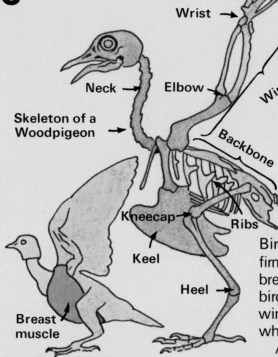

False wing
Wrist
Neck
Elbow
Wing
Lung
Air sacs
Skeleton of a Woodpigeon
Backbone
Tail
Kneecap
Ribs
Keel
Heel
Breast muscle

Inside a Bird

Birds have many hollow bones and these keep them light in the air. The bones are strong, because they have lots of slender struts inside them which criss-cross the hollow spaces. These act rather like the girders which hold up a building.

Birds have powerful muscles firmly anchored between a large breast bone and each wing. When birds fly, these muscles pull the wings down. The wings go up when the muscles relax.

A bird needs to breathe in a lot of air when it is flying, so it has extra sacs or bags for air, as well as lungs. These also help to keep the bird light.

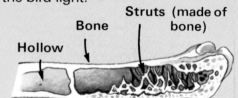

Struts (made of bone)
Bone
Hollow

The parts inside a bird that digest and break up food are similar to ours. The food passes from the mouth down a tube into the crop (see the drawing below). The crop in many birds is mainly a storage bag and some birds bring up food for their young from the crop.

The food then passes to the first part of the stomach where it mixes with digestive juices.

Birds have no teeth, so most of the "chewing" is done in the second part of the stomach, or gizzard, where it is ground to a pulp. Some birds swallow pebbles or grit to help this grinding process in the gizzard.

The digested food then goes down the intestine, and its goodness passes through the wall of the intestine into the blood. The waste passes to the cloaca and out of the body.

Beaks and Eating

Birds' beaks are specially suited to the ways they feed. Here are some examples of different types of beak.

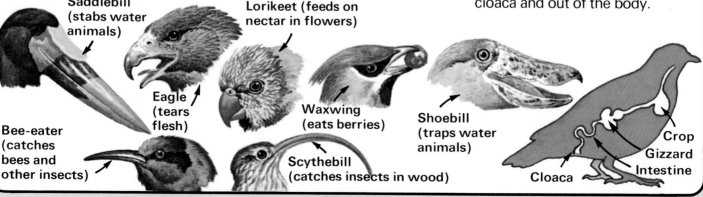

Saddlebill (stabs water animals)
Lorikeet (feeds on nectar in flowers)
Eagle (tears flesh)
Waxwing (eats berries)
Shoebill (traps water animals)
Bee-eater (catches bees and other insects)
Scythebill (catches insects in wood)
Crop
Gizzard
Intestine
Cloaca

Feathers

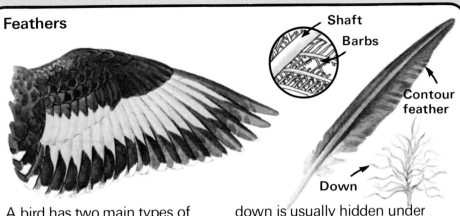

Shaft
Barbs
Contour feather
Down

A bird has two main types of feathers: contour feathers and down. Contour feathers cover the bird, overlapping each other, and help waterproof it. The down is usually hidden under the contour feathers, and helps keep the bird warm. All a bird's feathers together are called its plumage.

Starling in breeding plumage

Ptarmigan camouflaged against patchy snow.

Adult birds moult regularly. That is, they shed their old feathers and grow new ones. When some birds moult, they grow feathers of a different colour specially for the breeding season.

When a bird's colour blends in well with its background, it helps hide the bird from enemies. This is called camouflage.

Birds spend a lot of time keeping their feathers clean and in order. They nibble at their feathers, pulling each one through the beak. This is called preening. Birds bathe often too, in water or dust.

Treecreeper preening

Migration

The most common kind of migration is the twice-yearly journey made by many birds between their summer and winter feeding grounds. Most migrations are by birds that live in the northern half of the world. When winter comes, they fly south, where summer is just beginning. At the end of the southern summer, they fly north again. This way they never have to suffer a harsh, cold winter, and they have a better chance of finding food.

Arctic Terns migrate from the Arctic to the Antarctic every year.

Taking Off

Greylag Goose

Most birds take off by jumping into the air, but many find this difficult. Swans, Geese and some Ducks need long runways to get up enough speed to take off, rather like most aircraft. (See page 19 for a picture of Flamingos taking off.) Some birds, like Ostriches and Penguins, cannot fly at all.

In the Air

Albatross gliding

Once in the air, smaller birds, like Sparrows, flap their wings fast. Hummingbirds can hover in the air. Larger birds, like Eagles, glide and soar. Soaring birds ride up on warm air currents, and glide downwards with stiff wings. This saves energy. Some birds, like this Albatross, hardly flap their wings at all.

Landing

Herring Gull

To land, most birds glide within range of their target, then drop their feet, cup their wings, and spread their tails. This slows them down and also helps them keep their balance.

5

How Do Birds Know What to Do?

Many birds find food, fly, mate, rear their young and migrate over long distances without having to be taught. They do all these things by instinct. For example, it is instinct that guides all the birds of one species to build their nests in one particular way. Experiments have shown that chicks brought up separately from other birds behave exactly like other members of their species.

Birds need to repeat many of the instinctive things they do to make them perfect. Birds are also able to learn from their mistakes and by copying others. Blue Tits, for example, have learnt to peck through milk bottle tops to drink the milk. One bird discovered this way of feeding and others copied it.

The different stages in a bird's life are all ruled by instinct and learning. The pictures below explain some of these stages.

1

Robin defending his territory

Many birds have an area called a "territory" for the breeding season. They guard their nests from enemies and threaten other birds if they come inside the territory for food. Actual fights are quite rare.

2

Sage Grouse displaying

To attract a mate, many birds "display" to each other. The male may show off his brightly coloured plumage. Some birds fly or jump about in special ways, while others sing. Mating cannot normally happen until after this display.

3
Black-winged Stilts mating

The male climbs on the female's back to mate. He sends a liquid containing sperms into her body through an opening. Some sperms reach the eggs inside the female. When a sperm and an egg join, it is called fertilization. Only fertilized eggs can grow into chicks.

4

Little Ringed Plover on nest

Eggs laid in holes are usually white or a plain pale colour. But eggs laid on the ground must be camouflaged (see page 5) to hide them from enemies. Birds sit on their eggs to keep them warm while the

Kingfisher's egg (laid in hole)

chicks are growing. This is called incubating the eggs.

5
Egg tooth

Moorhen chick hatching

The chick has to break open the hard egg shell. It makes the first crack with the sharp egg tooth on the tip of its bill. It moves about and jerks its legs to hatch out.

6

Herring Gull chick

Wryneck chick

Birds that hatch inside the protection of a nest or hole are normally blind and naked. Those hatched on the ground can see and have some feathers. They can usually feed themselves and walk soon after hatching.

7
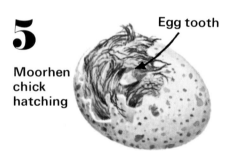
Dunnock

Chicks beg for food by opening their beaks, which are often brightly coloured inside, or by pecking at the parents' bills. This gives the parents a strong urge to feed the young.

The Names of Birds

Scientists have given names to different groups of animals and plants. All birds are in the **Class** of animals called Aves, which is the Latin word for birds. Scientists use Latin or Greek names so that people all over the world, whatever language they speak, will know what bird or group of birds they are talking about.

Birds are divided into 27 **Orders.** One order is called Falconiformes. In this order there are five **Families,** for example the Family Accipitridae. In this Family are Eagles, Hawks and some Vultures. They are grouped in **Genera** (singular: **Genus**), and there are 64 Genera in the family Accipitridae.

One Genus is called *Accipiter,* and it includes 47 **Species**. One of these Species is the Northern Goshawk (its Latin name is *Accipiter gentilis).*

Northern Goshawk (*Accipiter gentilis*)

Class: Aves (Birds)	
Order: Falconiformes	26 other ORDERS
Family: Accipitridae	4 other FAMILIES
Genus: Accipiter	63 other GENERA
Species: Accipiter gentilis	46 other SPECIES

What is a Species?

The Mauritius Kestrel is one of many species in danger of becoming extinct.

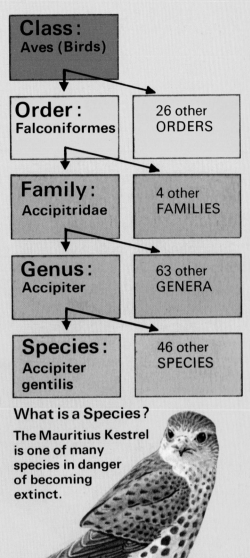

There are over 8,600 species of birds in the world. Members of the same species all look alike and behave in the same way For example, all White Storks have red bills. Sometimes the males of a species look different from the females, but all the females look alike, and all the males look alike.

The members of a species can breed together, but members of two different species do not normally produce young.

Many species, like the bird above, are now very rare. When there are no more members of a species left, the species is said to be extinct.

Why are there Different Species?

Warbler Finch

Large Tree Finch

Cactus Ground Finch

Large Ground Finch

Darwin's Finches

The many different species of birds have developed over millions of years. The way that different birds look and act has changed very slowly. This slow process of change is called evolution.

Here is one way this can happen: imagine a group of seed-eating birds living in a particular area. One day, just by chance, one chick hatches which has a slightly stronger beak than the rest. This means that it can eat hard seeds that the others cannot break. It thrives and breeds, and some of its young are born with the same strong beak. Gradually the birds with strong beaks grow in numbers and a new species evolves. This new species eats different food from the first species, so there is still enough food to go round.

Any accidental change may start a new chain of evolution —longer legs or brighter colours, for example. But the change will only be passed on if it helps the animal to survive. Most accidental changes are not helpful, and the animal dies without passing on the new feature.

A great naturalist called Charles Darwin confirmed this pattern of evolution when he studied Finches in the Galapagos Islands in 1835. The pictures above show some of the species that he realized had developed from one original species.

Ostriches

Ostriches and their relatives cannot fly, but, apart from the Kiwi, they have long strong legs and can run fast. Their soft plumes are more like hair than feathers.

Male

Female

Ostriches can be three metres high and can weigh 140 kilos.

Their good eyesight and height help them to spot enemies, like lions, hyenas and jackals, before it is too late to run away.

Male Ostriches were killed for the white plumes in their tails and wings.

They use their strong legs to kick their enemies.

Ostriches have only two toes on each foot.

Ostriches are the tallest and heaviest of all birds. They live in Africa on grass or scrubland, where they move about in flocks of about twelve birds, sometimes with herds of zebra or wildebeest. They feed on leaves, berries, seeds and small animals like locusts or mice, and also swallow pebbles to help grind up their food. They drink a lot of water and eat juicy plants, like cacti, which contain water. Adult Ostriches can run up to 56 kph.

1 How Ostriches Breed

The male Ostrich mates with two or three females. He performs a mating dance to attract them. He waves his head and neck around and shows off his plumes.

2

Each female lays about seven eggs in a nest. The male sits on them at night and his dark plumage hides him from jackals and other animals that might eat the eggs.

3

Chick

Ostrich's egg

Hen's egg

Ostrich eggs are about 15 cm long and about 20 times bigger than hens' eggs. Kalahari Bushmen eat them and use the shells to make water containers.

4

Almost immediately after hatching, the chicks are able to run about. When they are frightened, they lie flat on the ground where they are well camouflaged.

Other Flightless Birds

Cassowary

Cassowaries live in rain forests in Northern Australia and New Guinea. Their strange horn and spiky feathers protect them as they move through the jungle.

Emu and chick

The Australian Emu lives on grasslands and eats leaves, seeds and insects. The male sits on the eggs, which are green. These hatch into stripy chicks.

Plumes

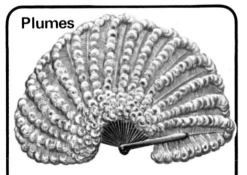

In the 19th century, Ostriches nearly became extinct. Millions were killed for their plumes, which were used to decorate hats and to make fans like this one.

Rhea

The Rhea of South America has a dull grey plumage. Several females lay their eggs in the same nest. The male Rhea incubates them and looks after the chicks.

Kiwi

The Kiwi of New Zealand's forests is nocturnal (active at night). Its nostrils at the tip of its beak help it to smell berries, worms and insects, which it eats.

Penguins

Penguins cannot fly, and their short legs make them clumsy on land. When they have to move fast, they toboggan on their bellies. But Penguins can swim faster than any other birds.

All Penguins live by the sea in large groups, called rookeries. They catch fish and squid to eat.

They can live 25–30 years, but sea lions and whales hunt them and Skuas swoop down to attack their chicks.

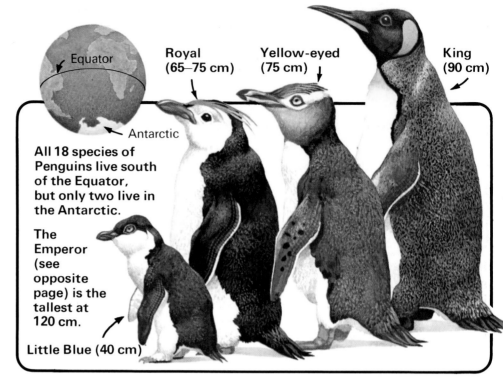

Equator

Antarctic

All 18 species of Penguins live south of the Equator, but only two live in the Antarctic.

The Emperor (see opposite page) is the tallest at 120 cm.

Little Blue (40 cm)

Royal (65–75 cm)

Yellow-eyed (75 cm)

King (90 cm)

Keeping Warm

Jackass Penguin

Penguins have oily, thickly-packed feathers which keep heat in and water out. If they get too hot they fluff up their feathers and hold out their wings.

Rockhopper Penguins

Rockhoppers are small, noisy and playful. They do not live on ice, but on rocky coastlines.

Their name comes from their skill in hopping from ledge to ledge.

They make nests in clumps of grass between rocks or in caves.

They use their sharp claws and hooked bills to help them climb up the rocks.

Pairs of Rockhoppers greet each other by lifting their bills and squawking.

1 Emperor Penguins

In winter, Emperors waddle in single file to the nesting grounds inland. They are fat from eating all summer at sea. The fat layer under their skin protects them from the cold.

2

Each year the same pair meet and mate. The female lays a single egg on the ice. Then she travels many miles to feed at sea. The male stays to care for the egg.

3

He keeps the egg warm by putting it on his feet and covering it with his loose belly skin. The egg is completely hidden. The male hardly moves and does not eat while the female is away.

4

In eight weeks the egg hatches. The mother returns and looks after the young. The chick crouches on its mother's feet. The hungry father, now half his normal weight, goes off to feed.

5

The parents take turns to go and hunt for food. They feed the chick by regurgitating, or bringing up, partly digested fish from their crops.

6

The older chicks huddle together to keep warm while their parents are feeding. Parents and chicks go back to the sea in the summer.

Swimming and Jumping

Penguins' bodies are streamlined like torpedos. They "fly" through the water using their wings as flippers. They can shoot out of the water on to land in one leap.

Gentoo Penguins

Grebes and Divers

Grebes and Divers are water birds. They have streamlined bodies, long necks and sharp beaks. They dive for fish and small water animals.

Their legs are set far back, so they swim well but walk with difficulty.

Different species of Grebes are found all over the world, often on inland waters. Divers, or Loons, live mainly on northern seas, normally coming inland only to breed.

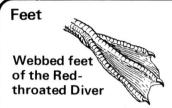

Feet

Webbed feet of the Red-throated Diver

Toes of the Great Crested Grebe

Flaps of skin open and push away water.

Flaps of skin fold up to let water flow between toes.

Divers have webbed feet, but Grebes do not. Both use only their feet for swimming under the water, and not their wings

as Penguins do. Grebes have separate toes with flaps of skin between them. These flaps fold up against the toes when

they draw the feet up for the next stroke, or when they dive. This allows the water to pass between the toes easily.

Great Crested Grebes

Non-breeding plumage

Breeding plumage

The dance often starts and ends with a bout of head-shaking. The pair face each other and waggle their heads from side to side.

Here a Grebe is crouching low in the water, with its wings spread and its chest puffed out.

1 The Dance

In the breeding season, the Great Crested Grebe grows a dark brown frill of feathers round its neck, and two black ear tufts. When two Grebes meet, they often get very excited, and they spread out these frills and tufts like a ruff.

Great Crested Grebes are well known for their courtship dance, which includes many different positions and actions. Three of them are shown here: crouching, head-shaking and diving for weeds. The dance means that two

birds have paired up, and will probably mate. It is also performed by Grebes at other times. Some of the positions are used as signals or warnings to rival birds.

Black-throated Divers

The Black-throated Diver cannot walk very well. It has to drag its body on land, so it builds its nest near the bank. It shuffles down a runway made of flattened grass into the water.

Great Northern Divers

Breeding plumage

Non-breeding plumage

Birds often have much brighter coloured plumage in the breeding season, and Great Northern Divers become a completely different colour. This special breeding plumage can help birds attract a mate. The rest of the year, there is no need for their colours to be so striking, so they become more drab and dull. This helps them to avoid their enemies.

Sometimes a pair will dive to the bottom and pull up some weed. When they surface they swim towards each other. They may rise out of the water, paddling hard with their feet to stay up. When they meet they bring their chests almost together and offer the weed to each other.

2 Nest-building

The birds lay their eggs on a floating platform, made of piled-up weed and sticks. They trample the weed to make a solid nest and wall it up round the edge to make a hollow in the centre for the eggs.

3 Chicks

The striped chicks can swim as soon as they hatch. But often they prefer to be carried on the parents' backs. The parents feed them on insects and small fish. They do not begin to dive for food until they are six weeks old.

13

Pelicans and Cormorants

Pelicans and Cormorants are fishing birds and usually live in colonies, or large groups. They are found all over the world on both freshwater lakes and sea coasts. Although they fly well, their short stumpy legs make them move slowly on land. After diving for fish, Cormorants stand with their wings spread out to dry.

The other birds on these pages belong to the same Order, or group, as Pelicans and Cormorants.

White Pelicans

White Pelicans fly and fish together. They glide over lakes with their huge wings, and use their great bills to scoop up fish. The bill pouch can hold 13 litres of water. Sometimes Pelicans form a horseshoe-shaped line and swim towards each other, joining up to make a circle. Then they dip their beaks at exactly the same time to catch as many trapped fish as possible. Adult Pelicans can catch nine kilos of fish a day.

1

Brown Pelicans

These sea birds are the smallest Pelicans. They dive-bomb into the water and catch fish in their pouches.

2

The Pelicans surface and then swallow the fish whole. Gulls gather round fishing Pelicans hoping to steal some of the catch.

3

Adult Pelicans bring up fish they have swallowed to feed to their young. The chicks put their heads right inside their parents' beak pouches.

14

1 Shags

Shags nest in crowded colonies on rocky cliffs. Their nests are made out of twigs and seaweed.

2

The female lays about three eggs and the parents take turns to sit on them until they hatch.

3

Chicks

The chicks are born naked. After a few days they begin to grow dark brown downy feathers and open their eyes. After seven weeks they have learnt to fly.

Guano Islands

There is a group of islands off the coast of South America where thousands of Guanay Cormorants live. The ground is covered with deep layers of the birds' droppings. This is called guano, and it is rich in a chemical called nitrate. People collect the guano and use it as a fertilizer for farmland.

Frigate Bird

Frigate Birds live on coasts and islands. The male has a bright red patch of loose skin under his beak. He can blow it up like a balloon to attract females.

Gannets and Boobies

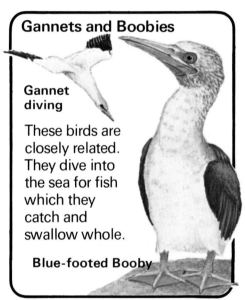

Gannet diving

These birds are closely related. They dive into the sea for fish which they catch and swallow whole.

Blue-footed Booby

Snake Bird

The Anhinga is called the Snake Bird because it moves its head and neck above the water in an S shape. It stabs fish with its sharp beak, tosses them into the air and then catches and swallows them. The Anhinga also eats frogs, newts, salamanders and crayfish.

Storks and Herons

Storks and Herons belong to the same group as Flamingos (see page 18), Ibises and Spoonbills. All these birds have long legs, large wings and a short tail. Most of them feed in shallow water and marshes. They nest in colonies.

White Storks

Storks make a clattering noise when they meet. They throw back their heads and clap the two halves of their bills together fast.

White Storks often nest on house roofs or chimneys. In Holland, people put up poles with a cartwheel laid flat on top for Storks to build on.

(see page 18)

The Migration of the White Storks

EUROPE

Istanbul

Gibraltar

AFRICA

→ Routes taken by White Storks in late summer

Most White Storks leaving Europe cross the sea to Africa at one of its narrowest points (Gibraltar or Istanbul). They avoid long sea crossings because there are no currents of hot air over the water for them to glide on. They mostly glide and soar and only occasionally flap their wings.

At the end of the summer, both adults and young leave the nest and migrate to a warmer place.

The nest is built of sticks, paper, rubbish and often horse manure. The Storks often go back to last year's nest. They repair it, so it grows bigger every year.

Eight chicks may hatch, but those hatched last often do not get enough food to live. The adults feed the chicks on chewed-up mice, frogs and other small animals.

White Storks breed in Europe, Central Asia and North Africa. Hundreds of them used to migrate from Africa to Europe in early spring each year, and people would welcome them as bringers of good luck. But there are fewer and fewer White Storks nesting in places where they were once regular visitors.

Nowadays they have to face many dangers—factory chimneys, high power lines, hunters and aeroplanes. There are a few White Storks left in Asia, and in eastern Europe they still nest in large numbers. But in Japan, where they once lived, they are now extinct.

Grey Herons

Grey Heron in nest with young

Grey Heron in flight

Herons can be recognized by the curve in their necks when they fly. The Grey Heron eats fish, frogs and small mammals. It nests in trees.

Black Herons

The Black Heron can make an umbrella shape with its wings, which shades the surface of the water from the bright African sun. This helps the bird to catch fish, perhaps because it can then see them more clearly.

Egrets

Hat decorated with Egret feathers

Male Egrets were hunted for these long back feathers.

Egrets are closely related to Herons. In the 1900's thousands of Egrets were killed for their fine feathers. These were used to decorate fashionable hats.

Great White Egret (or Great White Heron)

Ibises

Scarlet Ibis

Ibises use their curved bills to probe for and catch prey. The Scarlet Ibis lives in rain forests in South America.

Marabou Storks

The Marabou has a fleshy bag under its beak. Like Vultures, Marabous eat dead flesh left by lions and other hunters.

Spoonbills

Roseate Spoonbill

The Spoonbill wades in shallow water, moving its spoon-shaped bill from side to side. It traps small fish and animals as water flows through its bill.

Sacred Ibis

The ancient Egyptians thought the Sacred Ibis was a god who had come back to life as a bird. It is now extinct in Egypt but lives in other parts of Africa.

Flamingos

There are several different species of Flamingos. The ones shown here are Greater Flamingos. They live in large groups in places where the water is shallow and salty. Compared with the size of their bodies, their necks and legs are longer than those of any other birds.

Flamingos are so big that they need a lot of space to take off into the air. It is hard for one bird to take off alone because its neighbours are crowded too close. The whole flock usually flies off together.

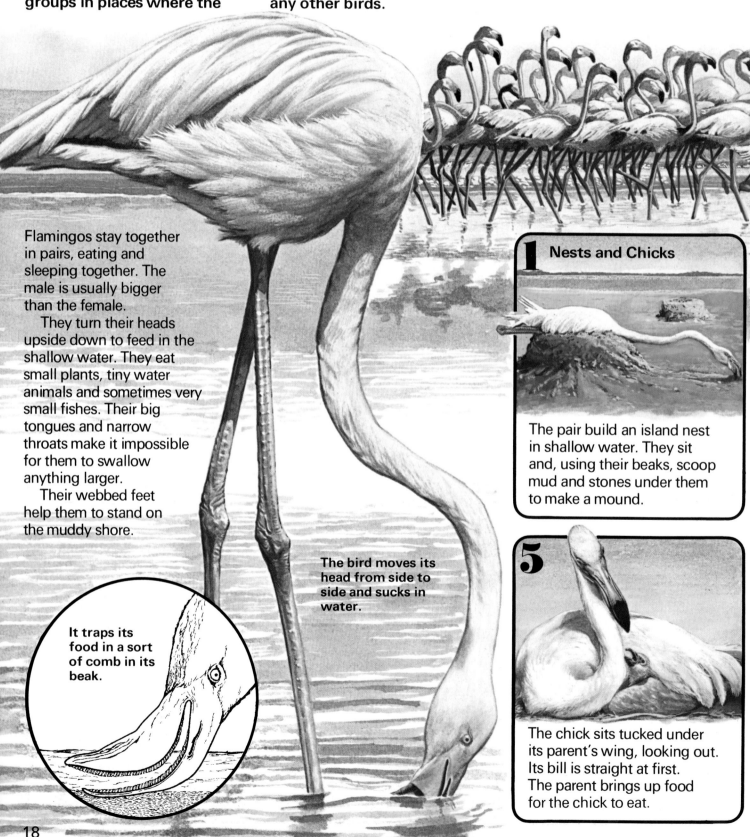

Flamingos stay together in pairs, eating and sleeping together. The male is usually bigger than the female.

They turn their heads upside down to feed in the shallow water. They eat small plants, tiny water animals and sometimes very small fishes. Their big tongues and narrow throats make it impossible for them to swallow anything larger.

Their webbed feet help them to stand on the muddy shore.

It traps its food in a sort of comb in its beak.

The bird moves its head from side to side and sucks in water.

1 Nests and Chicks

The pair build an island nest in shallow water. They sit and, using their beaks, scoop mud and stones under them to make a mound.

5

The chick sits tucked under its parent's wing, looking out. Its bill is straight at first. The parent brings up food for the chick to eat.

Flocks are easily frightened away by low-flying aeroplanes. Unfortunately, airports are often built near the flat areas where Flamingos live. Colonies are sometimes completely deserted because of this disturbance.

Flamingos fly in long lines with their necks and legs stretched out straight. They make honking noises as they fly.

2 The birds make a hollow in the top of the mound and the female usually lays one egg. The hollow stops it from rolling out of the nest.

3 The adult Flamingos take it in turns to sit on the egg. They fold their long legs under their bodies while sitting on the nest.

4 When it rains, the Flamingo spreads its wings to stop the mud nest from being washed away. After about a month, the chick hatches.

6 At first the chick is grey. The pink colour comes later from a natural chemical in its food. Scarlet Ibises also get their colour from their food.

7 When the young leave the nest they form flocks of their own, but their parents still feed them for some time. Slowly the chicks' bills grow and they begin to feed themselves.

Swans

Swans are large birds that live on and by ponds, lakes and rivers. They have stout legs and webbed feet so they swim well, but they waddle on land.

They eat mostly water plants and use their long necks to reach down for food. Most Swans live in flocks, except in the breeding season when they make pairs.

When Mute Swans fly, their wing beats make a loud creaking noise.

The cob guards the nest and will attack another Swan that comes too close.

The nest is built of grasses and rushes on raised ground, though it is usually surrounded by water.

Whooper Swan

Trumpeter Swan

Because they are so heavy, Swans need a long run across the water before taking off.

Bewick's Swan

There are eight kinds of Swans. The male is called a cob, the female a pen, and the young are called cygnets.

This Swan is looking for food on the water bed.

This Swan is preening its feathers.

Cygnets are often carried on their parents' backs.

Mute Swan

Black Swans

Black Swans of Australia gather in huge flocks. They have white wing feathers which can only be seen when they fly.

Geese

Geese are strong, stocky birds that feed on grasses, grain and other plants. They live in flocks called gaggles. Although they have webbed feet, they spend most of their time on land, usually near rivers and lakes. The female is called a goose, the male a gander and the chicks goslings.

Geese have been kept for food for thousands of years and were popular with the Romans, Greeks and Egyptians in ancient times.

Néné or Hawaiian Goose

Red-breasted Goose

Canada Goose

Snow Goose

Domestic Geese

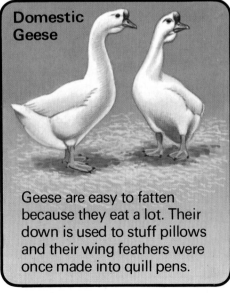

Geese are easy to fatten because they eat a lot. Their down is used to stuff pillows and their wing feathers were once made into quill pens.

Greylag Geese

In early spring, a goose follows a gander about, watching him out of the corner of her eye. He gets very excited.

The gander rushes to attack any other young ganders in the gaggle. He honks loudly and beats his wings.

When they back away, he hurries back to his mate calling triumphantly. He impresses her by this show of strength.

Together they dip their necks, lowering and pointing their heads. This means they are getting to know each other better before mating.

Like all birds, Geese have no language. But they make noises, and can also "talk" to each other with positions and movements of the body.

Imprinting

When goslings hatch they become attached to the first large moving object they see. This is called "imprinting". Goslings hatched by hens, or even by people, accept them as "mother" and follow them everywhere.

Ducks

Ducks, like Swans and Geese, are waterfowl. They can be recognized by their flattened bill, short legs and webbed feet. They have thick waterproof feathers covering a layer of down which keeps them warm. Ducks have been domesticated and eaten for centuries and they are still hunted for sport.

Male and female Ducks, unlike most Geese and Swans, look different—the male, called a drake, is usually more colourful than the female, called a duck. Most Ducks nest near the water's edge.

Shelduck

Goosander ducklings can swim as soon as they get into the water for the first time. The eggs are often laid in holes high up in trees. After hatching, the young jump out. They are so light that they do not hurt themselves.

The Shoveler has a broad, shovel-like beak. Like the Flamingo, it has a sort of comb in its beak which strains very tiny water animals out of the water. Shovelers often feed closely together because groups stir up more food in the water.

Shoveler duck

Goosander duck

Shoveler drake

Mandarin drake

Ducks use oil from a gland near their tails to keep their feathers in good order. They spread the oil all over themselves with their beaks.

Feeding

Pintail up-ending

Pochard diving

Gadwall dabbling

Wigeon grazing

Some Ducks feed on or just under the water. They eat small plants and animals by sucking up water and sieving the food through their beaks. They can also up-end, or tip up, to reach down further.

Diving Ducks can dive down to the water bed to feed on plants and small creatures. They can stay under the water for half a minute or more before bobbing up to the surface.

Wigeon graze on grasses and other plants on salt marshes near sea coasts. Wigeon that live in the far north also eat berries from bushes.

In the winter many Shelduck fly south to warmer areas. Those in Scandinavia fly as far as the Mediterranean, and those in northern Asia fly to India, Pakistan and Burma.

When Ducks land on water they put out their feet to act as brakes.

Mallard drakes

Mallard duck

Goosander drake

This Duck is asleep with its head under its wing. In winter it keeps its nostrils warm like this. It stands on one leg and warms the other leg against its body.

Goldeneye duck

Goldeneye drake

Tufted drake

The Goldeneye displays in the water when he has chosen a mate. He throws his head back and splashes with his feet.

Nesting

Eider Duck

Eider Ducks live near northern seas. They nest in colonies. The nest is a hollow in the ground and the female plucks down from her breast to line it. When the ducklings have left, people collect the down to fill eiderdowns and duvets.

Moulting

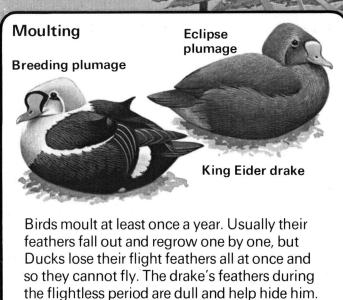

Eclipse plumage

Breeding plumage

King Eider drake

Birds moult at least once a year. Usually their feathers fall out and regrow one by one, but Ducks lose their flight feathers all at once and so they cannot fly. The drake's feathers during the flightless period are dull and help hide him. Later he moults this "eclipse plumage".

Birds of Prey

Birds of prey are hunters and feed on other birds, small mammals, snakes, fish and insects. Their eyesight is much better than ours and they have powerful wings and strong hooked beaks. The largest bird of prey is the Andean Condor, which has a wingspan of three metres. The Pygmy Falconet is the smallest and is only 16 cm long.

Condors can soar to a tremendous height on their enormous wings. They ride on a rising current of warm air called a thermal.

Eagles can kill animals three times their own weight, but usually their prey is much smaller.

The Golden Eagle builds its nest, called an eyrie, on a rocky crag or in a very tall tree. Every year the pair returns to the same nest and add to it. It can be as large as two metres across. Sometimes the nest becomes so heavy that it falls out of the tree.

Condors, like Vultures, do not kill their prey, but eat only carrion, or dead flesh.

Californian Condors are very rare birds. Cattle farmers poison dead animals to kill scavengers, like wolves and coyotes. Sometimes Condors eat the poisoned bait and die. Many others have been shot or have been unable to find food, because the cattle ranches in the area where they live have been changed into fruit farms. The few Condors left alive are now guarded in a reserve.

1 African Fish Eagles

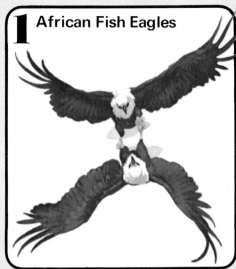

Before they mate, African Fish Eagles display together in the air. A male and a female link claws and tumble through the air, whirling round and round in cartwheels.

2

Chicks

They return to last year's stick nest high in a tree, and add to it. The female lays two or three eggs and incubates them. The parents feed the young with fish or sometimes small water birds.

3

Eaglet

When their feathers have grown, the eaglets exercise their wings. They rush about the nest flapping them. After ten weeks the eaglets are strong enough to make their first flight.

Feeding

Vultures

Flocks of Vultures feed on the remains of prey left by other animals. Their featherless heads do not get sticky with blood.

Ospreys

The Osprey hunts for fish. It circles above the water and dives feet first when it spots one. It plunges in and seizes the fish in its claws.

Falconry

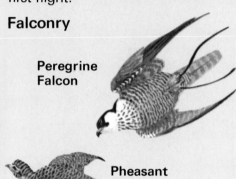

Peregrine Falcon

Pheasant

Hood

Secretary Birds

These birds kill snakes by stamping on them, jumping back, and stamping again. Their crests look like quill pens behind a secretary's ear.

Kites

Kites are scavengers and often live near towns. They turn and swoop in the air and then drop down to pick up scraps from the street.

Falcons and Hawks can be trained for hunting in a sport called falconry. Falconers cover the birds' heads with hoods to calm them. Some Falcons can dive at up to 320 kph, which makes them superb hunters for Partridges and Pheasants.

Pheasants, Grouse and Chickens

All these birds belong to the group that includes the domestic chicken, the most common bird in the world. The group also includes one of the rarest—the Imperial Pheasant. People hunt many of these species.

The Yokohama chicken has been bred for its long tail feathers.

The cock has sharp spurs, which he uses when fighting rivals.

Domestic chickens like this Ross Brown can lay an egg a day.

The Silver Sebright is a breed of domestic chicken.

Turkeys

Female

The male puffs out his chest to attract a female.

Wild Turkeys first lived in America and were brought back to Europe by explorers. In the wild they live in woods and eat nuts, acorns, berries and insects. At night they roost (or sleep) in trees.

There are many kinds of domestic chickens, but they have all been bred from the same species—the Red Jungle Fowl of South-East Asia. It looks like a farmyard cockerel, but has much shinier feathers. It still lives in forests and jungles where it makes its nest out of dry leaves and grass. Like many other birds, it breeds once a year.

Black Grouse

Male

The adult male is called a Blackcock. His tail normally looks like this.

The female is called a Greyhen, although her feathers are brown and help hide her when she is sitting on the nest.

The displaying Blackcocks fan out their tails and make a "roocooing" call.

Black Grouse live on the edges of forests and on moors. The males have a special area of ground, called a lek, where 10–30 of them gather at the beginning of spring. There each Blackcock displays his feathers, hisses, crows and puffs out his chest as a challenge to other males. As the females arrive at the edge of the lek they are attracted by the males' display. Then they mate.

Pheasants

The Peacock's lovely train grows from his lower back. It is not his tail.

The Blue Peafowl from India belongs to the Pheasant family. The male, called a Peacock, shivers his long feathers and holds them up in a huge fan to attract the female, called a Peahen.

Male Pheasants are brightly coloured, but the females are a mottled brown.

Male

Female

The female Common Pheasant lays her eggs in a scrape in the ground, lined with leaves and grass. She is difficult to see in the long grass or brambles. If the eggs are stolen or destroyed, she will lay more. The chicks leave the nest with their mother soon after they hatch.

Partridges

Red-legged Partridges live on farmland, rocky mountain sides, and scrubland. If you disturb a covey, or group, of Partridges, they will all fly off together, beating their wings noisily.

They nest in hollows scraped in the ground and lined with dead leaves and grass. After hatching, the chicks stay close to their mother, and at night shelter for warmth under her wings.

1 Mallee Fowl

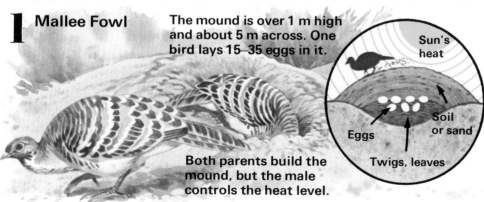

The mound is over 1 m high and about 5 m across. One bird lays 15–35 eggs in it.

Both parents build the mound, but the male controls the heat level.

Sun's heat

Eggs

Soil or sand

Twigs, leaves

2

The chicks have to struggle out from the egg chamber in the centre of the mound.

Instead of sitting on its eggs to incubate them, the Mallee Fowl of Australia lays them inside a huge mound made some weeks before from twigs, leaves and soil or sand. The leaves rot and make the mound warm, just like a compost heap. The Mallee Fowl keeps the temperature just right. If it is too hot during the day, it piles on more earth to keep out the sun's rays. In the evening it scrapes the earth off to let the heat escape. It tests the temperature by pushing its beak into the mound.

Waders

Most Waders are birds of the shore. Many have long legs and wade without getting their feathers wet. In the summer, many fly from Africa to breed in Europe, where there is usually plenty to eat and to feed the young.

Most Waders make their nests on the ground on beaches or pasture land. The speckled eggs are difficult for enemies to spot among the pebbles or grasses.

Phalaropes

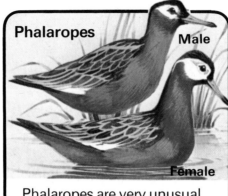

Male

Female

Phalaropes are very unusual. The female is more colourful than the male and she displays to attract him. The male sits on the eggs and looks after the chicks.

Woodcocks

The Woodcock's plumage is mottled brown, grey and black. When it sits on the ground surrounded by dead leaves, it is almost invisible to enemies.

All birds have beaks which have become adapted to finding and eating particular foods. Birds that live in the same area often eat different foods, so there is enough to go round.

All the birds in this picture are in their summer plumage.

Dotterels

This Dotterel is leading the fox away from her nest. She pretends to be injured and drags her wing so that the fox follows her. If the fox pounces, she will fly away.

Redshanks make quick pecks in the mud to eat small shrimps, snails and worms. Their prey is small so they need to eat a lot and may feed on moonlit nights as well as in the daytime.

Dunlin eat worms and shrimps. They make quick little jabs in the mud with their beaks. This is called "stitching" because the rows of little holes look like sewing stitches.

Oystercatchers use their strong bills to prise open cockle and mussel shells, and to hammer at shells to break them.

Curlews live on mudflats and pasture land. They probe for food in the mud with their curved bills. They pull out worms and other small animals.

Ruff in normal plumage

Ruffs

Reeve

Ruff in breeding plumage

The male Ruff gets his name from the ruff of feathers he grows to attract the female. Like Blackcocks, Ruffs display in groups on a lek. The female is called a Reeve.

Cranes

Cranes are tall birds with long legs and long necks. There are 14 species and most live near marshes or rivers. They eat grain, berries and other plants as well as frogs, small reptiles and mice. They live in large flocks, except in the breeding season when they make pairs. They fly with their necks and legs stretched out straight.

Crowned Cranes live in Africa. They are noisy birds and shriek when they fly. They feed in marshes and stamp their feet to disturb frogs, which they stab with their beaks.

Pairs of Cranes put their beaks in the air and call together.

Before mating, Cranes perform an exciting dance. These Sarus Cranes stretch up and bow down, leap about and flap their wings.

Knots migrate north in autumn. In winter vast flocks gather to feed in estuaries.

Turnstones turn over stones and pull apart seaweed looking for small crabs and sandhoppers.

Dunlin

Turnstones

Snipe push their bills deep in the mud and swallow worms and insects whole.

Avocets stand in shallow water to feed. They sweep their upward-curved bills from side to side, sifting insects and shellfish out of the water.

29

Gulls, Terns and Auks

Most seabirds are basically black, white or a mixture of both. They have webbed feet and strong bodies, and they fly well. Many have harsh, squawky voices.

The groups shown on these pages behave in different ways. Auks, such as Puffins and Guillemots, dive and swim under the water to catch their food, while Gulls and Terns feed mainly from the surface. Many Gulls scavenge inland for food as well.

Puffins

A Puffin can carry as many as 20 fish in its beak.

Puffins use their feet as rudders when landing and changing direction.

When Puffins meet, they shake their bills to greet one another.

Puffins make a burrow for their single egg in grassy places or under rocks, often in the soft soil on the top of cliffs. They dig with their beaks and use their clawed feet as shovels. Sometimes they chase out rabbits and nest in their burrows. The parents bring beakfuls of fish to their chick, which stays in the burrow until it is about six weeks old.

1 Gulls

Before mating, male and female Black-headed Gulls run side by side with their heads down.

The male also coughs up some food for the female to eat.

Gulls usually breed with the same mate for life. Every year they return in large groups to the same breeding ground. Males and females perform a courtship dance together when they are ready to mate. They gather straw, moss and bits of paper, trampling it down to make a nest.

2

Black-headed Gull with chick

Herring Gull with chick

Gulls lay up to three eggs. The parents take it in turns to sit on them and to guard against rats, foxes, dogs and other birds which might steal the eggs.

When the chicks have hatched, they beg for food from their parents. Some Gull chicks do this by cheeping and pecking at a red spot on the parent's bill.

3

Adult Black-headed Gull in breeding plumage (summer)

Three-week-old Black-headed Gull chicks

Juvenile Black-headed Gull

In winter, Black-headed Gulls have white heads with a dark blotch behind the eye.

Young Gulls learn to fly when they are about six weeks old. Until they are mature (old enough to breed), their plumage is different from the adults'. They live in the same Gull colony as their parents.

Terns

The spotted eggs are difficult to see among the pebbles and broken shells on the beach.

A male Little Tern offering food to a female.

The chicks are also well camouflaged.

Terns are sometimes called Sea Swallows because of their pointed wings and forked tails. They usually nest in large colonies, but the Little Tern prefers smaller groups. The nest is just a hollow scraped in the sand or shingle. The male courts the female with gifts of fish, which he feeds to her. After mating with him, she lays two or three eggs.

Fairy Terns

The Fairy Tern breeds on islands. It builds no nest. The female lays her eggs on a bare branch or ledge. The chicks have large feet which help them cling to the branch.

Cliff Colonies

Many seabirds live in large groups, sometimes of a thousand or more birds. They build their nests on rocks, cliffs and islands, just out of pecking distance of each other. Each bird keeps its neighbours away by stretching out its neck and aiming blows at them with its beak.

Kittiwakes build nests of seaweed, grass and mud on narrow ledges where they are safe from enemies.

Gulls, like birds of prey, can soar upwards in circles. They ride on currents of air that rise up near cliffs.

Guillemots lay their eggs on bare rock ledges. The eggs are pointed at one end, and this pear shape stops them from rolling off the ledge. If they are touched, they just roll round in a circle.

Razorbills rear their single chick in gaps between the rocks on cliff faces. They do not build any kind of nest.

Herring Gulls are often seen inland, and some hardly ever go near the sea. They find plenty of food in cities and on farmland.

Great Black-backed Gulls kill and eat Puffins, rabbits and the chicks of other birds, as well as fish.

31

Pigeons

Pigeons are found all over the world, except where it is very cold. They are rounded birds with short legs and soft feathers. There are nearly 300 species of Pigeons. Some are also called Doves, although it means the same thing.

Most Pigeons live on seeds and fruits. All of them can suck up water with their beaks, unlike other birds that have to tilt their heads back to drink.

Rock Doves

All domestic Pigeons have developed from the wild Rock Dove, which lives on cliffs and ledges. The female builds a shallow twig nest in a dark cave.

Racing Pigeons

Message tied to leg

For centuries people have kept Pigeons and built dovecots for them. As Pigeons almost always find their way home they were used to carry messages. People still breed them for racing.

Dodos

The Dodo was a flightless bird related to Pigeons. Settlers on the island of Mauritius killed Dodos for food and by 1681 there were none left alive.

Show Pigeons

Kormoner

Fantail

Some Pigeons are specially bred as show birds. Sometimes their shapes are changed so much that they cannot feed their young.

City Pigeons

Most city Pigeons are descended from domestic Pigeons that have escaped or been released. They nest on ledges on buildings and eat what they find or are fed in streets and parks. They can be black, grey, brown, white, or a mixture of colours.

1 Woodpigeons

Woodpigeons live on farmland. The male puffs up the shimmery purple and green feathers on his neck to attract a female.

2

The male croons and the pair nibble each other's feathers and caress. Then they are ready to mate. Together they build a stick nest where the female lays two white eggs.

3

Birds have a bag in their gullet called a crop (see page 4). Pigeons make a type of milk in the crop and bring it up to feed to their chicks.

Cuckoos

Some members of the Cuckoo family are called parasites because the female lays her eggs in other birds' nests. Every spring, the Common Cuckoo lays about twelve eggs, each in a different nest. The bird in whose nest she leaves the egg is called the host. The host is usually a small bird, like a Warbler or a Dunnock.

Some other birds are parasitic, like the Honeyguides, the Cowbirds and the Black-headed Duck.

1

Female Cuckoo

The Common Cuckoo watches the Reed Warbler's nest until it is unguarded. Then she takes out one of the eggs, swallows or drops it, and lays one of her own.

2

Cuckoo's egg

The Cuckoo's egg is larger than the Reed Warbler's, but it is nearly the same colour. Cuckoos lay eggs that look like the eggs of their host, so the host does not notice the new egg.

3

The Cuckoo's egg hatches before the others. When the chick is a few days old, and still naked and blind, it heaves the Reed Warbler's eggs out of the nest.

4

The adult Reed Warblers bring insects to feed the young Cuckoo. They put the food into its huge gaping beak. They believe the Cuckoo is their own chick.

5

Reed Warbler

Cuckoo chick

The Cuckoo grows very fast and it is soon bursting out of the nest. It is now much bigger than its foster parents, who have to stand on its back to feed it.

Roadrunners

This bird lives in hot dry places in North and Central America. It runs fast and uses its tail as a rudder to swerve quickly and change direction. It eats insects, lizards and snakes.

Turacos

Schalow's Turaco

Turacos live in dense forests in Africa. They run along branches, hopping from tree to tree, and fly the short distances which are too far to jump. They live on fruits, berries and insects.

Parrots

Parrots are very noisy, brightly coloured birds. There are over 300 species and most live in tropical jungles. They have hooked beaks which they can use when climbing. Most Parrots live in trees and many have loud, shrieking voices.

Scarlet Macaw (1 m long)

Nesting

Western Rosella

Most Parrots nest in holes in trees or termite mounds where the chicks are well hidden from enemies. They often use holes left by Woodpeckers or other birds.

Monk Parakeet

Groups of Monk (or Quaker) Parakeets collect thorny twigs and branches to build a huge shared nest. Each pair has its own nest chamber and entrance hall.

Macaws are the largest Parrots. They have very long tails which stream out behind them when they fly. Macaws live in South America and eat nuts, berries and fruits.

Pygmy Parrots

Finsch's Pygmy Parrot (10 cm long)

The six species of Pygmy Parrots are tiny. Their long claws and stiff tails help them climb up and down trees like Woodpeckers.

Budgerigars

Wedge-tailed Eagle

Budgerigars at a water hole

Budgerigars live in Australia and collect in enormous flocks. Each Budgerigar stays with the group because, as part of a great mass of flying birds, it is less likely to be caught by a bird of prey.

Budgerigars feed on grass seeds and drink at water holes together. Sometimes thousands of them die because a drought dries up the water holes and prevents their food from growing.

Budgerigars were first brought to Europe in 1840 and they became popular pets. Blue and yellow Budgerigars have been specially bred—in the wild they are always green.

1 Feeding

Black Cockatoo

Most Parrots have a thick, fleshy tongue. They hold a seed or nut in the top part of the beak with their tongue, and crack it with the lower part of the beak.

2

Rainbow Lorikeet

Lorikeets feed on nectar in flowers. The brush-like hairs on their tongues pick up pollen too. The Lorikeet brushes this pollen on to another flower and so helps pollinate it.

3

Greater Sulphur-crested Cockatoo

Cockatoos, like other Parrots, can use their claws like a hand to pick up food. Cockatoos live in flocks, and feed and roost together.

Talking

African Grey Parrot

The African Grey probably imitates human speech better than any other Parrot, but it does not understand the meaning of the words it copies.

Keas

The Kea of New Zealand is more like a bird of prey than a Parrot. As well as eating leaves and berries, it eats dead flesh which it tears with its long, curved bill. It gets its name from its call— ''Kea-ea-ea''.

Kakapos

The Kakapo or Owl-Parrot is nocturnal and has a flat owlish face. By day it sleeps in hollows under trees. It cannot fly and so is in danger from stoats and rats. It is one of the world's rarest birds.

Owls

Owls never gather in flocks. They are meat-eaters and catch all sorts of animals—small mammals, insects, frogs, snakes and fish. There are about 130 species of Owls and different ones are found in most parts of the world. Some Eagle Owls are almost a metre high and some Least Pygmy Owls are only 12 cm high.

Owls seize their prey with their sharp claws and kill with their strong hooked beaks.

Barn Owl with Field Mouse

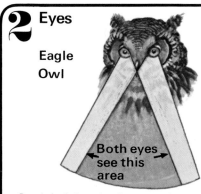

Tengmalm's Owl

Some Owls nest in tree holes made by Woodpeckers. During the day they roost in these holes.

Most Owls hunt by night. Some can catch their prey in total darkness, by sound alone. They hoot to warn other Owls away from their territory and to call to each other. When food is scarce, they may hunt in the daytime.

How Owls Hunt at Night

1 Feathers

Scops Owl

Tawny Owl's wing

Many Owls have drab brown plumage which camouflages them from their prey. Their dull feathers do not catch the light.

The wing feathers have a soft, fringed edge, which helps make Owls' flight silent. This picture shows the edge of a Tawny Owl's wing in close-up.

2 Eyes

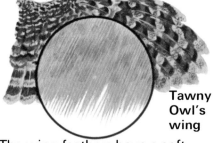

Eagle Owl

Both eyes see this area

Owls' vision is sharper than that of most birds. Their eyes are at the front of the head, not at the side. Owls use both eyes to look at the same area.

Snowy Owls

Arctic
Skua

Snowy Owls live in the far north where they hunt small mammals called lemmings, and Arctic hares. The female's plumage camouflages her on patchy snow. She lays her eggs in a scrape in the ground. The male brings her food while she sits on the eggs. Although the parents try to protect the chicks, many may be killed by Arctic foxes and Skuas.

Pellets

Whole Tawny Owl pellet containing:

Field Mouse skulls,

small mammals' ribs,

shoulder bones,

legs, feet and back-bones.

Owls swallow their prey whole. Later they cough up the parts they cannot digest in a pellet. The pictures above show the contents of a Tawny Owl's pellet.

Short-eared
Owl

Owls cannot move their eyes in their sockets at all, but they can turn their heads in almost any direction—even upside down!

3 Ears

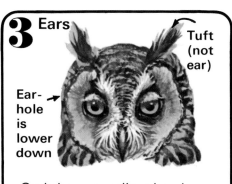

Tuft (not ear)

Ear-hole is lower down

Owls have excellent hearing. Their ear holes are very big and can pick up tiny sounds, like the squeaking of a mouse. The tufts on their heads are nothing to do with ears.

Elf Owls

The adult Elf Owl is smaller than a Sparrow. It often nests in an empty Woodpecker hole made in the huge Saguaro cactus. When the Elf owlets hatch they are only about 25 mm long.

Swifts, Swallows and Martins

Swifts, Swallows and Martins all behave in the same way, although Swifts belong to a different Family.

They all have long, swept-back wings and streamlined bodies and spend most of their time in the air where they catch flying insects in their gaping beaks. Many species migrate thousands of miles north from Africa and South America to breed in Europe and North America.

To save making lots of trips when they are feeding their young, Swifts collect hundreds of insects in their throats. They take this food ball back to the nest.

Swifts have been known to fly up to 95 kph. They can easily escape from Hawks and other birds of prey.

Their eyes are set deep in their heads. This stops flying dust getting into them.

Common Swift

They tuck their short legs into their feathers, like aeroplane wheels. Their legs are weak and they can hardly walk.

When Swifts touch down, they cling to an upright surface like a wall or a tree. They climb with their toes pointing forwards and take off by dropping down into the air.

Swifts are believed to sleep on the wing. They only come down to nest.

Nests

The Common Palm Swift sticks feathers and plant material together with spit to make its nest on a palm leaf. It cements the eggs into the nest in the same way.

Sand Martins scrabble with their toes in sandy banks to scoop out their nest tunnels. The tunnel is about a metre long and has a little nest chamber at the end.

Swallows make their nests in buildings. They base the nest on a beam or a nail. They make pellets out of mud and build these up into a cup-shaped nest.

Hummingbirds

There are over 300 species of Hummingbirds and most are about 9 cm long from beak to tail. The Cuban Bee Hummingbird is the smallest known bird and measures only 5.7 cm.

Hummingbirds are only found in the Americas and most of them live in the tropical forests of South America. Their beautiful plumage reflects the light and changes colour as they dart about.

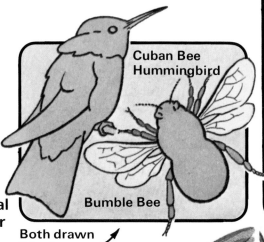

Cuban Bee Hummingbird

Bumble Bee

Both drawn life size

Flying

Hummingbirds can hover when they feed. They beat their wings back and forth in a figure of eight movement to do this, not up and down like other birds.

The special shapes of their long thin beaks are good for probing into different flowers for nectar.

Sword-billed Hummingbird

Buff-tailed Sicklebill

Broad-billed Hummingbird

1 Nests

Many female Hummingbirds spend a long time building their tiny nests. They make them with cobwebs, moss, leaves, petals and feathers.

2

When the two white eggs are laid, the female camouflages the nest with moss and lichen. She feeds the chicks on nectar. In most species, the male takes no part in rearing the young.

Hummingbirds get their name because they beat their wings so fast (over 100 beats per second) that they make a humming sound like a bee. They use up such an enormous amount of energy flying that they need to eat a great deal. They suck nectar from thousands of flowers and eat hundreds of insects every day.

Kingfishers

Kingfishers are small hole-nesting birds. There are more than 80 species and they are found all over the world, except in the far north and far south. Many live near water where they dive for fish, catching them with their spear-like beaks. Other species of Kingfishers, like Kookaburras, eat insects and reptiles.

Most Kingfishers are very brightly coloured, though if you see one flying, it moves so fast it is just a blur of colour.

Kookaburras

Kookaburras are well known in the Australian bush for their wild "laughing" chorus which is heard at dawn and dusk. One bird begins and others join in until they are all "laughing" loudly.

Bee-eaters

Rainbow
Bee-eater

Bee-eaters are colourful birds related to Kingfishers. Most species live in tropical places in Asia, Africa and Australia. They gather in large flocks and feed on bees and other insects.

1 Kingfishers

The male Kingfisher waits on a branch until he sees a fish in the water. In a flash, he dives down and seizes it in his beak. He may bash it on a branch to stop it flapping and kill it.

2

Female   Male

In early spring the male courts the female by giving her a fish. He offers it to her head first so that she can swallow it easily. Together they dig out a nest tunnel in the river bank.

3 Male

Female

The male hovers above the female and lands on her back to mate. He holds on to her neck with his beak and flaps his wings to keep his balance. After mating, the eggs start to grow inside the female.

4

The female lays about six white eggs in the nest chamber at the end of the tunnel. The eggs hatch in three weeks. The chicks are naked and blind. Their parents feed them with small fish.

5

The Kingfisher chicks grow fast. At first their feathers are covered in spiny quills. These soon split to let the feathers appear. Their first plumage is drabber than their parents', but after moulting in the autumn they grow bright new feathers. The young leave the nest about a month after they hatch.

Hornbills

Most Hornbills have a large bill and many have a casque on their bill. Although the casque can be bigger than the bill itself, casques are usually hollow and therefore light. Most species of Hornbills live in forests in Africa and Asia, although some are found in open country. Hornbills eat fruit, such as passion fruit, figs and berries, insects and lizards.

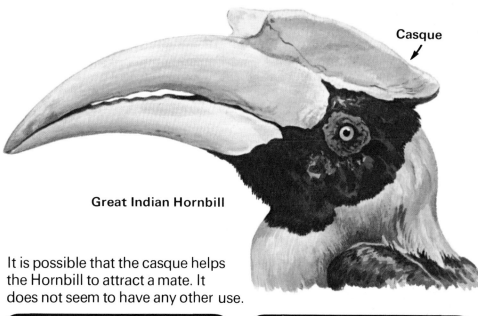

Casque

Great Indian Hornbill

It is possible that the casque helps the Hornbill to attract a mate. It does not seem to have any other use.

1 Red-billed Hornbills

Red-billed Hornbills make their nest in a hollow tree. They collect pellets of mud to wall up the tree hole. Then the female gets inside and seals up the hole with mud that has fallen into it, leaving only a narrow slit.

2

Male

Female

The female lays two to five eggs inside the tree. The male brings her insects, fruit and lizards, and feeds them to her through the slit. While she is inside the tree hole, she moults and pushes the feathers out through the hole.

3

Female

The Hornbill feeds her naked chicks with food which the male passes in to her. She keeps the nest clean by using the chicks' droppings to strengthen the mud wall. The chicks are safe from birds of prey and monkeys.

4

Female

When the chicks are old enough and her new feathers have grown, the female pecks away the mud wall. Then she flies out of the nest. She helps the male collect food to take to the young, who stay in the nest-hole.

5

Chicks

When their mother has left, the chicks seal up the hole again, still leaving a small gap through which food can be passed by the parents. The young birds' bills are pale orange, but will turn red by the time they are mature.

6

Adult

Chick

Six weeks after hatching, the chicks have grown their flight feathers. One of them breaks open the mud wall and makes its first clumsy flight. The others follow, while the parents sit on the tree squawking encouragement.

Woodpeckers

There are over 200 species of Woodpeckers in the world. Most of them make nesting holes in trees each year, but this is not the only cause of the loud tapping sounds that you can hear in woods. As well as using their bills for chipping away at tree trunks, Woodpeckers drum on hollow branches to attract a mate, and to warn off other birds.

Woodpeckers do not hurt themselves when they hammer at trees, because their heads and necks are specially adapted to take the shock.

Most Woodpeckers have two toes pointing forward and two pointing back on each foot. This arrangement is good for climbing and clinging on to tree trunks.

Greater Spotted Woodpeckers

Most Woodpeckers use their strong tails to help keep them upright when they are clinging to a tree.

1

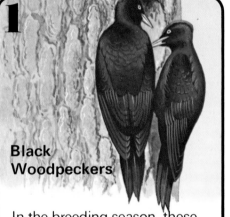

Black Woodpeckers

In the breeding season, these Woodpeckers make nesting holes in trees. The male and female take turns to bore into the trunk, or to enlarge a hole already there.

2

Some of the chippings from the hollowed-out tree form the lining of the nest. The eggs hatch in about twelve days and the chicks are blind at first.

3

The parents hang upside-down in the hole to feed the chicks. They stick their bills right down the chicks' throats.

4

When the chicks are older, they come to the hole to be fed. They leave the nest after about a month and do not return.

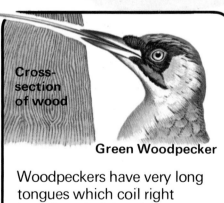

Cross-section of wood

Green Woodpecker

Woodpeckers have very long tongues which coil right back into their heads, not down their throats. When they poke their bills into wood, they flick their tongues out to catch insects and grubs.

Toucans and Barbets

Toucans live in the tropical forests of South and Central America. Although they look rather like Hornbills, they are not related to them as closely as they are to Woodpeckers and Barbets. Toucans' huge beaks are not as heavy as they look, even though they are sometimes longer than the birds' bodies.

The length of the bill makes it easier for the birds to reach fruits and berries. It is possible that its bright colour may help birds of the same species recognize one another.

Chestnut-eared Aracari (Aracaris are small Toucans.)

The Rainbow-billed, or Keel-billed, Toucan swings its body from side to side and makes a loud croaking noise.

Toco Toucan

Toucans eat mainly fruit and insects. They seize food with the tip of the bill and toss it down their throats by throwing back their heads.

Toucans are often found in groups of about a dozen. They seem to enjoy playing, jumping about on branches and knocking their bills together. They even throw berries to one another.

Gaudy Barbet

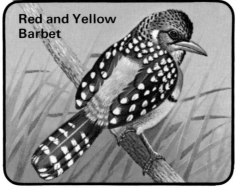

Red and Yellow Barbet

Crimson-rumped Toucanet (a small type of Toucan.)

Toucans fold their tails up over their backs when resting. Like this they can sit comfortably in tree holes, where they nest.

Barbets live in South America, Africa and Asia. They are small, brightly coloured birds and live mainly on fruits and insects. They make holes for nesting and sometimes for roosting.

D'Arnaud's Barbets burrow in sandy soil, and Red and Yellow Barbets dig holes in termite mounds or in sandy banks. Other kinds of Barbets hollow out rotten tree trunks.

43

Perching Birds

There are over 5,000 kinds of perching birds, including such different species as the Birds of Paradise and birds like Swallows and Martins (see page 38), Thrushes and Blackbirds.

All perching birds' feet are well adapted for perching, with three toes pointing forwards and one backwards They all have a similar bone structure and most of them are naked and helpless when they hatch. Scientists have grouped them together into an order (see page 7) called Passeriformes.

Birds of Paradise

The male birds perform a fantastic courtship dance.

Birds of Paradise are so beautiful that when they were first brought to Europe people believed they came from paradise. In fact, most of these birds live deep in the forests of New Guinea and neighbouring islands. The male is very colourful, but the female's plumage is a drab brown.

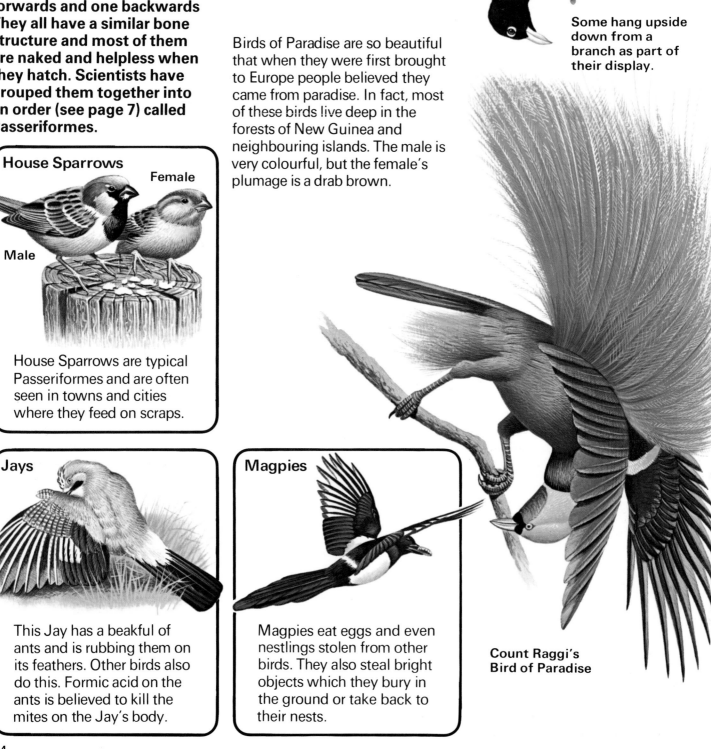

Count Prince Rudolph's Blue Bird of Paradise

Some hang upside down from a branch as part of their display.

Count Raggi's Bird of Paradise

House Sparrows

Female

Male

House Sparrows are typical Passeriformes and are often seen in towns and cities where they feed on scraps.

Jays

This Jay has a beakful of ants and is rubbing them on its feathers. Other birds also do this. Formic acid on the ants is believed to kill the mites on the Jay's body.

Magpies

Magpies eat eggs and even nestlings stolen from other birds. They also steal bright objects which they bury in the ground or take back to their nests.

Bowerbirds

Bowerbirds live in New Guinea and Australia. Most male Bowerbirds build a bower, or stage, on the ground to attract a female. They decorate it with colourful objects like flowers, shells, pebbles, shiny beetle cases and even bottle tops. The bower is not a nest. The male calls to the female and dances in front of the bower with a bright object in his beak. After mating, the female builds the nest in a tree.

The male Satin Bowerbird builds an avenue with twigs woven together. With a mixture of spit and charcoal, he paints

Satin Bowerbirds

Female

Male

the wall of the bower, using a piece of bark as a paintbrush.

He collects blue objects to decorate the bower's entrance.

Blue Tits

Blue Tits tear holes in milk bottle tops and drink the cream. This is a good example of a bird learning a skill which helps it survive.

Cocks of the Rock

This male bird has a crest on its head which almost covers its beak. To attract females, the males choose a clearing in the forest in which to show off their plumage.

Strange Nests

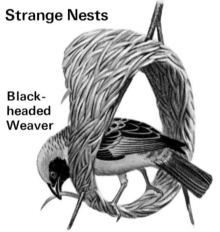

Black-headed Weaver

The male Weaver makes a nest out of grasses and strips of leaf. He builds outwards from a ring of grass until the nest is like a ball with a sock-shaped entrance-tunnel hanging down from it.

Dippers

The Dipper stands on rocks in streams, dipping its head and bobbing up and down. When it sees its prey, the Dipper

dives into the water. It can walk along the river bed, catching insects and fish in its beak.

Robin

In woodlands, Robins nest in hidden holes, but garden Robins often find that an old bucket or kettle makes a good nesting place.

Bird Facts and Figures

Species	Average size (Length = beak to tail tip)	Where the bird lives	Main foods	Nest	Average number of eggs laid
Ostrich	2 m high	Open bush country	Vegetation, small mammals	Scrape on ground	6–8
Emperor Penguin	1.3 m high	Antarctic sea ice	Fish	Makes no nest. Lays egg on ice	1
Great Crested Grebe	48 cm long	Lakes	Fish	Floating reed nest	3–6
Great Northern Diver	75 cm long	Northern seas	Fish	Reed nest on bank of lake	2
White Pelican	1.5 m long	Shallow rivers and lakes	Fish	Nest of debris on ground	1–2
Guanay Cormorant	75 cm long	Coasts of Chile and Peru	Fish	Nest of debris scraped in guano	3
White Stork	1 m long	Open grasslands and marshes	Frogs, reptiles, small mammals, insects	Stick nest, often on building	3–5
Grey Heron	90 cm long	Rivers and ponds	Fish, frogs	Stick nest in tree	3–5
Greater Flamingo	1.5 m long	Flat coastal waters and inland lakes	Tiny water animals	Mud nest in shallow water	1–2
Mute Swan	1.5 m long	Rivers, lakes and ponds	Water plants	Large nest on ground by water	5–7
Greylag Goose	80 cm long	Lakes, marshes and grasslands	Seeds and small water creatures	Plant nest on marshy ground	4–8
Mallard Duck	58 cm long	Inland water, ponds in parks	Water and land plants	Nest on ground or sometimes in tree	7–14
Golden Eagle	85 cm long	Mountains and moorlands	Mammals and birds	Stick nest on cliff or in tall tree	2
African White-backed Vulture	80 cm long	Open plains	Dead flesh of zebra, antelope, etc.	Stick nest in tree	1
Common Pheasant	male 80 cm female 60 cm	Farmland	Plants, seeds and berries	Hidden scrape on ground	6–19
Red Jungle Fowl	male 70 cm female 30 cm	Forests	Grain, bamboo, seeds, insects	Hidden scrape on ground	5–6
Oystercatcher	43 cm long	Mudflats, seashore	Mussels and other shellfish	Scrape on beach, lined with shells or pebbles	3
Sarus Crane	1.5 m long	Grassy plains and marshes	Grain, berries, insects, fish	Plant nest on marshy ground	2
Herring Gull	60 cm long	Sea cliffs and dunes, farmland	Fish, shellfish, scraps	Shallow nest on cliff or sand	2–3
Little Tern	24 cm long	Sandy beaches and dunes	Small fish	Scrape on beach, edged with pebbles	2–3
Puffin	30 cm long	Rocky islands and coasts	Small fish	Burrow on cliff top	1
Woodpigeon	41 cm long	Woods and farmland	Grain, seeds, berries and buds	Twig nest in tree	2
Common Cuckoo	33 cm long	Woods, farmland, heaths	Caterpillars and other insects	Lays eggs in other birds' nests	6–18
African Grey Parrot	35 cm long	Forests	Seeds and fruit	Tree hole	2–4
Barn Owl	34 cm long	Woods and farmland	Small mammals, small birds and insects	In tree or building	4–7
Common Swift	16 cm long	In the air	Flying insects	Under eaves of building	2–3
Ruby-throated Hummingbird	9 cm long	Woods, gardens	Small insects and nectar	Cup nest in tree	2
Kingfisher	16 cm long	Rivers and streams	Fish	Tunnel in river bank	6–7
Great Indian Hornbill	1.3 m long	Forests	Fruit	Large hollow in tree	2
Green Woodpecker	32 cm long	Woodlands	Insects and insect larvae	Hole drilled in tree	5–8
Keel-billed Toucan	38 cm long	Tropical forests	Fruit	Tree hole	3
House Sparrow	14 cm long	Towns, farmland	Scraps, seeds, grain, insects	Grass and debris nest in trees and buildings	3–6
Count Raggi's Bird of Paradise	35 cm long	Forests	Fruit	Nest in fork between branches of tree	1–2

BIRDS QUIZ

You can find the answers to all these questions somewhere in the "How Birds Live" part of this book. When you have done the Quiz, check your answers with the list on page 239.

1. Which of these statements is *not* true about an ostrich?
   a) It has long legs and can run fast.
   b) It has only two toes on each foot.
   c) It is the tallest and heaviest of birds.
   d) It flies long distances to migrate.
   e) Ostrich eggs are about 15 cm long.

2. Which of these birds can not fly?
   a) Penguin
   b) Toucan
   c) Emu
   d) Parrot
   e) Pheasant
   f) Ostrich
   g) Pelican
   h) Flamingo
   i) Kiwi
   j) Rhea

3. Some birds beaks are suited to how they eat. Match the beak with the way of eating.

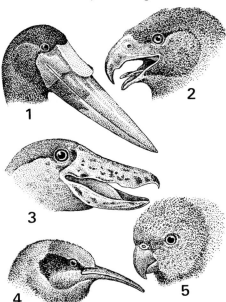

   a) Tears flesh.
   b) Catches insects.
   c) Feeds on nectar in flowers.
   d) Stabs water animals.
   e) Traps water animals.

4. The Anhinga is called the snake bird because
   a) it eats snakes.
   b) it looks like a snake.
   c) it moves its head and neck above the water in an "S" shape.
   d) it slithers along the ground.

5. All of these statements about a stork are true except one. Which one?
   a) They make a clattering noise when they meet.
   b) They build nests of sticks, paper, rubbish and horse manure.
   c) They fly with their babies in their beaks.
   d) They are extinct in Japan.

6. One of these statements is not true. Which one?
   a) Storks nest on house roofs.
   b) Shags nest on rocky cliffs.
   c) Penguins nest in igloos.
   d) Woodpeckers nest in a hollowed-out tree trunk.

7. Match the hatching time of the eggs with the bird.
   1) 8 weeks   a) Penguins
   2) 12 days   b) Kingfishers
   3) 3 weeks   c) Flamingoes
   4) one month   d) Woodpeckers

8. Match the food to the bird.
   1) Scraps   a) Vulture
   2) Fruit and   b) Toucan
      berries   c) Owl
   3) Field mice   d) Humming-
   4) Nectar   bird
   5) Prey left by   e) Sparrow
      other animals

9. Which of these three statements is *always* true about birds?
   a) All birds can fly.
   b) All birds build nests.
   c) All birds lay eggs.

10. A cuckoo is called a parasite bird for which of these reasons?
   a) It eats other birds.
   b) It lays its eggs in other birds nests.
   c) It eats the food of other birds.
   d) It flies on the backs of other birds.

11. Which two of these birds are now extinct all over the world?
   a) Stork
   b) Rhea
   c) Dodo
   d) Archeopteryx
   e) Ibis

12. Which two of these statements are *not true* about all budgerigars?
   a) They come from Australia.
   b) They always live in cages.
   c) All budgerigars are blue and yellow.
   d) All wild budgerigars are green.
   e) They feed on grass seeds and water.

13. Which of these words are the names for female birds?
   a) pen
   b) goose
   c) cock
   d) cob
   e) drake
   f) duck
   g) hen
   h) gander
   i) greyhen
   j) blackcock

14. Identify the bird by the shape.
   1) Toucan
   2) Owl
   3) Swift
   4) Flamingo
   5) Penguin

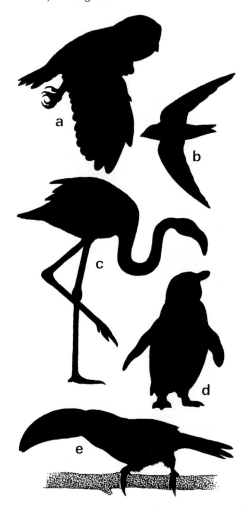

In real life, some of these animals are much bigger or smaller in proportion to each other than they look here.

PART 2
HOW
ANIMALS
LIVE

Brown Bat

Introduction to Part Two

This part of the book is all about how animals live in the wild. It is full of exciting pictures and every page is packed with interesting and unusual facts—from the huge African elephant to the tiny vampire bat. It shows you how animals have their babies and how they look after them.

It shows how animals live in different parts of the world—which ones sleep during the day and feed at night, how some stalk and kill their food, and how some choose their mates.

You can read how polar bears teach their young to catch fish and how a camel survives in the desert without water. You can find out how long a hippo can stay under water, how fast a cheetah can run, and how bats find their way in the dark.

A map of the world on pages 92 and 93 shows all the different parts of the world where the animals live. On page 94 a special chart gives more than 300 easy-to-understand facts about their lives and habits.

Giant Panda

Beavers

Baby Zebra

Tiger with Cubs

Red Stags Fighting

Written by Anne Civardi and Cathy Kilpatrick

Illustrated by George Thompson

Special Consultant: Michael Boorer, Writer and Broadcaster

Contents of Part Two

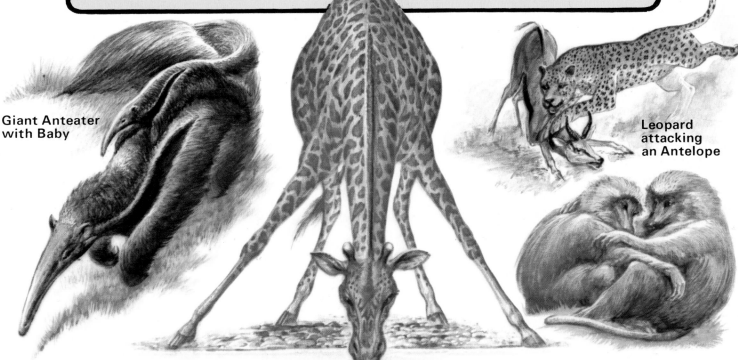

Giant Anteater with Baby

Leopard attacking an Antelope

Giraffe drinking at Water Hole

Baboons cleaning each other

51

Chimpanzees and Other Apes

Chimpanzees are clever and are the animals most like people. They are a kind of ape. An ape is different from a monkey because it does not have a tail.

Chimps eat leaves, fruit and seeds. Sometimes they kill and eat small animals. Most of their day is spent on the ground cleaning each other and playing.

They use sticks and stones as tools to get food and to fight with. A big chimp might throw stones at an approaching enemy or hit it with a stick.

When chimps meet, they often hold hands, kiss and hug each other. If one is very upset or frightened, it runs to the other chimps for comfort. They touch and pat it to calm it down.

They talk to each other by making grunting and hooting noises. When they are very excited, chimpanzees bark loudly and jump up and down waving their arms in the air.

A mother chimpanzee takes great care of her baby. She feeds and cleans it and teaches it to do lots of different things. The baby suckles and sleeps close to her for at least four years.

Making Faces

This chimpanzee is thinking.

This one wants to play.

This chimp is hooting hello.

This one is very frightened.

Most grown-up chimps know that insects, called termites, make a delicious meal. This one has found a big termite mound and is poking a long stalk of grass down the holes to catch some.

After a while, he pulls the grass out and licks the insects off the end. Chimpanzees also use grass stalks and long, thin sticks to collect honey from bees' nests and to get ants out of ant-hills.

This chimp is sleeping high up in the tree top. Every night all chimps, except the babies, make nests of twigs and branches to sleep in. Sometimes they make pillows out of clumps of leaves.

Chimpanzees often get together to clean each other. They comb one another's hair with their fingers and pick off seeds, bits of dirt, scabs and ticks.

This baby chimpanzee is only a few months old. He rides about clinging to his mother's stomach. When he gets a bit older he will ride piggy-back.

Chimps usually walk and run on all fours. Sometimes they run downhill swinging their legs between their arms. They can go much faster like this.

Other Kinds of Apes

Gorillas are the biggest and strongest kind of ape. Usually they are quiet and shy, but if they get excited or angry they stand up and beat their chests.

This ape is called a siamang. He can fill a big sac under his chin with air to make a booming noise. When he lets the air out, he makes a loud shriek.

Gibbons are very acrobatic apes with extra-long arms and hooked fingers. They use them to swing between branches and to leap from tree to tree.

Giraffes

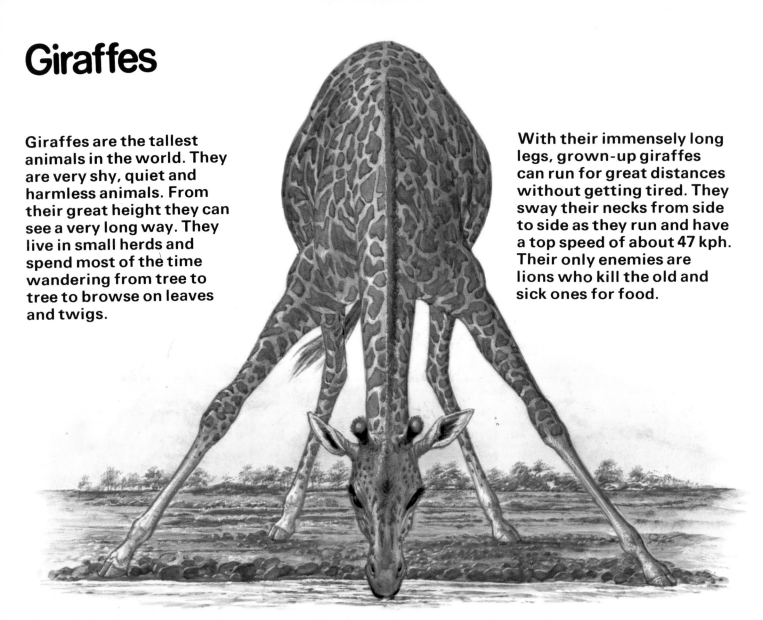

Giraffes are the tallest animals in the world. They are very shy, quiet and harmless animals. From their great height they can see a very long way. They live in small herds and spend most of the time wandering from tree to tree to browse on leaves and twigs.

With their immensely long legs, grown-up giraffes can run for great distances without getting tired. They sway their necks from side to side as they run and have a top speed of about 47 kph. Their only enemies are lions who kill the old and sick ones for food.

A giraffe has a very awkward time getting his head down to drink. He has to spread his front legs apart, like this, and lower his neck between them. His front legs are longer than his back ones. A giraffe sucks in water and then uses his throat to squeeze it up his neck and into his stomach.

1 Baby Giraffes

2

A mother giraffe gives birth to her baby while she is standing up. The baby, which is born feet first, drops gently from its mother down on to the ground.

It is not often hurt by the fall and can run and walk when it is a few hours old. The baby drinks milk from teats between its mother's back legs.

Big giraffes usually sleep standing up, for only a few minutes at a time. A young one may curl up on the ground to sleep, guarded by its mother.

Eyes, Ears and Noses

A giraffe has very good eyesight. His huge eyes are on the sides of his head so he can see all round him.

His hearing is very acute and he can twist his ears right round to listen to sounds from all directions.

The giraffe has special nostrils which he can close up to stop dirt and dust getting up his nose.

Fighting

These two big male giraffes are having a fight. They swing their necks together and butt each other with their heads and knobbly horns.

A giraffe's big, heavy hooves can kill a lion with a single blow.

Giraffes have two, three or four horns on top of their heads. Some have another knob which grows between their eyes.

By stretching his long neck, a big giraffe can reach leaves high up in the treetops. Acacia leaves are his favourite food. He strips them off the branches with his tongue, which is 45 cm. long, and tough hairy lips.

The Okapi

The okapi is the giraffe's only relative. Its patterned coat helps it to hide in the rain forests where it lives. Okapis were first discovered only 75 years ago.

Brown Bears

Brown Bears are found in Asia and parts of Europe. The biggest ones, Grizzlies and giant Kodiaks, live in North America.

Bears eat all kinds of food—fruit, ants, roots, honey from wild bees' nests, berries, meat and fish.

Sleeping in Winter

Most brown bears spend the cold winter months resting. They dig dens in the earth or find a quiet, warm spot, such as a cave or hollow tree to live in.

Some of the big female bears wake up in January or February to have their babies. The tiny cubs are born blind with no teeth and hardly any hair.

Playing

The mother bear and her cubs leave the den when the weather is still quite cold. They play together in the snow and slide down slopes as if they are tobogganing. The cubs can climb trees but the mother bear is much too heavy.

She watches them all the time to make sure that they do not get into any trouble.

This is a giant Kodiak bear. Usually he walks about on all four legs. Sometimes, to show how big and strong he is, he stands up on his back legs, like this.

1 Fishing

This mother bear is teaching her cubs how to catch a fish to eat. They are standing very quietly in the shallow water waiting for one to swim by.

2

When she sees a fish, the bear quickly grabs it in her huge paw and puts it into her mouth. Sometimes she will flip a fish out on to the bank.

Polar Bears

Polar Bears live on the cold icy shores of the Arctic ocean. In winter they live where the pack-ice meets the sea.

They are one of the biggest and strongest animals in the world. Standing on its back legs, a polar bear is taller than most elephants.

The females dig dens in the snow to have their babies in. The cubs stay with their mother for about ten months.

A polar bear feeds mainly on meat. It catches a seal by creeping over the ice and pouncing on it while it is asleep. Sometimes it waits for one to swim up for air where the ice is broken. As soon as the seal's head pops up out of the water, the bear reaches down and bites it with his huge teeth. He then hauls it out of the water on to the ice to eat it.

Keeping Warm

A polar bear has a thick, shaggy coat and a layer of fat under his skin to keep him warm. Hairs on the bottom of his feet stop him sliding about on the ice.

In the Water

Baby polar bears do not seem to like the cold water at first. By the time they are six months old, they are expert swimmers and follow their mother about in the water.

Sometimes they rest their heads on her back if they are very tired. When swimming, polar bears use their front legs to paddle with and they steer with their back legs.

Other Bears

This is a spectacled bear. He has this name because of the white fur around his eyes. It makes him look as if he is wearing glasses. He lives in South America.

The sun bear is the smallest kind of bear and has a very long tongue. He often tears open trees with his claws to lick the honey out of the wild bees' nests.

Sloth bears will sleep almost anywhere and they snore loudly. Baby ones ride around on their mother's back, clinging to her shaggy fur with their long claws.

Tigers

Tigers are found in many countries in Asia. Some live in steamy jungles and swamps. Others live in cold mountain country.

Like most big cats, they spend the day resting and sleeping. At night they hunt for food.

A grown-up male tiger is the biggest cat in the world. The female, who is called a tigress, is smaller and lighter than the male.

A tiger's striped coat is a good camouflage. It makes it very difficult to see in long grass, shady places and in moonlight when it is hunting.

Tiger cubs are born in a den. They are quite helpless until they are about two months old. Until then, they are looked after and fed by their mother.

Growing Up

A tigress usually has three or four babies at the same time. At first they drink her milk to make them strong. The father tiger does not help look after the cubs. He leaves the tigress to teach them all the things they need to know. The cubs fight and play with each other and their mother. They practise how to stalk and pounce. Soon they must kill for themselves. By the time they are two years old they will be expert hunters.

1 Tiger Talk

Tigers talk to each other by roaring. A male roars to tell other tigers to keep away. A tigress roars to call to her cubs or to attract a male.

2

A big male tiger lives by himself on a special, large piece of land known as his territory. He marks it by spraying urine over the trees and bushes.

He also leaves droppings and scrapes grooves in the ground. This lets other tigers know that the land belongs to him and warns them to keep away.

The cubs hide in caves or thick scrub and grass while their mother goes off hunting for food. When she has killed an animal, she brings back the meat.

When the cubs are about three months old, the mother leads them to the meat. She makes a den nearby so that they can eat when they are hungry.

After they have eaten as much as they can, the cubs rest in the den. When the mother kills more food, she leads them to it and makes another den for them.

Keeping Cool

Tigers hate being too hot and often sit in shallow water to cool down. They are good swimmers and sometimes catch fish and turtles to eat.

Keeping Warm

In very cold places, tigers grow thick, shaggy coats to keep themselves warm. They are usually bigger than the jungle tigers.

Their coats are paler with fewer stripes than other tigers. A grown-up male, like this one, has a ruff of long hair round his face.

3

If he is very angry, a tiger wrinkles up his nose, snarls and twists his ears round to show two white spots. This is a warning to keep away from him.

4

A tiger flicks his tail from side to side when he is stalking an animal. He lashes it about as he charges and pounces. It shows that he is very excited.

The tiger swallows his food in big chunks without bothering to chew it properly. Sometimes he eats so much, he does not have to feed again for several days.

Rhinos

Two kinds of rhino live in Africa—black rhinos and the bigger white rhinos. Both are really a greyish-brown colour, but the black ones are slightly darker.

They look alike, with thick leathery skin and two big curved horns growing just behind their noses. Their mouths and heads are a different shape.

Rhinos usually live near to water. They move about and feed during the night when it is cool. They sleep either standing up or lying down during the day.

Feeding Together

A Black Rhino's Mouth

Black rhinos have rubbery, pointed lips for plucking leaves off bushes.

A White Rhino's Mouth

White rhinos have wide, flat mouths made specially for grazing off the ground.

Black and white rhinos sometimes feed together in the same place. They never fight over food because they like different things to eat.

The black rhino eats the leaves, twigs and shoots of small bushes. The white one eats only grass. His neck is longer because he has to bend down to get his food.

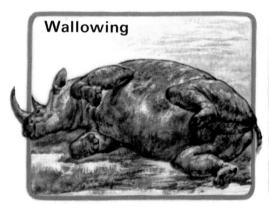

Wallowing

The Great Indian Rhino

This rhino is having a mud bath. Every day rhinos wallow in muddy pools to keep cool and get rid of insects. Sometimes they roll over on their backs, like this.

This kind of rhino lives in India, sleeping and feeding in tall elephant grass or swampy jungles. His thick, bumpy skin is folded in places and makes him

look as if he is wearing a suit of armour. Unlike African rhinos, he only has one horn. Indian rhinos fight only with their teeth and do not use their horns.

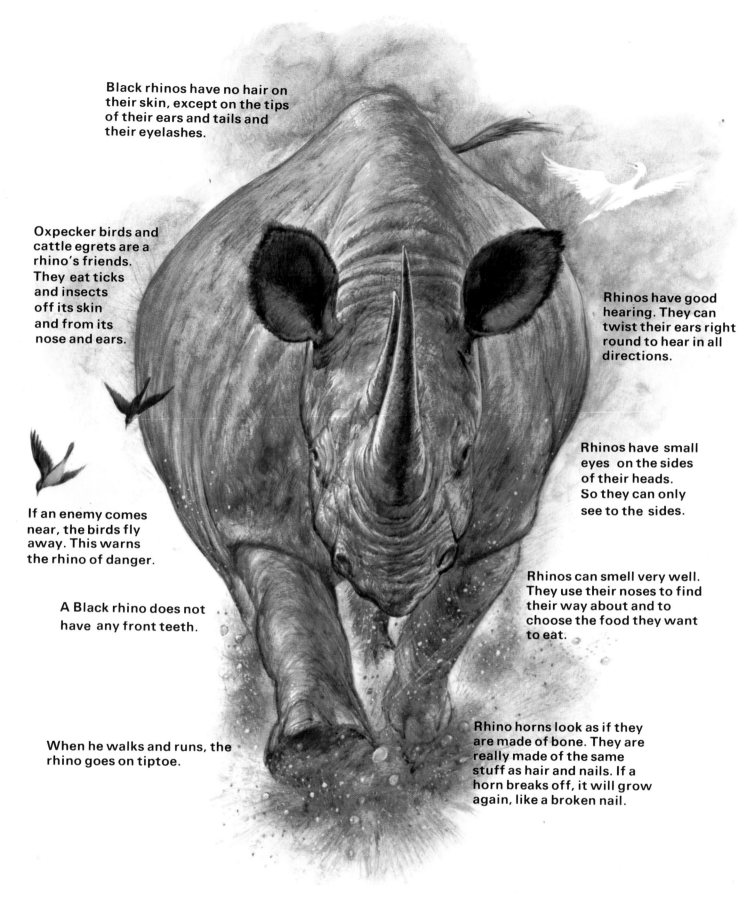

Black rhinos have no hair on their skin, except on the tips of their ears and tails and their eyelashes.

Oxpecker birds and cattle egrets are a rhino's friends. They eat ticks and insects off its skin and from its nose and ears.

Rhinos have good hearing. They can twist their ears right round to hear in all directions.

If an enemy comes near, the birds fly away. This warns the rhino of danger.

Rhinos have small eyes on the sides of their heads. So they can only see to the sides.

A Black rhino does not have any front teeth.

Rhinos can smell very well. They use their noses to find their way about and to choose the food they want to eat.

When he walks and runs, the rhino goes on tiptoe.

Rhino horns look as if they are made of bone. They are really made of the same stuff as hair and nails. If a horn breaks off, it will grow again, like a broken nail.

Most black rhinos seem to have bad tempers. They charge when they are frightened or become suspicious. This is probably because they cannot see very well ahead of them.

They grunt and squeal when they are excited. This black rhino is charging an enemy. He uses his ears and nose to hear and smell where the danger is and they help him to go the right way.

Rhinos can gallop round corners and change direction very quickly, although they are so heavy and bulky. They can run very fast—sometimes at 45 kph. over a short distance.

Sloths, Anteaters and Armadillos

These strange animals live in South America. They all use their strong, curved claws to defend themselves against their enemies.

A sloth also uses his claws to hang from the branches of trees. He reaches out with long arms to collect the food he wants to eat.

Anteaters and armadillos feed on ants and termites. Sometimes an armadillo catches snakes, worms and spiders to eat. Sloths prefer fruit and leaves.

Sloths

Sloths are the slowest furry animals in the world. They spend their lives moving lazily along the branches of trees or just hanging upside-down asleep.

They never clean themselves or move unless they have to and they even sneeze slowly. Sloths eat, sleep and have babies while they are upside-down.

As soon as the baby is born, it grips tightly to its mother's fur with its tiny claws. The mother sloth carries her baby about on her chest, like this.

Sloths cannot stand up on their arms and legs. It is very difficult for them to move on the ground at all. Out of a tree a sloth is completely helpless.

This one is trying to crawl to the nearest tree. It might take him hours to reach it. He drags himself along on his stomach, using his long, front claws.

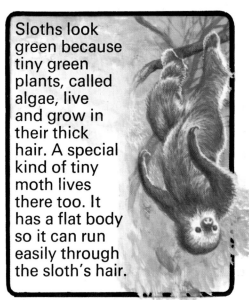

Sloths look green because tiny green plants, called algae, live and grow in their thick hair. A special kind of tiny moth lives there too. It has a flat body so it can run easily through the sloth's hair.

Anteaters

The Giant Anteater

Giant anteaters always seem to have their long snouts close to the ground, sniffing for food. They have to walk on their knuckles, like this, to protect their long, sharp claws.

This baby anteater will ride about on its mother's back until it is about a year old. When she is ready to have another baby, it will go off and live by itself.

A giant anteater usually takes off at a slow, clumsy gallop when it sees an enemy. If it is forced to fight, it rears up on its back legs and lashes out with its claws.

Tamanduas

A tamandua is a small anteater that spends most of its life in trees. Like other anteaters, its favourite foods are ants, termites and squashy grubs.

Tamanduas tear open anthills and termite mounds with their sharp, front claws. Then they poke their snouts into the holes to catch the insects.

This tamandua has collected lots of ants on his long, sticky tongue. He shoots it in and out of the ants' nests to catch them and put them into his mouth.

Armadillos

1

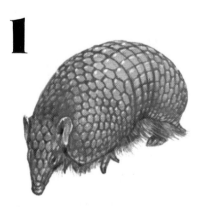

2

Armadillos are covered with lots of bony plates, which protect them like armour. This giant one is digging a burrow with its claws.

The small, three-banded armadillo walks about on the tips of its strong, front claws. It has a very good way of protecting itself.

If it is frightened, it rolls itself up into a tight ball, about the size of a melon. Only its enemy, a jaguar, is strong enough to rip the ball apart.

Elephants

Elephants are the biggest land animals. There are two kinds, the African elephant and the Indian one. These two pages are all about African elephants.

If an elephant gets too hot, it flaps its huge ears backwards and forwards to cool itself down.

Elephants have very strong teeth to chew branches and roots of trees. They grow six sets of teeth in a lifetime. New teeth grow as the old ones are worn down.

Elephants live in small family groups called clans. In each clan there are a few grown-up female elephants, their babies and teenage children, and other young elephants.

The oldest and biggest female is the leader of the clan. Big bull elephants live by themselves or in their own groups. They join the females at mating time.

A mother leaves the clan to have her baby One or two elephants may go with her. After the baby is born, she helps it to stand by lifting it up with her feet and trunk.

Mud Baths

1

2

3

Every day elephants roll about in the mud, like this, to get rid of insects and to keep their skin in good condition.

After a mud bath, elephants suck dust and sand up their trunks and then blow it out to stick it to their muddy bodies.

Then they rub themselves against a termite hill or a big tree. This squashes any insects which are left on their skin.

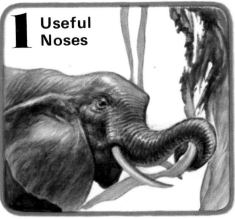

1 Useful Noses

An elephant's trunk is a very useful thing. He uses it to pick berries, gather tufts of grass, tear down leaves and branches and strip bark off trees.

2

He also uses his trunk for drinking. He sucks up water through the two long nostrils and squirts it into his mouth. A trunk holds about 2 litres.

3

This elephant is using his trunk as a snorkel so he can breathe under the water. He also smells, feels and breathes with it when he is out of the water.

4

Elephants lift heavy things and push big trees over with their trunks. They scoop out holes, dig for water and even rub their eyes with their long noses.

She feeds the baby with her milk several times a day. It stays very close to her, for the first few months of its life, often walking between her front legs for safety.

Fighting

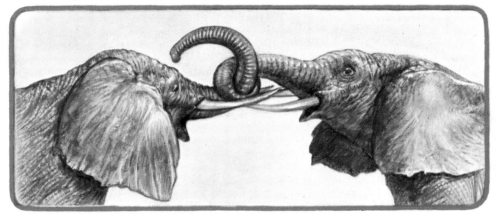

Bull elephants often fight each other at mating time. They use their trunks and tusks as weapons, to hit and jab each other. Tusks are really very long teeth.

The fights do not last very long. The elephants stop as soon as one proves he will win. He then goes off to mate with a female elephant, called a cow.

Indian Elephants

Indian elephants are not as big as African ones. They have smaller ears and tusks and only one lip on the end of their trunks. African elephants have two.

65

Beavers

1 Baby Beavers

Inside the lodge, the mother beaver lies on a soft bed of bark and twigs to have her babies. The tiny kits are covered with soft brown fur.

2

Kits can walk at birth but they have to practice a lot before they become expert swimmers. This mother beaver is holding a kit's tail to steer it in the right direction.

3

When a baby beaver is very tired, its mother may help it back to the lodge. She carries it in her arms, like this, or picks it up by the scruff of its neck with her mouth.

Beavers are excellent builders. They make their houses, called beaver lodges, on the edges of lakes and rivers.
Like rats, mice, rabbits and squirrels, beavers are rodents. All rodents have two big, sharp front teeth to gnaw with.

Mother and father beavers stay together all their lives. They have three or four babies, which are called kits, every year.
A young beaver lives with its parents until it is about two years old. Then it goes off alone to start a family and build a lodge of its own.

Beavers eat the bark, twigs, branches and leaves of trees. They like aspen, birch and willow trees the best.

Beavers bite down trees with their sharp teeth to get food and to make their lodges. They sit on their broad, flat tails to gnaw at a tree trunk.

A beaver's teeth grow all the time as they get worn down by gnawing. If they grew too long, they might prop open its mouth.

These two beavers are grooming each other with their teeth and claws. They have a special split claw on their back feet for combing through fur.

All summer, the beavers collect food and put it into the foodstore for the cold winter months.

Beavers are very good swimmers. They paddle with their webbed back feet and use their flat tails as rudders to steer.

Grooming

A beaver has oil glands at the base of its tail. It grooms itself to spread oil over its coat to make

1

First it cleans its nose with its front paws.

itself waterproof. At first, baby beavers get very wet whenever they swim.

2

Then it scratches its head, chest, arms and stomach.

Their mother teaches them how to oil their coats. This beaver knows just what to do.

3

It leaves the cleaning of its legs and back until last.

Beavers put their food into their mouths with their front paws.

The beavers chop the tree into pieces and drag or roll them, one by one, to the place where they are building the lodge.

Beavers are always scurrying about finding sticks and twigs to repair their lodges.

This beaver is slapping its tail on the water to warn the others of danger. It makes a very loud noise.

Big beavers bunch lots of twigs together and bite off the leaves. Baby beavers eat one twig at a time.

A Beaver Lodge

The lodge is made of sticks and twigs, packed together with mud and stones.

Before they make their lodges, beavers build a dam of sticks to make the water deeper.

The beaver family live in one big room above the water. A hole in the roof lets air in and out of the lodge.

All the entrances are under the water to stop other animals getting into the lodge. The beavers store their food close to one of the entrances.

Lions

The lion is called the king of beasts because he is so fierce and powerful.

Lions are the only wild cats that live together in family groups. A family of lions is called a pride.

In each pride there are two or three grown-up lions, five or six grown-up lionesses and lots of cubs. There may also be several young lions and some lionesses.

Family Life

Cubs chase about and spring on each other's tails. They learn to do things, like stalking and pouncing, which will be useful when they have to look after themselves and catch their food.

They play with their mother and nuzzle her face. This keeps her friendly and stops her from getting cross and hurting them. Their father does not play with them very much.

1 The Head of the Family

Grown-up lions have big, shaggy manes round their heads and necks. This one is roaring to warn all the other lions to keep away from his pride.

2

If another lion comes too close, then they will fight. The fight goes on until one of them is hurt and runs away. Sometimes two or three younger lions will attack an older lion all together.

1 The Kill

The lionesses do most of the hunting. Sometimes they hunt alone but usually two or three hunt together. Zebras and gnus are their favourite food.

2

First they stalk an animal, keeping well hidden. Then they rush out and spring on it. A lioness can make a spring of over 10 metres through the air.

3

She sinks her fangs into the animal's throat to kill it. Sometimes she will drag the body to a sheltered place where the pride can feed on the meat.

The cubs are much more lively than the big lions. They play and explore even when it is very hot. Their mother leaves them hidden in the bushes and long grass while she goes off to hunt. Their spotted coats make them very difficult for an enemy to see.

The cubs start eating meat before they are three months old. After a year, they are able to hunt and kill for themselves.

The big lions usually eat first while the rest of the family watches. If the animal is only small and they are very hungry the big lions may eat it all.

But if the kill is big, there will be enough for the whole pride. The lionesses and cubs wait until the lions have had enough before they start to eat.

As soon as the whole pride has left the kill, hyenas, jackals and vultures come to finish it off. They pick every single scrap of meat off the bones.

Zebras

Zebras live in small family herds which are usually led by one big, strong male. He is called a stallion. Female zebras are called mares and baby ones, foals.

They are fat and healthy because they normally have enough to eat. They like the coarse, stringy grass that other animals will not touch. Herds of zebra are often seen grazing peacefully with giraffes, wildebeests and ostriches.

There are usually five or six mares and their foals in each family group. The stallion protects them and keeps all the other stallions away.

If he is alarmed, he gives a loud bark to warn his herd of danger and they gallop off. He will even fight young lions if they attack the group.

1 Having a Baby

The mother zebra lies down in a quiet spot to have her baby. It is born inside a big bag full of water, called the birth sac. The foal's head comes out first.

2

The baby struggles out of the birth sac as soon as it is born. Its mother, who is very tired now, lifts up her head and licks it dry.

3

At first it is very wobbly on its legs and it falls over a lot. But when it is about 15 minutes old, the foal is steady enough to walk with its mother to join the herd.

Zebras like to stay close to each other in small groups. They often rest, standing in pairs like this, during the hottest part of the day.

They groom each other to get rid of ticks and other itchy insects. The zebras use their teeth to bite the insects off one another's skin.

Grown-up male zebras fight a lot, especially during the mating season. They gallop round and round, kicking and biting each other's legs and necks.

Bushbabies

Bushbabies are small furry animals with long back legs and huge eyes. They move very fast among the trees and can jump over 4 metres from branch to branch. Small kinds of bushbabies hop along the ground like kangaroos, using their tails to balance.

They are called bushbabies because the noise they make sounds just like a human baby crying. They are also known as galagos.

Senegal Bushbabies

All bushbabies are nocturnal. This means that they rest in the daytime and feed at night. Their enormous eyes help them to see in the dim light.

At dawn, bushbabies chatter together before they go to sleep. At night, they search for food. They catch insects with their hands and collect fruit and birds' eggs to eat.

This mother bushbaby hides her baby in the trees when she goes off to feed. The baby can already cling to branches with is long fingers and toes.

Other Night Animals

Lorises move about very slowly and never jump. They sleep with their heads tucked between all four feet. This baby slender loris is following its mother.

The aye-aye is a very rare animal, about the size of a cat. It has a special thin middle finger on each hand. It pokes this finger into holes to catch insects.

The tiny tarsier can swivel its head right round, like this, to watch out for danger. It uses its tail as a brake when it makes huge leaps from tree to tree.

Red Foxes

Red foxes live mainly in woods and bushy country. But some have learned to find food in towns, eating rats, mice and the scraps thrown into dustbins.

During the winter, red foxes have long, thick fur to keep them warm. They look much thinner in the summer when they lose their winter coats. Their big, bushy tails are called brushes and usually have white or black tips.

1 Growing Up

Red foxes live in dens, called earths. These may be under fallen trees, in hedges or on hillsides. They are often old warrens and burrows which were dug out by rabbits or badgers.

Female red foxes are called vixens. They have their babies in the earths during the spring. Usually four or five tiny cubs, covered with dark brown fluffy fur, are born.

2

When the cubs are about two weeks old, their eyes open and they begin to explore. They sniff and scratch at everything and tumble about the den.

3

After about six weeks, the cubs lose their baby fur and start to look more like their parents. Now they are more daring and go outside the earth to play.

They stalk and pounce on each other and on sticks and stones. When they are about six months old, they will be big enough to catch food for themselves.

Poaching

Farmers do not like foxes much because the foxes sometimes eat their turkeys and chickens. This fox has found a wild duck's nest and is eating the eggs.

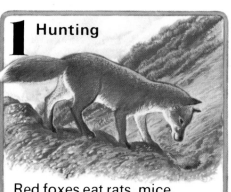

1 Hunting

Red foxes eat rats, mice, rabbits, frogs and insects. While the vixen looks after the cubs, the father fox, called a dog fox, goes off to hunt for food.

2

He is a very silent hunter. When he sees something to catch he keeps absolutely still. Then he pounces on it. This fox is taking a mouse back to his family.

Giant Pandas

Giant pandas live in China, high up on the mountain plateaux in the dense bamboo forests. It is very cold there but the panda's thick, rough hair helps to keep it warm.

A baby panda, like the one in the picture on the right, cannot move around on his own. He will start to crawl when he is about three months old. His mother takes great care of him. She makes sure he is always clean and has enough to eat.

Big pandas are very good at climbing. They will scramble up the nearest tree to get away from their enemies—leopards and wolves. Sometimes they sleep up trees, comfortably wedged between the branches.

Most pandas spend the whole day eating. Their favourite food is bamboo but they also like to eat other things, such as bamboo rats, small birds, snakes, flowers and fish. This one is feasting on a tasty bamboo shoot.

Wildebeests

Wildebeests are very strange looking antelopes with hairy faces, and beards which grow under their chins. They have long legs and run very fast. They are also called gnus.

There are more wildebeests living on the grassy African plains than any other kind of animal. But a lot of them are killed by hungry lions, hyenas and other meat-eating animals. Many die of a disease called rinderpest.

Little insects called bot-flies often lay their eggs in a gnu's nose. Usually he manages to sneeze the eggs out. But sometimes they hatch into flies inside his nose.

The flies bore their way into the gnu's brain and make him lose his balance. He turns round and round until he is so dizzy and exhausted that he falls over and dies. This is called 'turning disease'.

Hyenas lurk close to the gnus with turning disease. They wait for a gnu to fall over and then they kill and eat him.

If a wildebeest is upset or frightened he behaves in a very curious way. He prances about, paws the ground, thrashes his long tail about and pokes his horns into the earth.

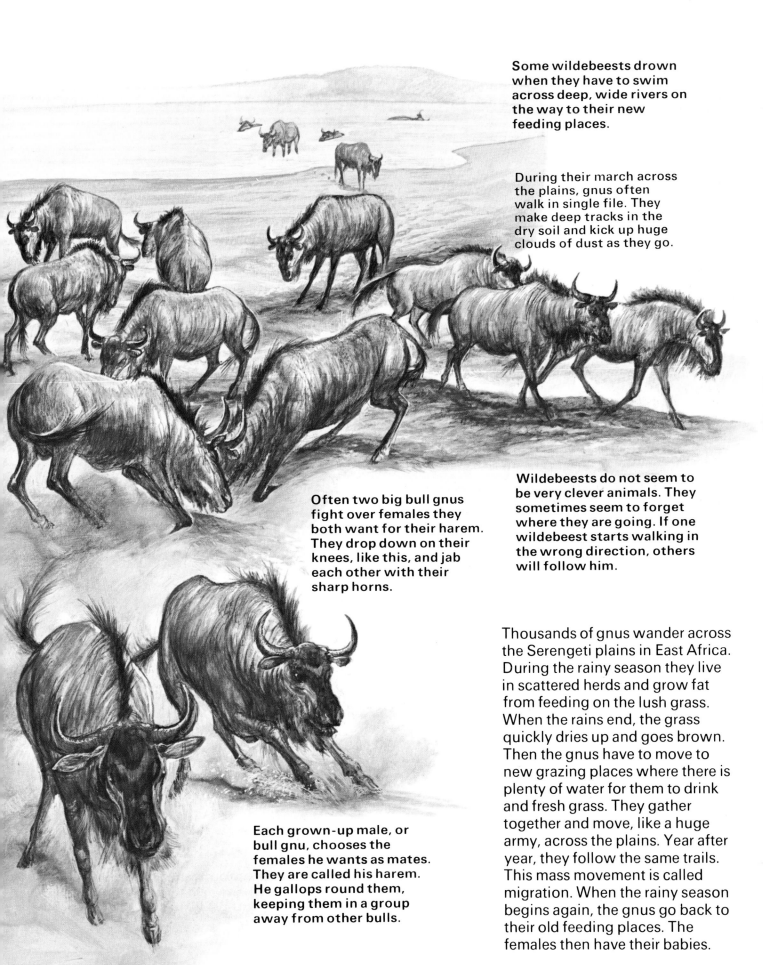

Some wildebeests drown when they have to swim across deep, wide rivers on the way to their new feeding places.

During their march across the plains, gnus often walk in single file. They make deep tracks in the dry soil and kick up huge clouds of dust as they go.

Often two big bull gnus fight over females they both want for their harem. They drop down on their knees, like this, and jab each other with their sharp horns.

Wildebeests do not seem to be very clever animals. They sometimes seem to forget where they are going. If one wildebeest starts walking in the wrong direction, others will follow him.

Thousands of gnus wander across the Serengeti plains in East Africa. During the rainy season they live in scattered herds and grow fat from feeding on the lush grass. When the rains end, the grass quickly dries up and goes brown. Then the gnus have to move to new grazing places where there is plenty of water for them to drink and fresh grass. They gather together and move, like a huge army, across the plains. Year after year, they follow the same trails. This mass movement is called migration. When the rainy season begins again, the gnus go back to their old feeding places. The females then have their babies.

Each grown-up male, or bull gnu, chooses the females he wants as mates. They are called his harem. He gallops round them, keeping them in a group away from other bulls.

Cape Hunting Dogs

Cape hunting dogs are very fierce and savage. They live together on the open plains of Africa in groups of up to 20 animals, called packs.

The dogs wander from place to place hunting for food. They will stay in one spot if there are plenty of animals, such as zebras or gnus to kill.

No two dogs have exactly the same markings on their coats. Only their tails are the same— with white tufts of hair on the ends.

1 The Kill

In the early morning or at dusk, most of the pack go off to hunt for food. A few stay behind to look after the young puppies.

The dogs walk silently towards a herd of animals and then start to chase it. The herd rushes off when it sees the dogs coming.

Soon one animal, usually ill or weak, is separated from the herd. The dogs chase it until it is too tired to run any more.

2

The animal has a horrible death as it is eaten alive by the savage dogs. Some of them attack its face. Others bite and snap chunks of meat from its rump and legs.

The dogs eat quickly before any hyenas and jackals come to steal their food. They hunt every day, often killing far more animals then they can eat.

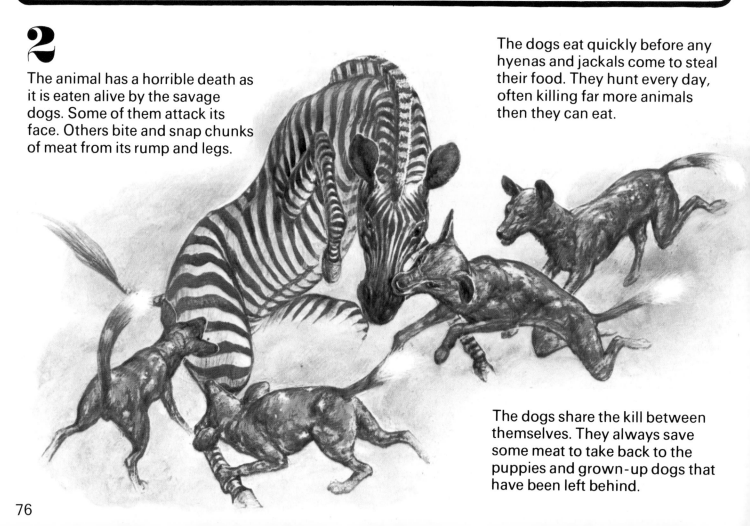

The dogs share the kill between themselves. They always save some meat to take back to the puppies and grown-up dogs that have been left behind.

1 Growing Up

Baby hunting dogs are born in burrows which have been left empty by other animals. The mother dog, known as a bitch, may have as many as twelve pups at the same time.

2

The puppies start eating meat when they are two weeks old. Their mother sicks up food she has swallowed to feed them. They squeak, wag their tails and nuzzle her mouth to beg for more.

3

When the pack moves to a new hunting ground, the puppies go too. The big dogs pick them up gently by the scruffs of their necks to carry them there. The herds move on when the dogs come.

Other Wild Dogs

Wolves also live and hunt in packs. A wolf pack is a family, with father as the leader, mother and, probably, the cubs from the last litter.

These two big male wolves are fighting to see which is the next leader after father. The loser has rolled over on his back to show he is beaten.

Coyotes usually live and hunt alone. In the evenings, they often meet on the prairies and howl together in chorus. From a distance, it sounds just as if they are singing together.

Dingoes are dogs which live in Australia. They were once tame dogs which escaped and bred in the wild. Sometimes they kill kangaroos and wallabies.

Hyenas and jackals hunt and kill when it gets dark. They do not like each other much. When they meet they often fight over bones and scraps of food.

During the day, jackals lurk in the shadows waiting to steal food. They are scavengers. A scavenger clears up the left-overs of another animal's kill.

Camels

There are two kinds of camels. One kind has two humps and is called the Bactrian camel. It lives in the Gobi desert in Asia. The other, the Arabian camel, which is called a dromedary, has one hump.

Camels eat all sorts of desert grasses and salty plants. If they get very hungry they will also eat meat, bones and skin. There are very few wild camels left in the world now. Most of them are tame and are used to carry heavy loads.

Floppy Humps

When a camel has not had enough to eat, his humps shrink and flop over to one side, like this.

Camels store fat in their humps. It gives them lots of energy. Their humps also help to protect them from the heat of the sun.

When camels are well-fed, their humps are plump and solid like these ones.

Camels never clean themselves and are always very smelly. They are sick at you if you annoy them.

Camels can close up their nostrils to stop sand and dust getting up their noses.

A camel has a big split in the middle of its upper lip. There is a groove from each nostril to the split, so that any dribble from its nose goes straight into its mouth and is not wasted.

A camel has hard leathery pads of skin on its front and back legs to rest on when it kneels down.

The two toes on each foot have big hard nails and are joined together by a tough bit of skin.

Soft fleshy pads on the bottom of its feet stop the camel from sinking into the soft sand dunes.

Camels are very well suited to desert life. They are able to live in hot, dry places because they can go without a drink of water for many days.

This picture of a Bactrian camel shows you some of the special parts of its body that help it to stay alive in the hot and cold deserts and on mountains.

Winters in the Gobi desert are very cold. To keep themselves warm, Bactrian camels grow thick woolly coats. In the summer this hair falls out.

Dromedaries

Arabian camels often make long journeys across the desert carrying heavy loads. Sometimes they have little to eat and drink for days.

Although a camel does not sweat very much, it loses some water through its breath and urine. At the end of a long journey it is often thin and weak.

These camels have come to a water-hole in the desert and are very thirsty. They may drink as much as 20 big buckets of water at a time.

Camels' Relatives

Vicuna

Guanaco

Alpaca

Llama

These animals are all relatives of the camel but none of them has a hump or lives in the desert. Vicunas and guanacos live in the wild in small herds.

They eat the green grass high up on the Andes mountains. Alpacas are tame and covered in valuable wool which sometimes grows all down their legs.

The wool is used to make very expensive cloth. Llamas are tame and have been trained to carry heavy loads. They are also kept for their milk and wool.

Kangaroos

Red kangaroos are one of the biggest and best-known kinds of kangaroo. They live on the inland plains over most of Australia. The herds are called mobs. The head of the mob is known as the old man.

Grown-up males are about 1.5 metres tall and usually a reddish-brown colour. Females are smaller with blue-grey coats. They have pouches low down on their stomachs for their babies.

How a Baby Kangaroo is Born

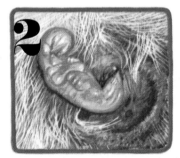

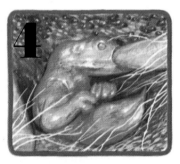

1 Just before the baby is born, the mother licks the inside of her pouch to clean it. She also licks the fur on her stomach. Then she sits like this to give birth.

2 A tiny newborn red kangaroo is about the size of a man's thumb nail. It is completely blind, has no hair and does not look like a kangaroo at all.

3 It grips its mother's hair with the claws on its front feet and crawls up her stomach and into her pouch. This only takes the baby about three minutes.

4 The baby stays in the pouch and sucks milk from the teats until it is fully formed. After about seven months, it is big enough to jump about and feed on its own.

Young kangaroos are called joeys. A joey goes on drinking his mother's milk for six months after leaving her pouch. This one has popped his head in to have a drink.

Until he gets too big, the joey often goes back to the pouch whenever he is tired or frightened. He jumps in head first and turns a complete somersault. Only his head and legs stick out.

A big kangaroo can make a jump of 3 metres in the air and 9 metres along. He springs off his strong back legs. His tail helps him to balance. The faster he goes, the further he jumps.

When male kangaroos fight, they rear up on their tails, and hold on to each other with their front feet. They give powerful kicks with their back feet. Their sharp claws can make very deep wounds.

Kangaroos spend most of the day sunbathing. When it gets cooler in the evening, they start to look for food and water. Red kangaroos can go without water for several days.

Other Animals with Pouches

Female koalas have upside-down pouches which open between their back legs. The babies crawl into them after they are born. Koalas live in eucalyptus trees and feed on the leaves and bark.

Animals that have pouches to carry their babies in are called marsupials. Only the females have them. This baby long-nosed bandicoot is trying to get into his mother's upside-down pouch.

Baby Virginian opossums ride about on their mother's backs after leaving the pouches. Sometimes, when opossums are frightened or hurt, they pretend to be dead so that their enemies leave them alone.

Bats

Bats are the only furry animals that can fly. There are about 1000 different kinds living all over the world. During the day, they rest in dark caves, hollow trees and empty buildings or hang from the branches of trees.

As they rest, bats clean themselves with their toes and tongues. At night, they fly about looking for food. Grown-up female bats usually have one baby every year. The baby clings to its mother with its teeth.

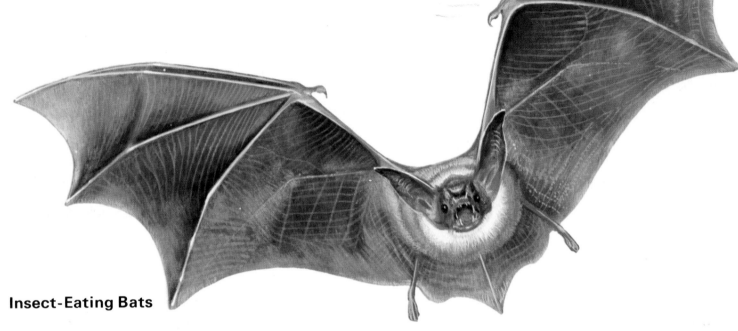

Insect-Eating Bats

A bat's wings are made of very thin, stretchy skin which grows between its long, bony fingers and its legs and tail. The back feet, with their sharp, curved claws, are free for grasping things.

This brown bat likes eating insects. It catches them while it flies about. Insect-eating bats have sharp teeth to scrunch up their food.

After a meal of many insects, the bat finds somewhere to rest. It hangs by its toes and folds up its wings. When it gets hungry again at dusk it goes off to hunt for more insects.

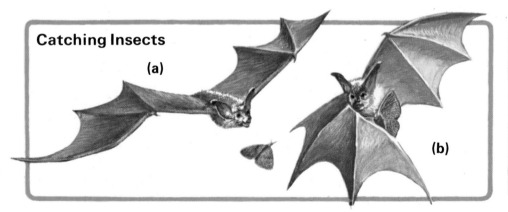

Catching Insects

(a)

(b)

Winter Sleep

Bats make high-pitched squeaks to catch flying insects and to find their way in the dark. The echoes of their squeaks tell them exactly where things are (a).

The bat catches the insect with its wings (b). It then pokes its head down to get the insect into its mouth. If it is a large insect, the bat will land to eat it.

Some bats sleep throughout the cold winter months. They hang upside-down, like this, and fold their wings round their bodies. This bat is covered with dew.

Fish-Eating Bats

At dusk, the fish-eating bat comes out of his hiding place to look for food. He flies very slowly above the water, swooping down to catch tiny fish with his sharp, hooked claws. As soon as the bat catches a fish, he lifts it out of the water and puts it into his mouth.

Vampire Bats

A vampire bat feeds only on fresh blood. He usually attacks an animal while it is asleep. The bat bites open the skin and laps up the blood with his long tongue. It is so quiet that the animal does not even wake up. Sometimes, vampire bats drink so much blood they cannot fly for several hours.

Flower-Feeding Bats

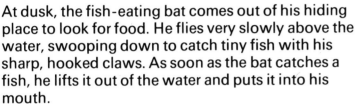

Flower-feeding bats are usually small with pointed heads and very long tongues. This one is poking its tongue down a flower to find something to eat. It hovers beside the flower. The pollen and nectar in flowers are the bat's favourite foods. They stick to the tiny hairs on the top of its tongue as it feeds.

Fruit-Eating Bats

These big bats are also called flying foxes because they have such fox-like faces. They eat ripe fruit, like bananas, wild figs, paw-paws and pineapples. Fruit bats often squabble and fight each other. They lash out with their claws and snap with their teeth. They fly out to eat at dusk and spend several hours feeding and resting on the fruit trees.

Leopards

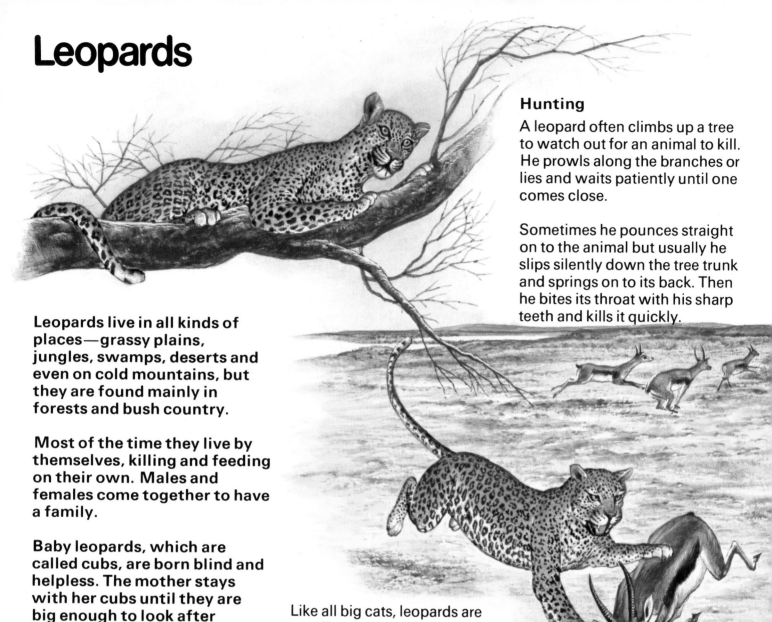

Hunting

A leopard often climbs up a tree to watch out for an animal to kill. He prowls along the branches or lies and waits patiently until one comes close.

Sometimes he pounces straight on to the animal but usually he slips silently down the tree trunk and springs on to its back. Then he bites its throat with his sharp teeth and kills it quickly.

Leopards live in all kinds of places—grassy plains, jungles, swamps, deserts and even on cold mountains, but they are found mainly in forests and bush country.

Most of the time they live by themselves, killing and feeding on their own. Males and females come together to have a family.

Baby leopards, which are called cubs, are born blind and helpless. The mother stays with her cubs until they are big enough to look after themselves and catch and kill their own food.

Like all big cats, leopards are excellent hunters. Their favourite kinds of food are small antelopes, wild pigs, baboons and porcupines.

Before the Kill

Leopards need to keep their claws sharp for climbing trees and killing animals.

This one has found a very good scratching post. It is sharpening its claws on the bark of a tree before it goes hunting for food.

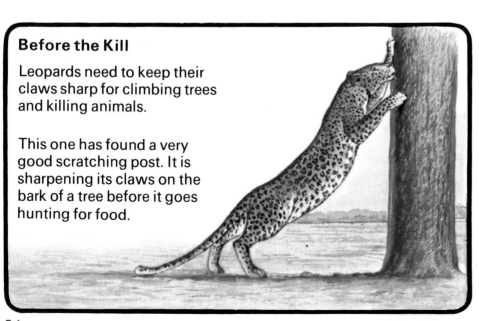

After the Meal

A leopard likes to have a drink of water after a meal. While he drinks, he keeps a watchful eye open for his main enemy—man.

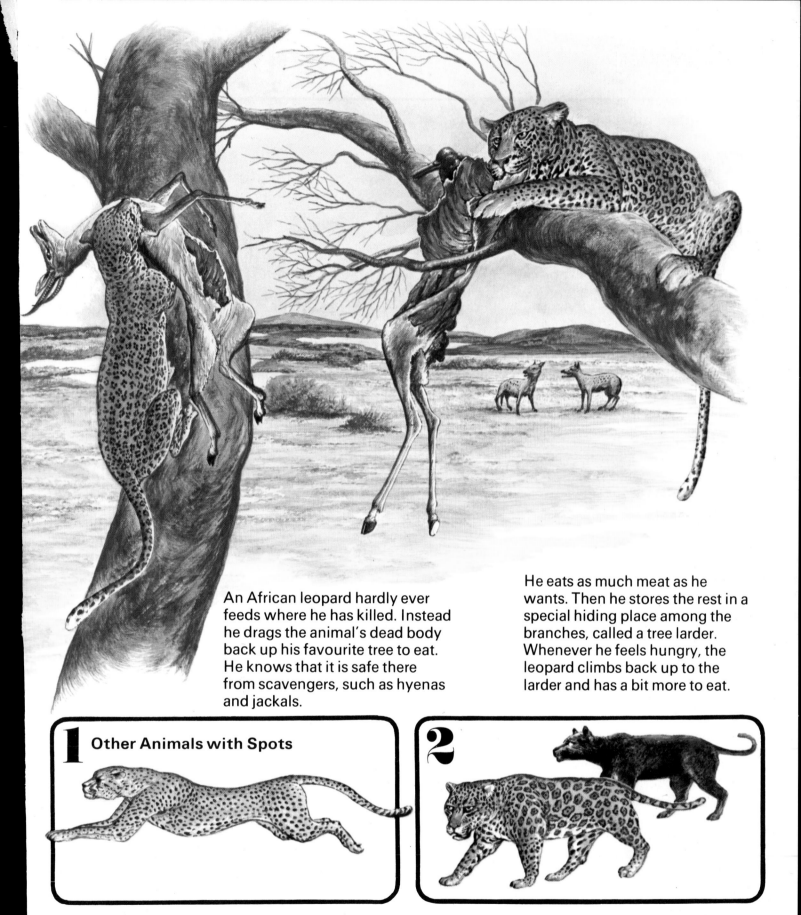

An African leopard hardly ever feeds where he has killed. Instead he drags the animal's dead body back up his favourite tree to eat. He knows that it is safe there from scavengers, such as hyenas and jackals.

He eats as much meat as he wants. Then he stores the rest in a special hiding place among the branches, called a tree larder. Whenever he feels hungry, the leopard climbs back up to the larder and has a bit more to eat.

1 Other Animals with Spots

2

Cheetahs are the fastest animals in the world and can run at over 110 kph. They are smaller and thinner than leopards and have longer legs. Unlike most big cats, they stalk and sprint after their prey to catch it.

Jaguars are stronger and fatter than leopards and their spots are a different shape. Indian leopards are called panthers. Sometimes they look completely black but really they have very dark spots all over their coats.

Red Deer

Red deer spend most of the day resting quietly in the shade. In the evening, they move to their favourite feeding places to eat leaves and grass.

Deer eat lots of food very quickly without bothering to chew it properly. While they are resting they bring the food back up into their mouths and chew it over and over again. This is called chewing the cud.

Grown-up male red deer are called stags and the females are known as hinds. Only the stags have big, bony antlers on their heads. Young red deer are called calves.

The deer's summer coats are sleek and red. In the winter they grow much thicker and turn a pale greyish-brown colour. Most red deer have a white patch under their tails. Other deer follow this when one scents danger and dashes away.

A Baby Red Deer

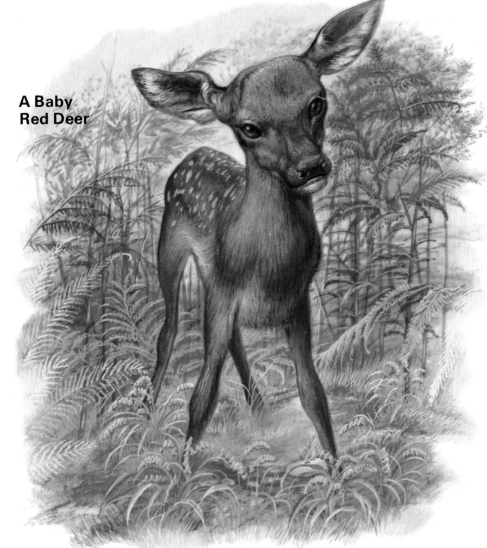

This baby deer is only a few hours old but he can already stand up and walk a little. Until he grows a bit older and stronger, he will rest, hidden in the grass and ferns.

The spots on his furry coat make him very difficult for an enemy to see. His mother feeds him several times a day on her milk. Soon she will take him to join the other hinds and their calves in the herd.

1 How Antlers Grow

A year-old male deer is called a knobber because he has two hairy knobs on the front of his head. His antlers will start to grow from these knobs when he is about two years old.

2

Every spring the antlers fall off. When they grow again in the summer, they are a bit bigger than the last ones. At first, they are covered with soft skin and hair, called velvet.

3

In the autumn, the velvet peels off, leaving a hard, bony part. Sometimes a stag rubs the velvet off against a tree. Fully-grown antlers, like these ones, have six or more spikes.

1 The Mating Season

The mating season, called the rut, begins in the autumn. Each stag rounds up the hinds he wants as his wives. He bellows to tell other stags to keep away.

2

The rut is a very tiring time for the stag. He is always rushing about trying to keep all his hinds close together in a group. They are called his harem.

He mates with each of them so that they will have babies in the early summer. Hardly any time is left for him to eat so he gets very thin and worn out.

3

During the rut, which lasts for about six weeks, a stag fights any other stag which comes near his harem of hinds.

The two stags lock their antlers together and try to push each other backwards. When one wins, he chases the other away.

After the rut is over, the stag is very tired and is hoarse through bellowing. Now it is time to leave his harem and join other stags.

Other Deer

The Moose

A moose is the biggest kind of deer and has huge antlers. In summer, it often wades into water to eat water plants, tearing them with rubbery lips.

The Chinese Water Deer

This tiny deer is very shy and hides in long grass and reeds. Instead of antlers, the males have two sharp tusks which poke out below their upper lips.

The Reindeer

Reindeer live in very cold places but their thick coats keep them warm. They have big flat hooves so they can walk on snow. Both males and females have antlers.

Hippos

Hippos live in Africa and spend up to 16 hours a day lazing about in rivers and swamps. They feed all the time on waterweed.

They are the second heaviest land animals and weigh so much that they cannot jump off the ground at all.

A big male hippo, which is called a bull, weighs about as much as 60 men. Female hippos are called cows, and babies are called calves.

Hippos can float with their bodies right under the water even though they are so big. They do this to keep cool and to stop insects biting them.

They are excellent swimmers and divers and can stay under the water for up to five minutes. A big hippo can even walk along the bottom of a lake or river.

Sometimes hippos sun-bathe on river banks. But they do not stay out of the water for very long as their skins dry up quickly in the hot sun.

Birds, such as egrets and brown hamerkops, are the hippo's friends. They peck biting insects and bits of river weed off his thick skin.

1 A Hippo's Head

A hippo's ears, eyes and nose are on the top of its flat head. It can keep most of its head under the water and still hear, see and smell very well.

2

He can see specially well in dim light and can swivel his ears round to hear in all directions. When he goes under the water, he closes his nose and ears.

This hippo looks as if he is yawning. He is really showing off his big teeth as a warning to any enemy. A hippo uses his teeth as weapons to fight with.

1 Out of the Water

Hippos spend the whole night looking for food. The bulls lead the way, the cows and calves follow. A new born baby walks just in front of its mother.

As they walk, the hippos trample down wide tracks. These tracks are called hippo trails. Night after night, they walk along the same trail searching for things to eat.

2

All healthy hippos have very big appetites. They feed on grass, leaves, roots and branches. At dawn, when they are full of food, they waddle back into the water.

3

Even though they are so heavy with such stumpy legs, hippos can run quite fast for a short way. This frightened mother and baby are rushing back to the water.

1 Baby Hippos

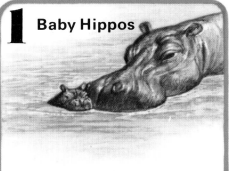

Baby hippos are born in the water. They learn to swim when they are only minutes old. Sometimes their mothers will hold their heads up out of the water.

2

Female hippos often babysit for each other. If one mother hippo wants to go off to feed or mate, she leaves her calves with another hippo.

Mud Baths

Hippos love to wallow and bask in muddy pools. They take mud baths to keep cool and to get rid of insects from their skin, just as an elephant does.

Monkeys

Monkeys usually live in family groups or big herds, called monkey troops. Most kinds spend their time feeding and sleeping in the trees.

They swing or leap from branch to branch looking for things to eat. Their favourite foods are fruit, nuts, plants and eggs.

Big, heavy monkeys like baboons prefer to live on the ground. At night they shelter near trees or rocks. They seem to be frightened of the dark.

Anubis Baboons

One strong grown-up male baboon is usually the head of the troop. All the other baboons have to obey him.

The boss baboon gets very cross if another baboon threatens him. He ruffles up his hair, bares his big teeth and barks to show he is not pleased.

Baboons mutter and grunt as they feed. They use their hands to put grass and plants into their mouths. Some baboons catch lizards, butterflies and grass-hoppers to eat.

When a baboon knows he has been defeated in a fight, he turns his rump towards the winner to show that he wants to give up.

A baby baboon has a pink face and ears and is covered with dark fur. It stays very close to its mother, clinging to the fur on her stomach when she moves about.

This baby baboon is about four months old. It rides about on its mother's back like a jockey. It holds on to her fur with its fingers and toes so it does not fall off.

These two baboons are cleaning each other. They pick and nibble bits of dirt, leaves, dry skin and salt off one another's hair and skin.

Young baboons are very playful. They chase each other about and pretend to have fights.

Baboons stay close together when they move from place to place. Some of the grown-up males walk on the outside of the troop to protect the others.

The grown-up males are very fierce and strong. They are always on the look-out for their enemies such as leopards, lions, wild dogs and hyenas.

If an enemy attacks the troop, they rush to the front to fight it off. All the other baboons quickly run away and hide among the rocks and trees.

Spider, woolly and squirrel monkeys live high up in the trees in the forests of South America.

Their long tails help the spider and woolly monkey to balance and to grip on to branches.

Spider monkeys often hang by their long, curly tails so they can reach out for fruit. Sometimes they use their tails to pick up things. They are very acrobatic and swing quickly through the branches of the trees.

Woolly monkeys can stand up on their back legs and walk along branches like tightrope walkers. They balance with their arms and tails. Usually, a woolly monkey sleeps curled up with his tail wrapped round his body.

Squirrel monkeys are very noisy and inquisitive. They chatter in the tree-tops as they leap from branch to branch looking for food. Often a group will huddle together and rest with their heads between their legs.

Other Monkeys

The red uakari is very shy. He hides in the trees where no one can see him. If he is excited, his bald head goes an even brighter red.

Male mandrill monkeys have the most colourful faces of all furry animals. They also have bright red, purple and blue bottoms.

A male proboscis monkey has a very big nose — proboscis means nose. It gets even longer and droopier as the monkey grows older.

Where the Animals in this Book Live

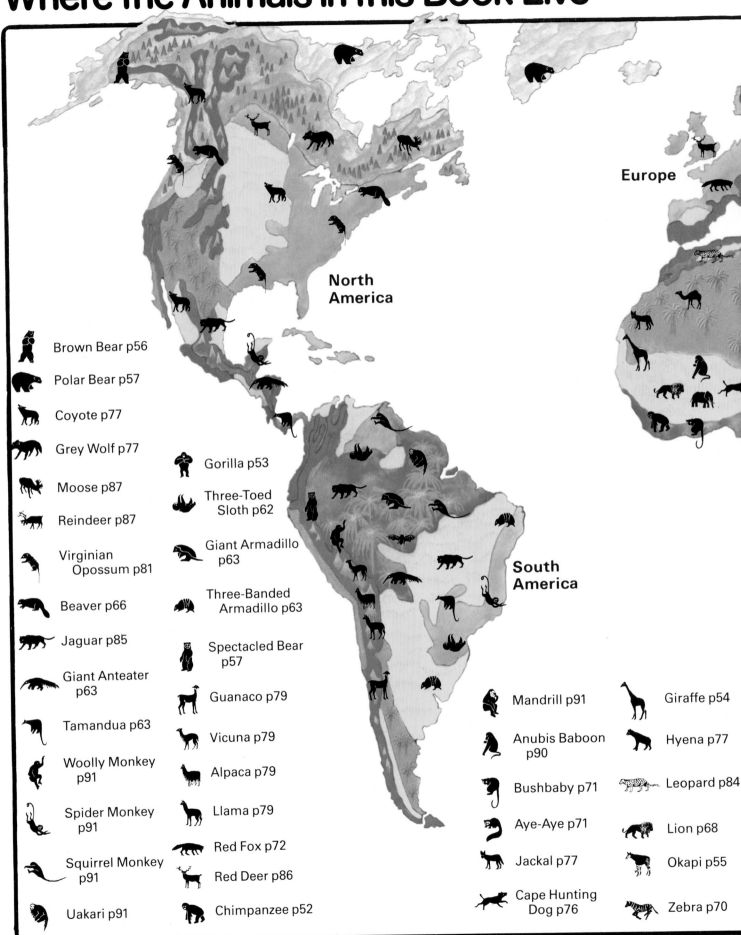

North America

Europe

South America

Brown Bear p56

Polar Bear p57

Coyote p77

Grey Wolf p77

Moose p87

Reindeer p87

Virginian Opossum p81

Beaver p66

Jaguar p85

Giant Anteater p63

Tamandua p63

Woolly Monkey p91

Spider Monkey p91

Squirrel Monkey p91

Uakari p91

Gorilla p53

Three-Toed Sloth p62

Giant Armadillo p63

Three-Banded Armadillo p63

Spectacled Bear p57

Guanaco p79

Vicuna p79

Alpaca p79

Llama p79

Red Fox p72

Red Deer p86

Chimpanzee p52

Mandrill p91

Anubis Baboon p90

Bushbaby p71

Aye-Aye p71

Jackal p77

Cape Hunting Dog p76

Giraffe p54

Hyena p77

Leopard p84

Lion p68

Okapi p55

Zebra p70

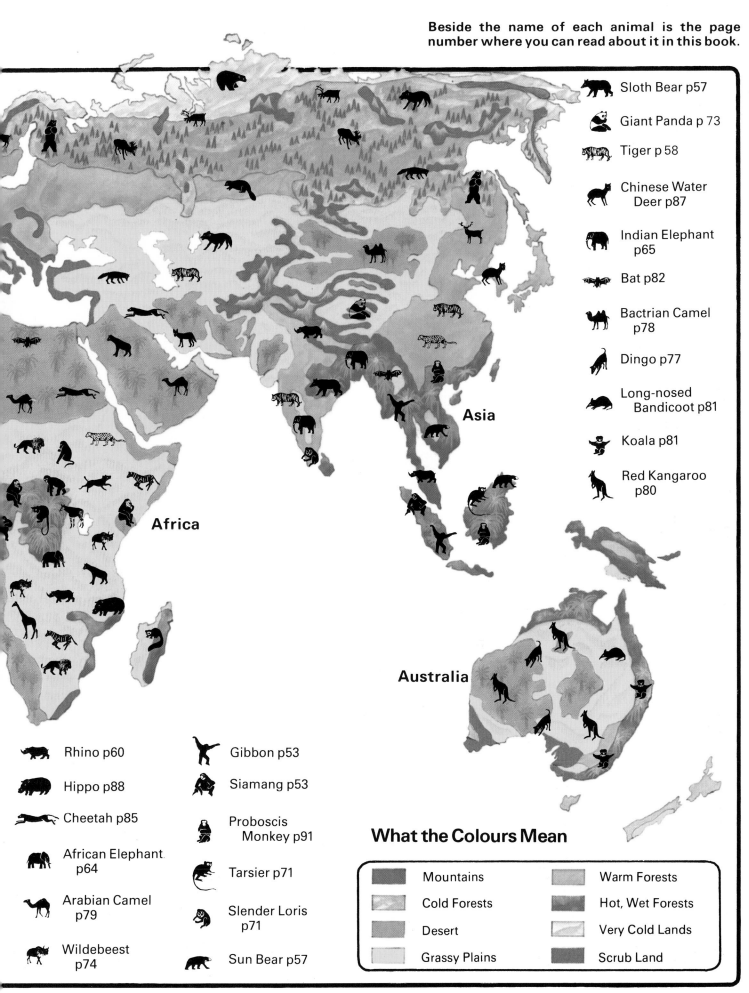

Beside the name of each animal is the page number where you can read about it in this book.

Sloth Bear p57

Giant Panda p73

Tiger p58

Chinese Water Deer p87

Indian Elephant p65

Bat p82

Bactrian Camel p78

Dingo p77

Long-nosed Bandicoot p81

Koala p81

Red Kangaroo p80

Asia

Africa

Australia

Rhino p60

Hippo p88

Cheetah p85

African Elephant. p64

Arabian Camel p79

Wildebeest p74

Gibbon p53

Siamang p53

Proboscis Monkey p91

Tarsier p71

Slender Loris p71

Sun Bear p57

What the Colours Mean

Mountains

Cold Forests

Desert

Grassy Plains

Warm Forests

Hot, Wet Forests

Very Cold Lands

Scrub Land

Animal Facts and Figures

Animal	Average Size of Adult Male	Weight of Male	Carnivore	Herbivore	Gestation Period	Size of Litter	When the Animal Feeds	Climber	Life Span
Chimpanzee	1.5 m high	80 kg	Yes	Yes	7½ months	1 baby	Day	Yes	40 years
Gorilla	1.75 m high	275 kg	No	Yes	9 months	1 baby	Day	Yes	20–45 years
Giraffe	4 m high	1,800 kg	No	Yes	14–15 months	1–2 babies	Dawn/Dusk	No	15–20 years
Brown Bear	2.8 m long	780 kg	Yes	Yes	6–8 months	1–3 babies	Dusk/Night	Yes	30 years
Polar Bear	2.5 m long	410 kg	Yes	No	9 months	1–4 babies	Day	No	34 years
Tiger	2.8 m long	272 kg	Yes	No	3½ months	3–4 babies	Mainly Night	Yes	20 years
Black Rhino	3.75 m long	1,800 kg	No	Yes	17½–18 months	1 baby	Night/Dawn/Dusk	No	50 years
Three-toed Sloth	60 cm long	4.5 kg	No	Yes	4–6 months	1 baby	Night	Yes	under 12 years
Giant Anteater	1.2 m long	23 kg	Yes	No	6½ months	1 baby	Day or Night	No	14 years
Giant Armadillo	1 m long	50 kg	Yes	No	Not confirmed	1–2 babies	Night	No	15 years
Tamandua	58 cm long	5 kg	Yes	No	Not confirmed	1 baby	Night/Dawn/Dusk	Yes	10 years
African Elephant	3–4 m high	7,500 kg	No	Yes	22 months	1 baby	Day	No	50–70 years
Beaver	1.3 m long	32 kg	No	Yes	3–4 months	3–4 babies	Dusk	No	15–20 years
Lion	2.4 m long	227 kg	Yes	No	3½ months	2–5 babies	Night/Dawn/Dusk	Yes	20–25 years
Zebra	2.4 m long	350 kg	No	Yes	11½–13 months	1–2 babies	Mainly Night	No	28 years
Bushbaby (Senegal)	20 cm long	300 gms	Yes	Yes	4 months	1–3 babies	Night	Yes	10 years
Red Fox	1.4 m long	6 kg	Yes	Yes	1½–2 months	4–10 babies	Mainly Night	No	12 years
Giant Panda	1.3 m long	160 kg	Yes	Yes	7–9 months	1–2 babies	Day	Yes	15–30 years
Wildebeest	2 m long	275 kg	No	Yes	8–9 months	1 baby	Dawn/Dusk	No	16 years
Cape Hunting Dog	1 m long	27 kg	Yes	No	2½ months	6–8 babies	Night/Dawn/Dusk	No	10 years
Grey Wolf	1.3 m long	70 kg	Yes	No	2 months	5–7 babies	Day	No	14–16 years
Hyena	1.6 m long	82 kg	Yes	No	3½ months	1–2 babies	Night/Dawn/Dusk	No	25 years
Camel (Bactrian)	3 m long	690 kg	No	Yes	12½–14½ months	1–2 babies	Day/Dusk	No	45 years
Red Kangaroo	1.5 m long	70 kg	No	Yes	1 month	1 baby	Night	No	10–20 years
Koala	85 cm long	15 kg	No	Yes	1 month	1 baby	Night	Yes	20 years
Virginian Opossum	50 cm long	5.5 kg	Yes	Yes	13 days	8–18 babies	Night	Yes	2 years
Vampire Bat	9 cm long	50 gms	Yes	No	3–4 months	1 baby	Night	Yes	12 years
Leopard	1.5 m long	91 kg	Yes	No	3 months	2–3 babies	Night/Dawn/Dusk	Yes	15–20 years
Cheetah	1.5 m long	65 kg	Yes	No	3 months	2–4 babies	Day	Yes	15–30 years
Red Deer	2.5 m long	250 kg	No	Yes	8 months	1–2 babies	Dawn/Dusk	No	15–18 years
Moose	3 m long	825 kg	No	Yes	8 months	1–3 babies	Day	No	20 years
Hippo	4.6 m long	4,500 kg	No	Yes	7½–8 months	1–2 babies	Night	No	40–50 years
Baboon (Anubis)	1 m long	34 kg	Yes	Yes	6–7 months	1–2 babies	Dawn/Dusk	Yes	20 years
Spider Monkey	63 cm long	6 kg	Yes	Yes	4½ months	1 baby	Day	Yes	20 years
Woolly Monkey	68 cm long	6 kg	No	Yes	4½–5 months	1 baby	Day	Yes	20–25 years

Animal Words

Browser—an animal that feeds on the leaves and twigs of small bushes and trees.

Burrow—the den that some animals make to live in during the cold winter months or when they have their babies.

Carnivore—an animal that eats other animals, birds, fish or insects.

Chewing the cud—the food an animal brings back from its stomach into its mouth to chew again.

Gestation period—the length of time a female animal carries her babies inside her before they are born.

Harem—a group of female animals that have been chosen as mates by one male animal.

Herbivore—an animal that eats grass, leaves and plants but not meat.

Herd—a group of animals that feed or move together.

Hibernation—the time when some animals sleep or rest during the cold winter months.

Litter—a group of babies born at the same time to one mother.

Marsupial—a female animal that has a pouch for her baby to live and feed in until it is old enough to look after itself.

Migration—the yearly movements of herds of animals from one feeding ground to another and back again.

Nocturnal animal—an animal that rests or sleeps during the day and hunts and feeds at night.

Predator—an animal, like a lion, that hunts and kills other animals for food.

Prey—the animal that is killed by a predator.

Suckle—when a baby animal is fed by its mother on her milk.

Territory—the patch of land or water where an animal lives and feeds, and defends against other animals.

ANIMALS QUIZ

You can find the answers to all these questions somewhere in the "How Animals Live" part of this book. When you have done the Quiz, check your answers with the list on page 239.

1. Five quick questions on Animal Facts and Figures.
   a) Which animal lives the shortest time?
   b) Which animal lives the longest time?
   c) Which animal's babies take the longest time to grow *inside* their mother?
   d) Name three animals which are both herbivores and carnivores.
   e) Which animal might have 18 babies at one go?

2. Which of these statements about bears is *not* true?
   a) Bears eat all kinds of food.
   b) Bears usually walk on all fours.
   c) Polar bears like to eat seals.
   d) A spectacled bear is short-sighted.

3. Which animal particularly likes bamboo?
   a) Brown Bear
   b) Giant Panda
   c) Rhino

4. Wildebeests are also called
   a) antelopes
   b) wild beasts
   c) gnus
   d) bulls

5. Why does a camel get floppy humps?
   a) It eats too much salt.
   b) It has not had enough to drink.
   c) Too many people have sat on it.
   d) It has not had enough to eat.
   e) It is too hot.

6. Which of these statements is not true about kangaroos?
   a) Herds are called mobs.
   b) The head kangaroo is called the old man.
   c) Babies are called joeys.
   d) Babies are born in pouches.
   e) They live in Australia.

7. Which of the Big Cats has
   a) spots?
   b) stripes?
   c) a shaggy mane?

8. a) Which of the Big Cats lives in a pride?
   b) Which of the Big Cat babies are called cubs?
   c) Which usually eats his kill up a tree?
   d) Who is the biggest enemy of all the Big Cats?

9. Rhino horns are made of:
   a) ivory
   b) bone
   c) nail-like material
   d) tooth-like material

10. The slowest and laziest of all the animals in this book is probably
    a) a monkey
    b) a sloth
    c) a camel
    d) a hippopotamus

11. Which of the following is *not* true?
    a) Gorillas are quiet and shy.
    b) All camels have two humps.
    c) Vampire bats feed only on fresh blood.
    d) Indian elephants are smaller than African elephants.

12. Which of these things do elephants and hippopotamuses have in common?
    a) Big ears.
    b) They live in Africa.
    c) They like mud baths.
    d) They both have tusks.

PART 3
HOW YOUR BODY WORKS

Introduction to Part Three

In many ways, your body is like a marvellous machine. It can do hundreds of different kinds of jobs. To show how it does some of its most important jobs, we have invented lots of different machines.

Our machines do not connect with each other. Each is separate, and each can do only some of the jobs your body can do.

For example, our Eating Machine (pages 100 and 101) shows what your body does to food after you have swallowed it.

EATING MACHINE

Out Teeth-and-Tongue Machine (pages 102 and 103) is a separate machine. We made it to show what different teeth do.

TEETH AND TONGUE MACHINE

Our Breathing Machine (pages 108 and 109) shows how your ribs work with a special muscle to make you breathe.

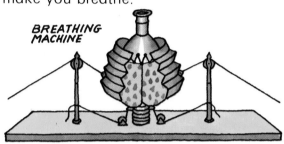

BREATHING MACHINE

We made up a mechanical man (pages 124 to 127) so that we could show how other muscles work to make your bones move.

MECHANICAL MAN

Real machines are much better than bodies at doing some things. Computers can calculate faster. Cranes can lift heavier loads. Cars can move faster.

But your body fits together so well that it can do many different jobs — and it can do lots of them at the same time.

No scientist has ever been able to make a machine as neat and light as your body that could do even half the things your body does. And no machine can have new ideas, or make jokes, or change its mind — or have babies.

Written by Judy Hindley and Christopher Rawson

Illustrated by Colin King

Designed by John Jamieson and Geoff Davis

Medical Adviser : Susan Jenkins, MRCP, DCH
Educational Adviser : Paula Varrow

Contents of Part Three

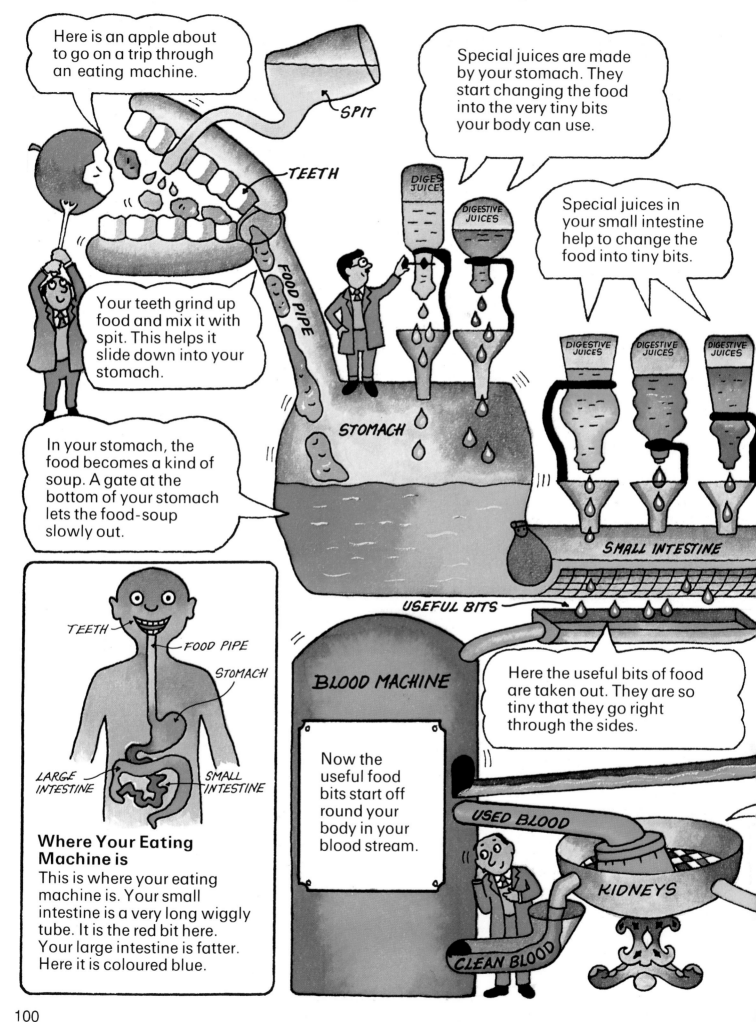

100

An Eating Machine

Here is a machine we have invented that shows the main things that happen to the food you eat.

In your food there are things your body can use and things it cannot use. In your eating machine, the food is chopped and churned and changed into tiny bits by special juices. This is called digestion.

Then the useful things can be sorted out and sent where they are needed.

To get rid of bad food, muscles in your chest and near your stomach squeeze together. The gate at the end of your stomach stays shut, so the food goes up.

CHEST SQUEEZES DOWN

Stomach juices mixed with the food make it taste sour.

MUSCLE SQUEEZES UP

GATE STAYS SHUT

LARGE INTESTINE

The rubbish is very sludgy by the time it gets here. You get rid of it when you go to the lavatory.

WATER

Water is taken out here. It goes right through the sides. It becomes part of your blood.

Used blood goes to the kidneys to be cleaned. Clean blood goes back into the blood stream. The waste water goes into the lavatory.

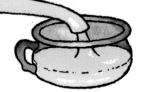

A Teeth-and-Tongue Machine

This teeth-and-tongue machine gets food ready to be swallowed. It does the main things your teeth and tongue do.

This machine has a chopper and some grinding wheels. You have special kinds of teeth to do what these parts do. Below you can see how they look.

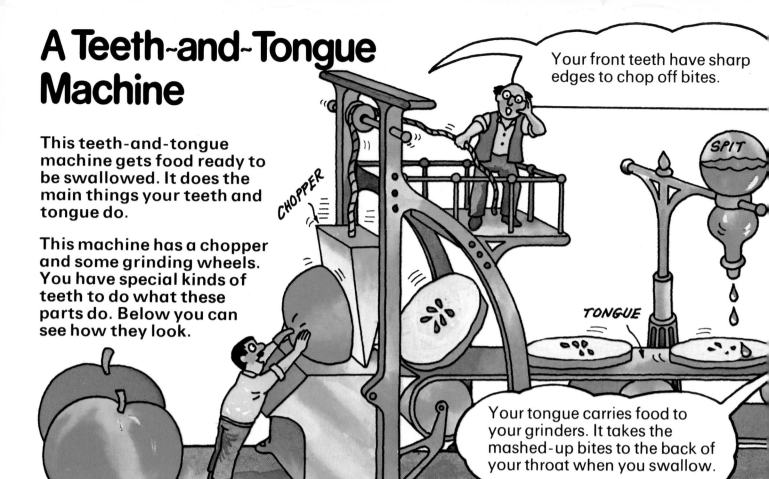

Your front teeth have sharp edges to chop off bites.

CHOPPER

SPIT

TONGUE

Your tongue carries food to your grinders. It takes the mashed-up bites to the back of your throat when you swallow.

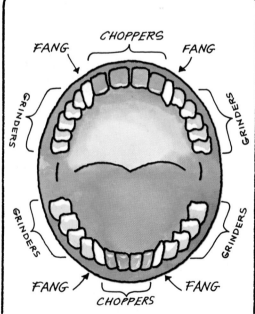

Count the Teeth
After your first teeth fall out, you will grow 32 big teeth. Your jaw has to grow too, so they fit in. This picture shows how many of each kind will grow.

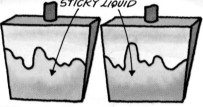

STICKY LIQUID

Why do Teeth go Bad?
Liquid from chewed food sticks to your teeth. You cannot see this. But if you slide your tongue round your teeth, they may feel gluey.

DRILL OUT THE BAD PART!

How are Teeth Mended?
Germs live in the holes of bad teeth. They eat the good part, which makes the holes deeper. Dentists have to drill out this germy part.

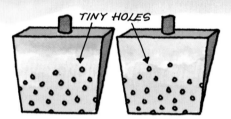

TINY HOLES

If the stickiness stays, it makes tiny holes in your teeth. This is a bit like the rust you get on metal tools when you leave them wet.

STOP UP THE HOLES!

The hard outside of teeth cannot grow back. Dentists have to fill the holes with metal to keep germs out.

102

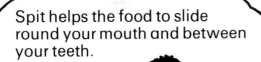

Spit helps the food to slide round your mouth and between your teeth.

A kind of trap-door at the back of your throat closes your windpipe when you swallow.

GRINDERS

TONGUE

TRAP DOOR

WINDPIPE   FOOD PIPE

Your back teeth are bumpy on top. You can feel it. They work together, grinding food between the bumps.

Your bumpy grinders need careful cleaning when they finish work. Food often sticks between the bumps.

FEELING PART

Germs in the air make the holes deeper and deeper. When they reach the feeling part under the hard part of your teeth, they hurt a lot.

Tongues and Tasting

SALTY HAM   SWEET ICE CREAM   SOUR LEMON   BITTER ORANGE PEEL

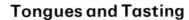

Nerves from your tongue carry messages to your brain. The nerves come from tiny spots called taste buds. They tell you about sweet, salt, sour and bitter tastes.

Your nose tells your brain about many food flavours. If you hold your nose while you eat, you can only taste sweet, sour, salt and bitter.

What are Fangs for?
Fangs are the pointy teeth beside your top set of choppers. Dogs use theirs to tear meat and gnaw bones. We do not use ours much.

There are patches of different kinds of taste buds on your tongue. There are lots of sweet-tasters on the tip.

Bitter-tasters are near the back of your tongue. Often you do not notice a bitter taste until you are ready to swallow.

What is Blood?

Most of your blood is a colourless liquid called plasma. The red cells in it make it look red.

Blood is crowded with special cells doing different kinds of work. This picture shows some of the things they do.

Your blood stream flows round your body like a river, to bring supplies to all the body cells.

The red blood cells bring oxygen from the lungs to the body cells. They take away the waste gas made by body cells as they work.

These fighting white cells kill germs that get into your body. They are bigger than red cells, but you do not have so many of them.

WHITE BLOOD CELLS

RED BLOOD CELLS

OUT   IN   OUT

OXYGEN

WASTE GAS

GERM →

PLASMA

HOW BLOOD GETS OXYGEN....

WASTE GAS

LUNGS

OXYGEN

WATER....

EATING MACHINERY

WATER →

Red blood cells bring waste gas to your lungs. They exchange it for oxygen.

The air you breathe into your lungs carries oxygen. The air you breathe out takes away waste gas.

Lots of water goes into your blood through the eating machinery. More than half of your blood is water.

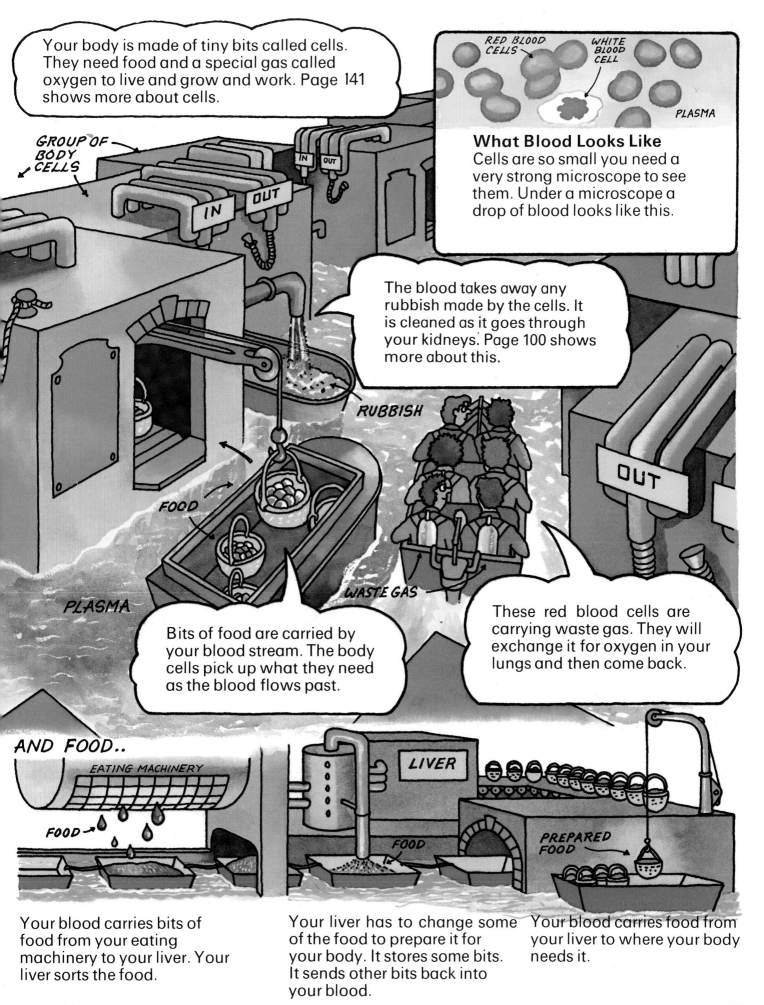

Your body is made of tiny bits called cells. They need food and a special gas called oxygen to live and grow and work. Page 141 shows more about cells.

What Blood Looks Like
Cells are so small you need a very strong microscope to see them. Under a microscope a drop of blood looks like this.

The blood takes away any rubbish made by the cells. It is cleaned as it goes through your kidneys. Page 100 shows more about this.

Bits of food are carried by your blood stream. The body cells pick up what they need as the blood flows past.

These red blood cells are carrying waste gas. They will exchange it for oxygen in your lungs and then come back.

Your blood carries bits of food from your eating machinery to your liver. Your liver sorts the food.

Your liver has to change some of the food to prepare it for your body. It stores some bits. It sends other bits back into your blood.

Your blood carries food from your liver to where your body needs it.

How Blood Goes Round

Your blood stream has many tiny branches. The branches join up so that the blood goes round and round. The map at the bottom of the page shows how this happens.

Your heart is a pump that keeps blood flowing round. It squeezes out blood like a squeezy bottle. It sends blood to your lungs to get rid of waste gas and pick up oxygen. It sends blood round your body to take oxygen to all the cells.

Your blood goes through rubbery pipes called blood vessels. Page 140 shows where your main blood vessels are.

How Your Heart Works
Your heart is a muscle with four tubes, like this. The tubes are big blood vessels. The picture shows where each of them leads.

A message from the brain makes your heart squeeze. This pumps blood out and sucks it in through different tubes. Tiny gates open and shut in your heart while this happens.

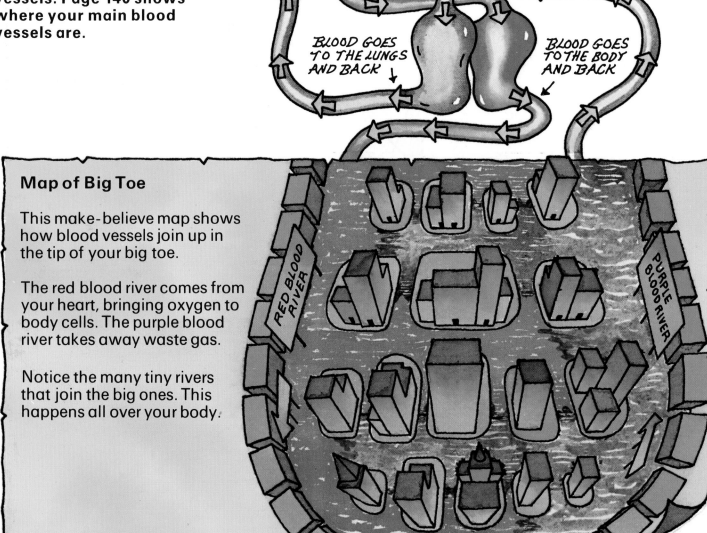

Map of Big Toe

This make-believe map shows how blood vessels join up in the tip of your big toe.

The red blood river comes from your heart, bringing oxygen to body cells. The purple blood river takes away waste gas.

Notice the many tiny rivers that join the big ones. This happens all over your body.

What Makes Your Heart Beat Fast?
Your body has to make lots of energy when you run or dance or play football.

Your heart has to pump very hard and fast. It has to get lots of blood up to your lungs and back to get the oxygen your body needs to make energy.

Put your hand on your chest like this when you have been running. Feel how fast your heart is beating. You breathe more quickly too.

Can Blood Run Backwards?
There are many tiny gates inside the blood vessels going to your heart. They can only move one way, like trap doors. The blood can only go up — it cannot fall back.

How to See Your Tiniest Blood Vessels
Look in the mirror. Gently pull your lower eyelid down. Under it you will see red threadly bits. These are some of your tiniest blood vessels.

You have many tiny blood vessels. If you could join them all up end to end, they would stretch more than twice around the world.

ZZZZZ WIGGLE

How Does Your Blood Get Back to Your Heart?
As you move about, your muscles help move blood back to your heart. When you slow down your blood slows down as well.

If you wiggle your toes you can keep your feet from going to sleep. The working toe muscles speed the blood along.

Watch Your Blood Move
The blue line on the inside of your wrist is blood. Rub your thumb up it, like this. You will see the blood stop — then follow your thumb.

How You Breathe

Your lungs are full of tiny holes, like sponges. They hang in your chest, in a space made by your ribs and a special muscle. When you breathe in, your chest swells up. Air fills your lungs like water in a sponge. This machine shows how it happens.

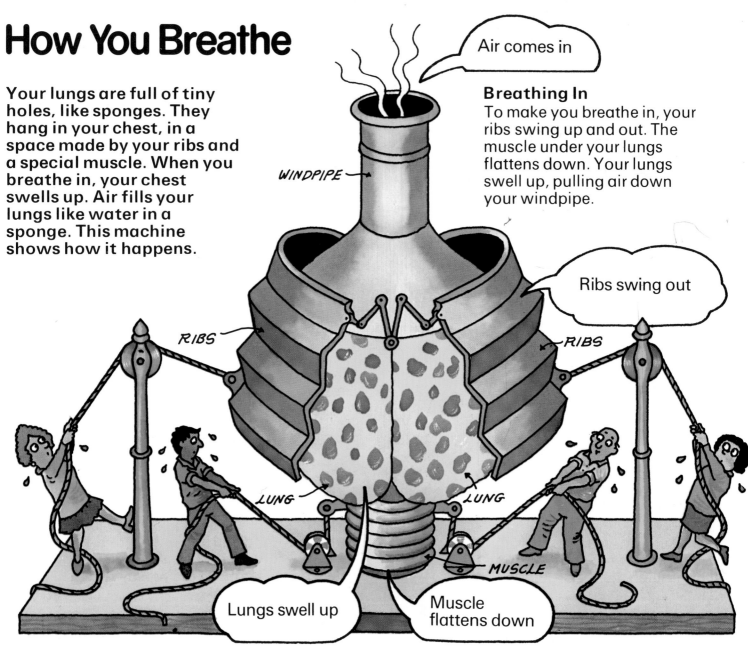

Air comes in

Breathing In
To make you breathe in, your ribs swing up and out. The muscle under your lungs flattens down. Your lungs swell up, pulling air down your windpipe.

WINDPIPE

Ribs swing out

RIBS

RIBS

LUNG

LUNG

MUSCLE

Lungs swell up

Muscle flattens down

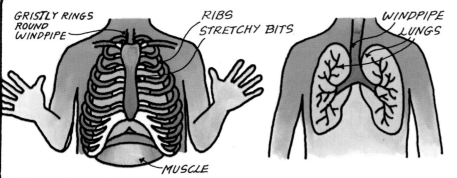

GRISTLY RINGS ROUND WINDPIPE

RIBS STRETCHY BITS

WINDPIPE LUNGS

MUSCLE

Your Breathing Machine
The muscle under your lungs is shaped like an upside-down saucer. When you breathe in, it flattens. Your ribs swell out, stretching the bits that join to your breastbone.

How Your Lungs Look
Your lungs are like sponges. They are made of tiny air sacs. Around each one is a net of blood vessels. They take oxygen from the air.

2·5 M. LONG

2·5 M. WIDE

2·5 M. HIGH

BREATHED OUT AIR

How Much Air Goes Through Your Lungs?
Lots of air goes in and out of your lungs each day. If you could trap all the air that goes out, it would nearly fill a room this big.

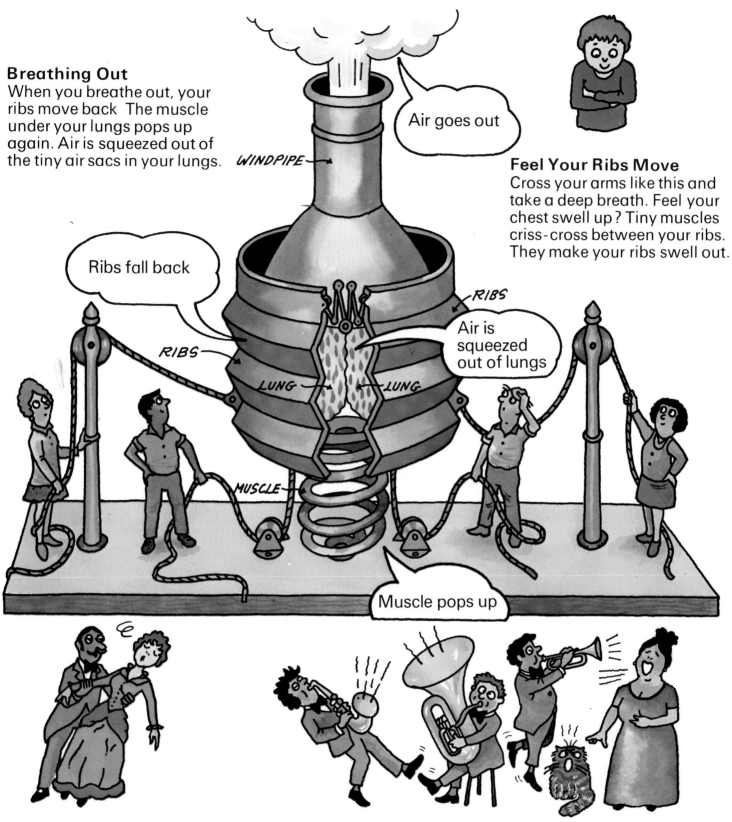

Breathing Out
When you breathe out, your ribs move back. The muscle under your lungs pops up again. Air is squeezed out of the tiny air sacs in your lungs.

Air goes out

Feel Your Ribs Move
Cross your arms like this and take a deep breath. Feel your chest swell up? Tiny muscles criss-cross between your ribs. They make your ribs swell out.

Ribs fall back

WINDPIPE

RIBS

Air is squeezed out of lungs

RIBS

LUNG   *LUNG*

MUSCLE

Muscle pops up

Tummy Breathing
The working muscle under your lungs pushes your stomach out and in. When ladies squeezed their waists with corsets, it could not work. They often fainted.

Getting More Lung Power
If you sing or play things like trumpets, you need lots of puff. Learn to use the muscle under your lungs to get more lung power.

To practise, push the top of your stomach out as you breathe in. Hold your hand just under your chest, like this, to feel it move.

A Talking Machine

This machine does the main things that you do when you talk.

You tighten your vocal cords to make them vibrate when you breathe out. This makes sound waves — special ripples in the air. You use your teeth and tongue and mouth to turn the sound waves into words.

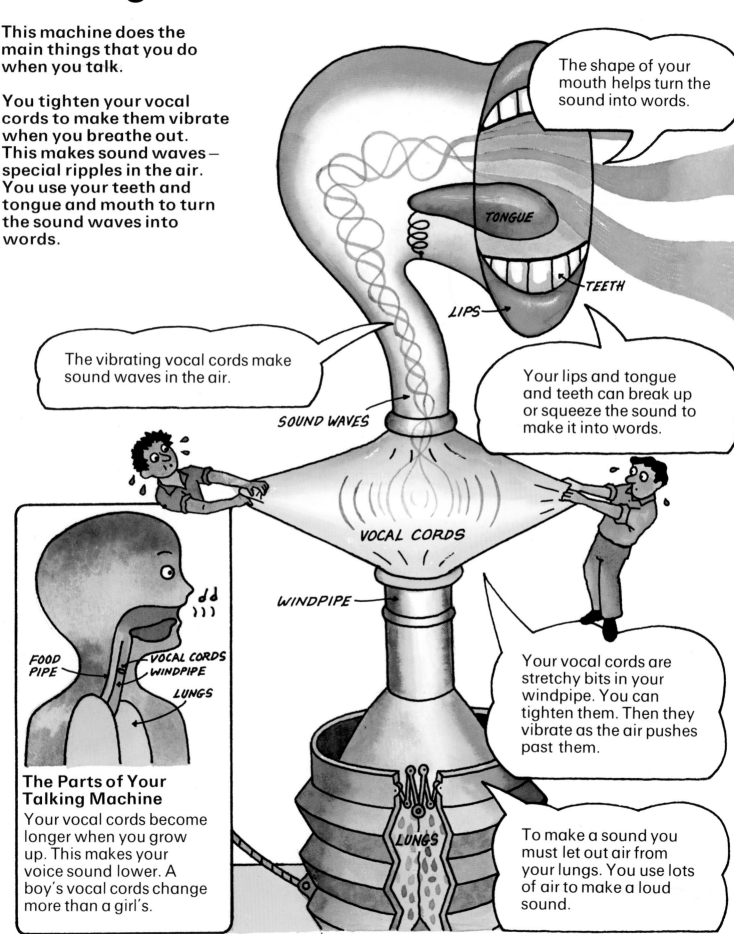

The shape of your mouth helps turn the sound into words.

TONGUE

TEETH

LIPS

The vibrating vocal cords make sound waves in the air.

SOUND WAVES

Your lips and tongue and teeth can break up or squeeze the sound to make it into words.

VOCAL CORDS

WINDPIPE

Your vocal cords are stretchy bits in your windpipe. You can tighten them. Then they vibrate as the air pushes past them.

FOOD PIPE

VOCAL CORDS
WINDPIPE

LUNGS

LUNGS

The Parts of Your Talking Machine

Your vocal cords become longer when you grow up. This makes your voice sound lower. A boy's vocal cords change more than a girl's.

To make a sound you must let out air from your lungs. You use lots of air to make a loud sound.

Making Words
The shape of your mouth changes to make different parts of words.

See how these people stretch and shape their mouths to make different sounds.

Watch yourself in the mirror while you talk. See how your own mouth changes shape.

Lip Reading
You can sometimes work out what people are saying from the shape of their mouths.

Think how useful this might be if you were a spy!

Making Sound Waves
Blow up a balloon and let it go. The rushing-out air will make the neck flap very fast. This is called vibration. Hear the sound waves it makes?

If you put a tube in the neck like this, there will be no sound as the air rushes out. The neck cannot vibrate and make sound waves.

Try stretching the neck to make high or low sounds. The wider you stretch, the lower the sound. Your vocal cords work like this.

What Ears Do

Your ear is a machine that picks up sound waves and turns them into messages to your brain. We have invented a machine that might be able to do the things your ear does. Part of it sends balance messages to your brain. Your ear does this too.

Sound waves go through a funnel to your ear drum. They make the drum vibrate.

EAR   FUNNEL   EAR DRUM

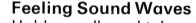

When you blow a trumpet you make sound waves. Sound waves are like ripples in the air. You cannot see them but you can feel them.

This funnel has wax and hairs to trap specks of dirt that might hurt the inside of your ear.

INNER EAR FILLED WITH LIQUID
BALANCE PART
EAR DRUM   NERVES
FUNNEL
THREE BONES   MIDDLE EAR

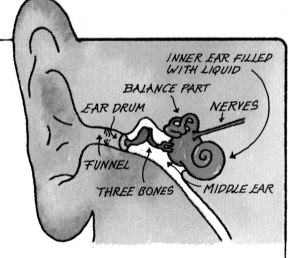

Feeling Sound Waves
Hold a cardboard tube against a balloon like this and speak into it. The sound waves will make the balloon vibrate. You can feel this with your fingers.

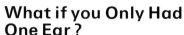

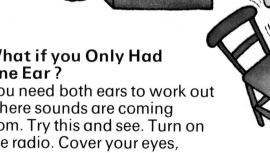

Your Ear Machine
Your inner ear is a curled-up tube with three extra loops. The liquid in the curled-up part picks up sound waves. The extra loops are to help you keep your balance.

What if you Only Had One Ear?
You need both ears to work out where sounds are coming from. Try this and see. Turn on the radio. Cover your eyes, cover up one ear, and turn around a few times. Where is the radio?

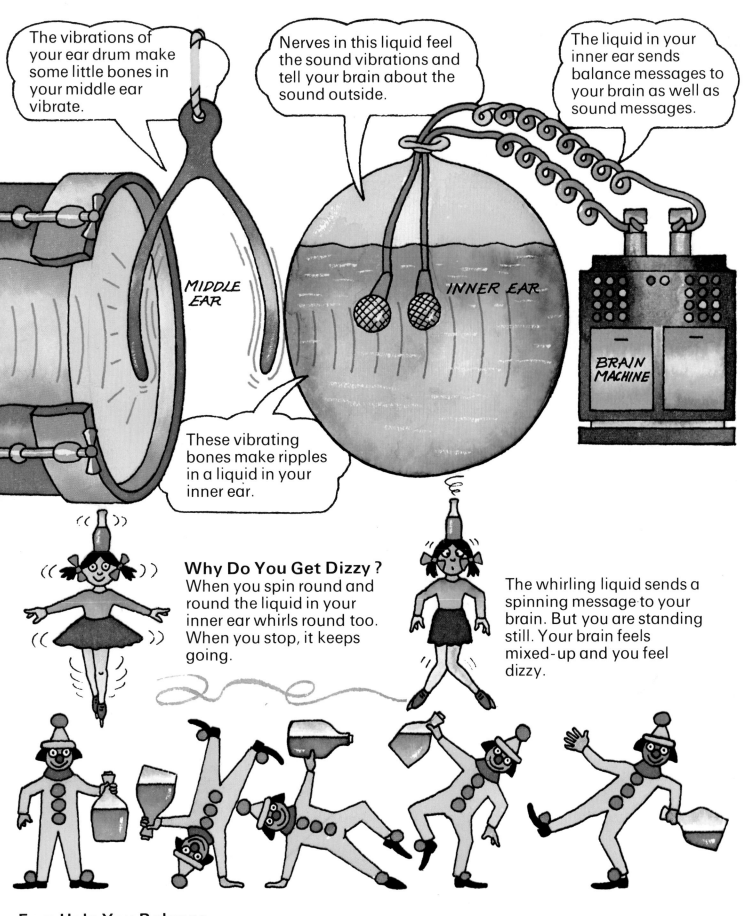

The vibrations of your ear drum make some little bones in your middle ear vibrate.

Nerves in this liquid feel the sound vibrations and tell your brain about the sound outside.

The liquid in your inner ear sends balance messages to your brain as well as sound messages.

MIDDLE EAR

INNER EAR

BRAIN MACHINE

These vibrating bones make ripples in a liquid in your inner ear.

Why Do You Get Dizzy?
When you spin round and round the liquid in your inner ear whirls round too. When you stop, it keeps going.

The whirling liquid sends a spinning message to your brain. But you are standing still. Your brain feels mixed-up and you feel dizzy.

Ears Help You Balance
The liquid in your inner ear stays level when you move, like the water in this jar.

See how the water sloshes round the jar when the jar tips and turns.

As the liquid moves around in your inner ear, nerves in the liquid tell your brain what is happening.

How an Eye Works

Your eye is very much like a camera. A camera takes in light rays from the outside world and squeezes them to fit on a small piece of film. Your eye gathers light rays into a very tiny picture that fits on the back of your eyeball. A nerve from this spot sends the picture to your brain.

On the right is a machine we invented to show the important parts of your eye and what they do.

Light rays from the spotlight bounce off the clown and make him see-able.

LIGHT RAYS

LIGHT RAYS

Light rays from the clown go through this lens. The lens bends the light rays.

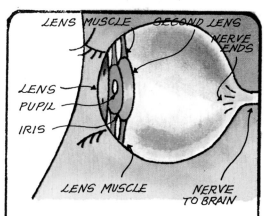

LENS MUSCLE · SECOND LENS · NERVE ENDS · LENS · PUPIL · IRIS · LENS MUSCLE · NERVE TO BRAIN

How Your Eye Looks

This picture shows where the different parts of your eye are. You can also see the muscles that change the shape of the lens inside your eye.

What a Lens Does

A magnifying glass is a lens. You can make it bend light rays into an upside-down picture. Try this.

Hold a magnifying glass between a torch and some white paper. Move the glass backwards and forwards until you see a clear pattern of light on the paper. You may have to move the paper.

Now hold your thumb over the torch, at the top, like this.

Where is your thumb in the pattern on the paper?

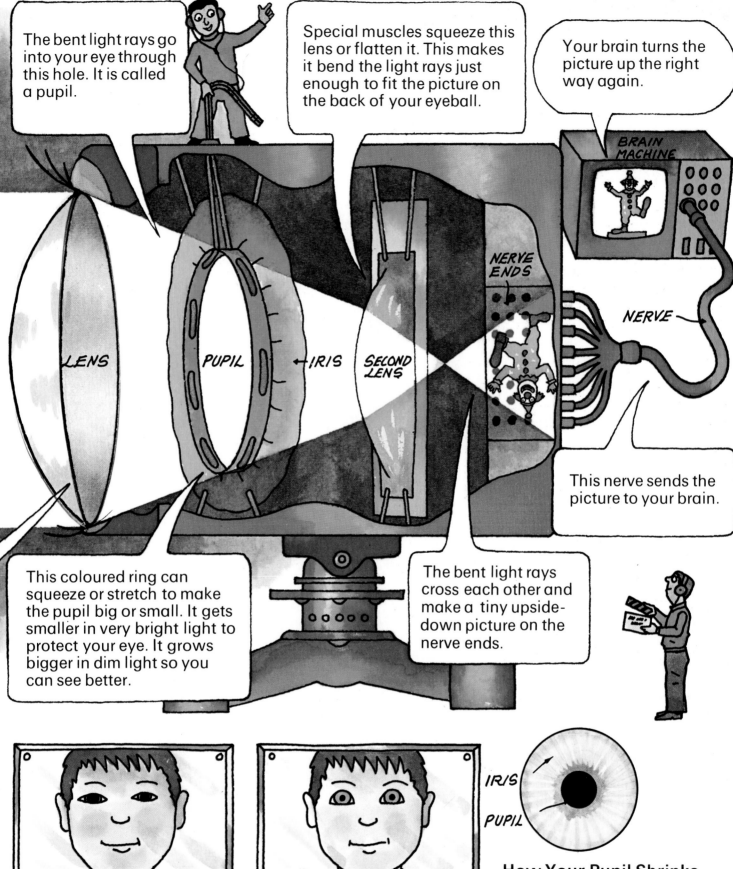

The bent light rays go into your eye through this hole. It is called a pupil.

Special muscles squeeze this lens or flatten it. This makes it bend the light rays just enough to fit the picture on the back of your eyeball.

Your brain turns the picture up the right way again.

BRAIN MACHINE

NERVE ENDS

NERVE

LENS

PUPIL

←IRIS

SECOND LENS

This nerve sends the picture to your brain.

This coloured ring can squeeze or stretch to make the pupil big or small. It gets smaller in very bright light to protect your eye. It grows bigger in dim light so you can see better.

The bent light rays cross each other and make a tiny upside-down picture on the nerve ends.

IRIS

PUPIL

Watch Your Pupil Shrink
Look in the mirror. Close your eyes nearly shut. Your pupils will get bigger.

Now open your eyes quickly. Watch carefully and you will see your pupils shrinking.

How Your Pupil Shrinks
The coloured ring round your pupil is called the iris. If you look closely, you can see rays. These are muscles that pull your iris in and out.

115

How Two Eyes Work Together

Each of your eyes sees a slightly different picture of the world. Your brain puts the two pictures together. On this page you can see how the picture changes in your brain.

When you look at something very close, it is easy to notice the difference in what your two eyes see. Just try this trick:

See-Through Pencil Trick
Print a word in large letters on some paper. Hold a pencil half-way between your eyes and the paper. If you close either eye, part of the word will be hidden. But if you stare hard at the paper with both eyes, you will see the whole word.

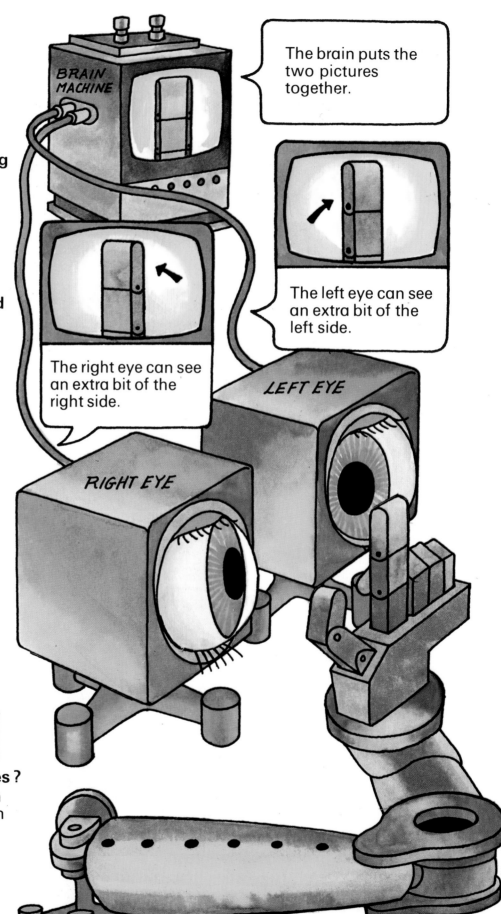

The brain puts the two pictures together.

The left eye can see an extra bit of the left side.

The right eye can see an extra bit of the right side.

BRAIN MACHINE

RIGHT EYE

LEFT EYE

Why Do You Have Two Eyes?
Close one eye. Hold a pencil in one hand. Stretch out your arm like this and try to touch something. Can you do it? Two eyes working together help you to see how close things are.

What Noses Do

This picture shows how your nose cleans and warms the air you breathe. The air is full of germs and tiny specks of dirt. We have made them into bugs so you can see how they get trapped.

A special gas floats away from things that have a smell. We have made it look like stars to show what happens to it.

BRAIN MACHINE

The smell gas hits some sticky feelers here. They send a message to the smelling nerve. The nerve tells your brain.

NERVE

SMELL FEELERS

BLOOD VESSELS

Tiny blood vessels in your nose act like a radiator. They warm cold air before it goes into your lungs.

STICKY PART

WARM CLEAN AIR

WINDPIPE

The hairs inside your nose help to clean the air. Germs and dirt get trapped in them.

The sticky lining of your nose traps dirt and germs. You clean them out when you blow your nose.

LUNGS

HAIRS

SPECIAL GAS

NOSTRIL

The air you breathe is full of germs and specks of dirt.

GERMS

A gas floats away from things that have a smell.

NERVE

SMELL FEELERS

WARM STICKY CAVE

HAIRS

NOSTRIL

WINDPIPE

Inside Your Nose
Your nostrils are two tunnels that lead to a warm, sticky cave behind your face. Here the air is cleaned and warmed before it goes into your lungs.

A Feeling Machine

Tiny nerves in your skin tell you if things are hot or cold, hard or soft, rough or smooth. Your fingers have many nerves. You use them a lot for finding out about things.

This machine explores the world, like your fingers. Its feelers act like the nerves in your skin. Each kind of feeler tests for something special.

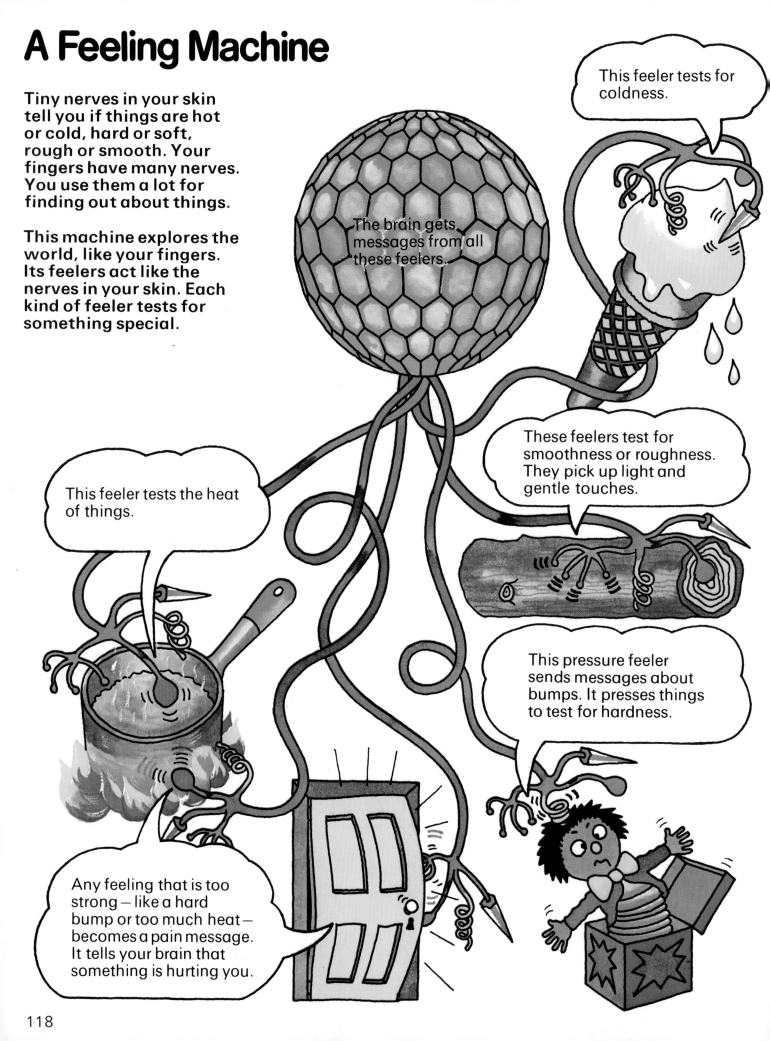

This feeler tests for coldness.

The brain gets messages from all these feelers.

These feelers test for smoothness or roughness. They pick up light and gentle touches.

This feeler tests the heat of things.

This pressure feeler sends messages about bumps. It presses things to test for hardness.

Any feeling that is too strong — like a hard bump or too much heat — becomes a pain message. It tells your brain that something is hurting you.

Touching, Feeling, Finding Out

Your brain gets feeling messages from nerves in your skin and nerves all through your body. These messages fool your brain sometimes. Read on and see why this happens.

The next pages show how your brain sorts out messages from your body.

Mysterious Pains
Tiny hurts on places like your feet and tongue can feel enormous. Why?

These places are crowded with feeling nerves. Your brain gets lots of pain messages — but they all come from one tiny spot.

Feely Box Trick
For this trick you need a box with two hand-holes and some things that feel funny.

Put the things inside, one by one, through your side. Get your friends to stick their hands through the other hole and guess what is inside.

Itchy Back Problems
The nerves on your back are far apart. A big space may have only one nerve. It is hard to tell just where a tickle itches.

Your Muscle Nerves
If someone wiggles your toe, you can tell without looking whether the toe is up or down. You get messages from feeling nerves in your muscles.

Why Do You Have Pains?
Nerves inside your body tell you when something is hurting your inside. This helps people to know what to do when you are ill.

Back Feeler Trick
Touch someone's back with a pencil. Then touch with two pencils at the same time. If the two pencils are closer than 2 cm, he may still think there is only one.

What Happens in Your Brain

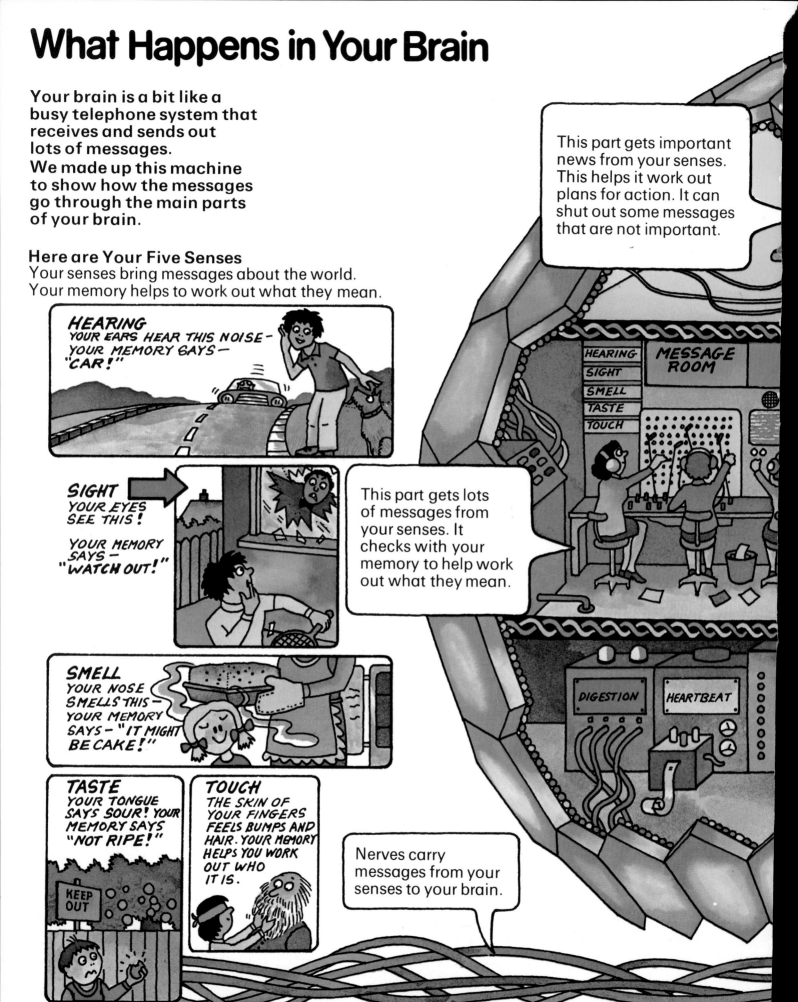

Your brain is a bit like a
busy telephone system that
receives and sends out
lots of messages.
We made up this machine
to show how the messages
go through the main parts
of your brain.

Here are Your Five Senses

Your senses bring messages about the world.
Your memory helps to work out what they mean.

HEARING
YOUR EARS HEAR THIS NOISE —
YOUR MEMORY SAYS —
"CAR!"

SIGHT
YOUR EYES
SEE THIS!

YOUR MEMORY
SAYS —
"WATCH OUT!"

SMELL
YOUR NOSE
SMELLS THIS —
YOUR MEMORY
SAYS — "IT MIGHT
BE CAKE!"

TASTE
YOUR TONGUE
SAYS SOUR! YOUR
MEMORY SAYS
"NOT RIPE!"

KEEP
OUT

TOUCH
THE SKIN OF
YOUR FINGERS
FEELS BUMPS AND
HAIR. YOUR MEMORY
HELPS YOU WORK
OUT WHO
IT IS.

This part gets important
news from your senses.
This helps it work out
plans for action. It can
shut out some messages
that are not important.

HEARING
SIGHT
SMELL
TASTE
TOUCH

MESSAGE
ROOM

This part gets lots
of messages from
your senses. It
checks with your
memory to help work
out what they mean.

DIGESTION   HEARTBEAT

Nerves carry
messages from your
senses to your brain.

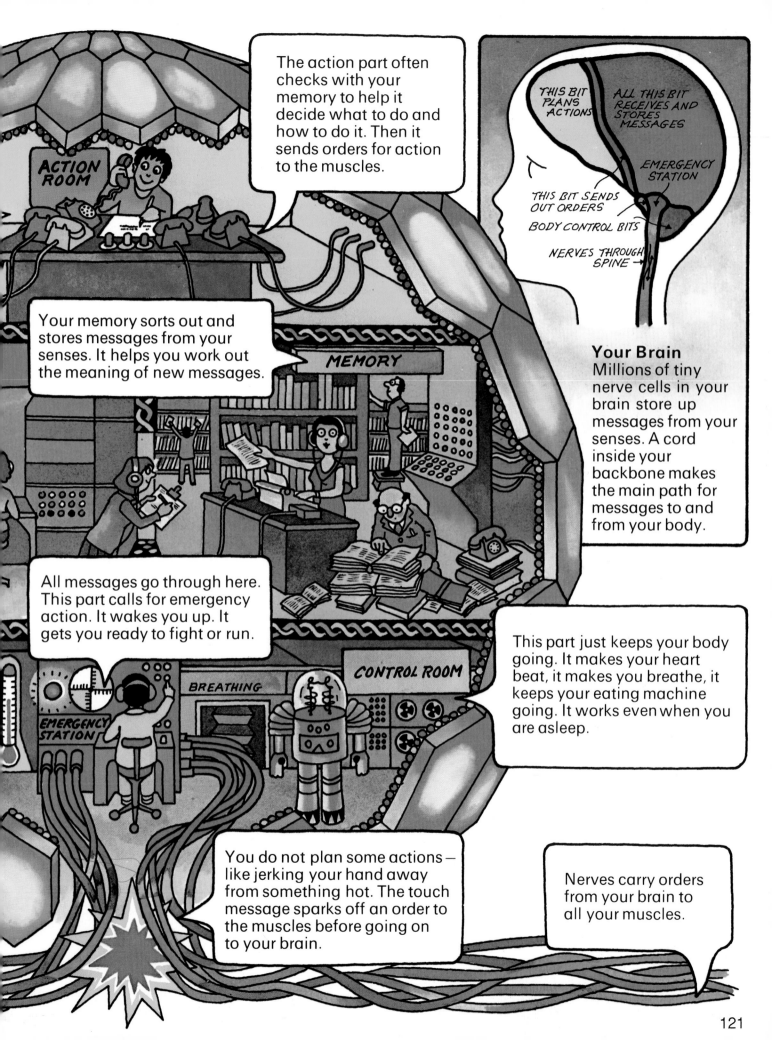

121

Alarm...

THIS IS YOU

You are sleeping soundly in a quiet room. Suddenly there is a scuffle at the open window.

You open your eyes and see a strange, dark shape. At first, you are terrified. You reach out and turn on the lamp.

THIS IS WHAT IS HAPPENING IN YOUR BRAIN

ACTION ROOM

ZZZZZZZZ

MESSAGE ROOM

ZZZZZZZZZ

MEMORY

ZZZZZ

EMERGENCY STATION

CONTROL ROOM

HEART KEEP GOING... LUNGS KEEP IT UP... GOOD WORK EATING MACHINE..

HEAR THIS! RED ALERT FROM EARS! EYES OPEN.... BODY ALERT..READY FOR ACTION....

EARS TO BRAIN! EMERGENCY, EMERGENCY!

EYES TO MESSAGE ROOM.. **DANGER,** GET HELP FAST!

EYES REPORT STRANGE FIGURE — TRY TO IDENTIFY —

ORDER TO HAND **QUICK!** REACH FOR THE LAMP SWITCH..

ACTION ROOM

MESSAGE ROOM

MEMORY

EMERGENCY STATION

CONTROL ROOM

Most of the brain is resting but the control room is always busy. And the emergency station is always ready for action. Just watch it now.

Now the newsroom can find out more about the strange noise. The action part can get the body's muscles going.

122

A Story of Your Brain in Action

Oh, it's only the owl that lives in the tree outside. He gives a hoot, to prove it, before he flies away.

You turn off the light and go to sleep again.

Here the brain is using messages from many senses to work out what is happening. It uses memories, too.

The emergency is over. Most of the brain shuts down. The emergency station will take over now, to watch over the body while it sleeps.

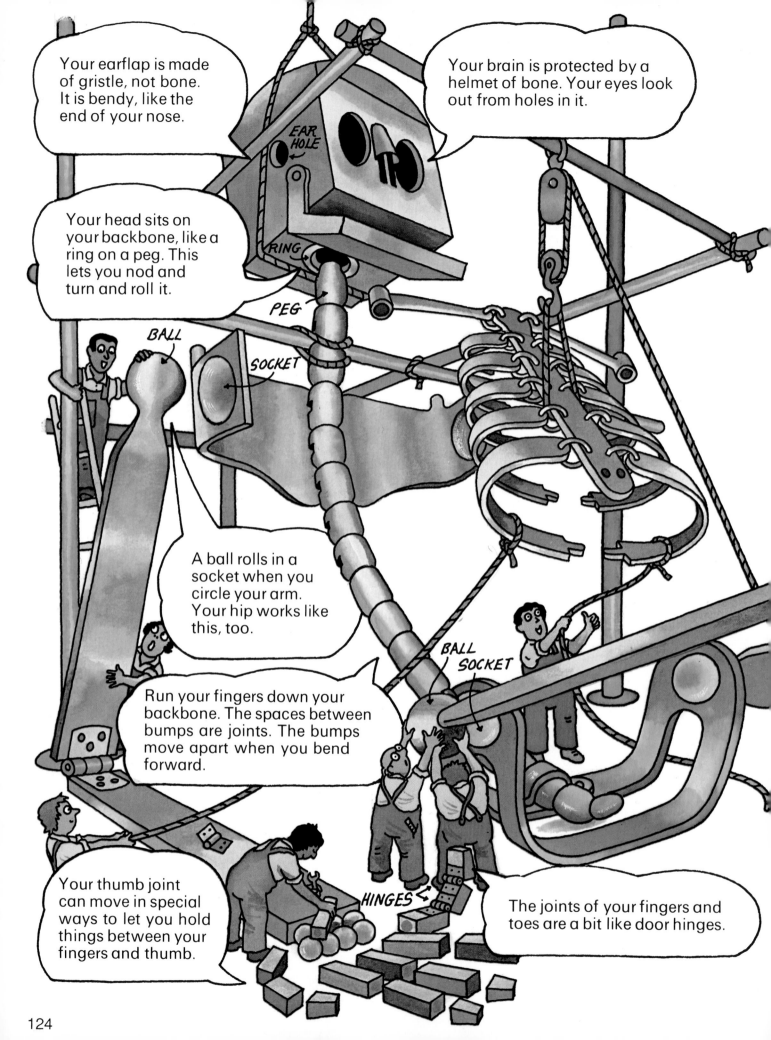

How Bones Fit Together

The places where your bones link up are called joints. This made-up skeleton shows how your main joints work.

This skeleton will not work as well as yours. Its metal pieces will be hard to move. Real bone is light. It is full of tiny holes, like honeycomb.

This is Your Skeleton
Muscles join these sticking-out bits. Pads of gristle make cushions between each two bones.

Many little joints in your feet and ankles move when you run. Try to run on your heels and see the difference.

You use these joints a lot. Try going stiff-legged and stiff-armed for half an hour. Can you eat? Can you throw a ball? Can you run? Or climb stairs?

OIL

Your body makes a special liquid that oils your joints. Otherwise you might creak.

LIGAMENTS

Special covers help hold joints together and keep in the oily liquid.

The little bones in your ankles and wrists let you make small, quick movements. The ends of the bones slide across each other.

Tough straps called ligaments hold the joints in place.

Your elbows and knees are special hinge joints. They can move in more ways than the joints in your fingers.

SPECIAL COVER

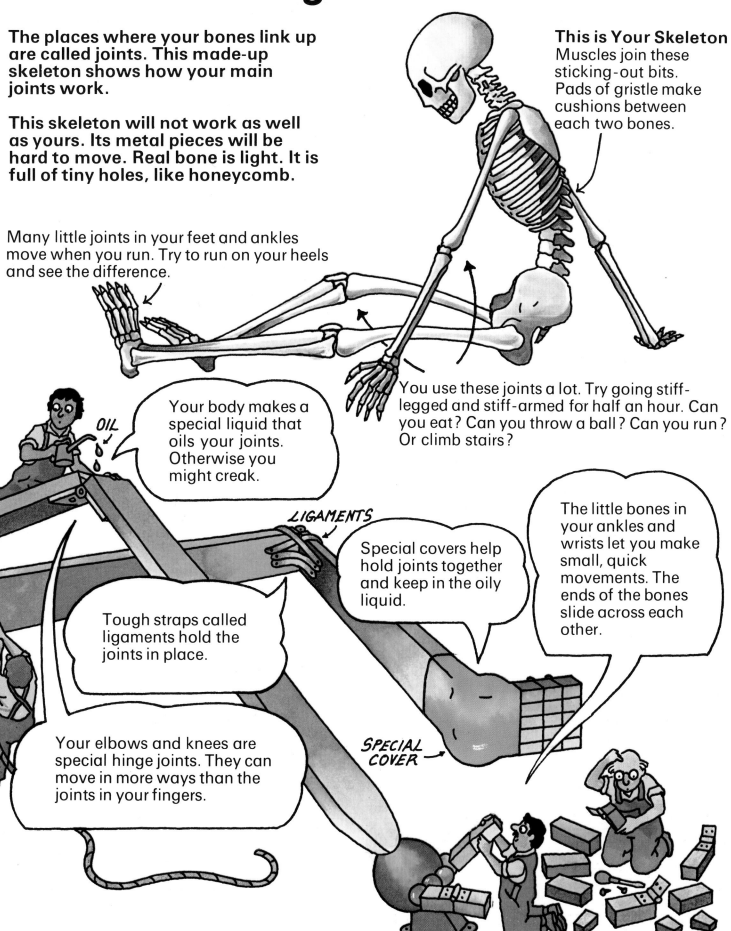

125

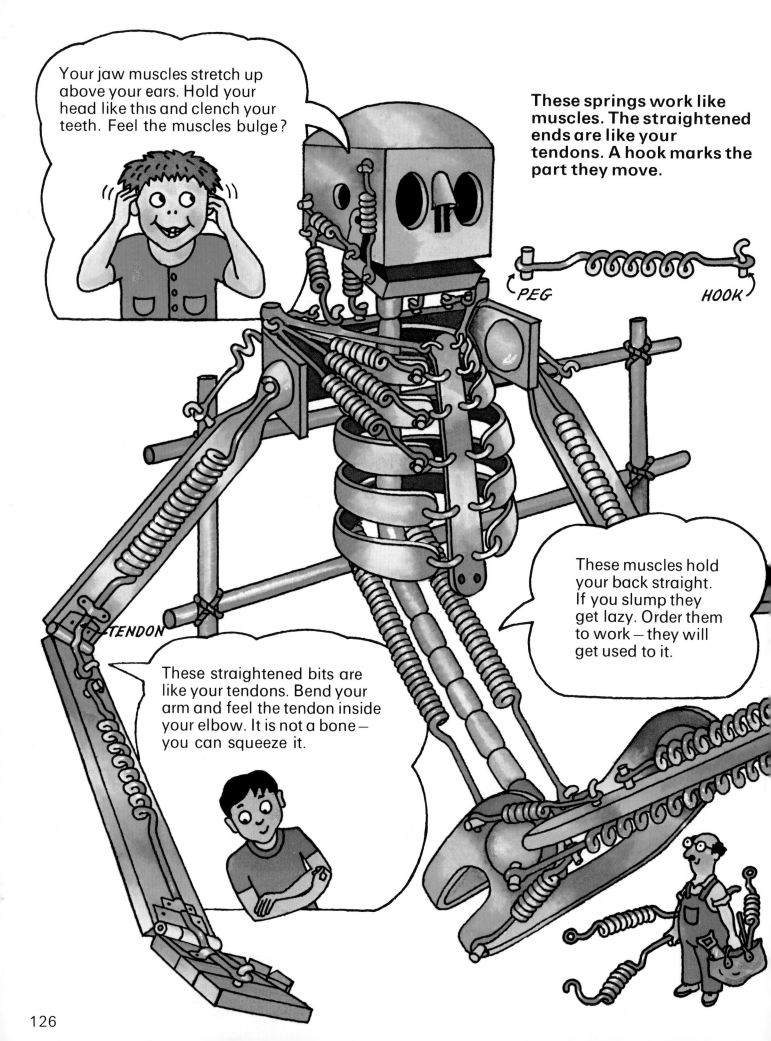

How Muscles Work

The springs on this skeleton work like muscles. Look to see how they join the movable parts. They work these bits the way your muscles work your bones.

Nerves connect these muscles to your brain. Messages from your brain make them work. Your brain can send many messages and work many muscles at the same time.

Other muscles work things inside you, like your heart and eating machinery. A special part of your brain keeps these muscles going.

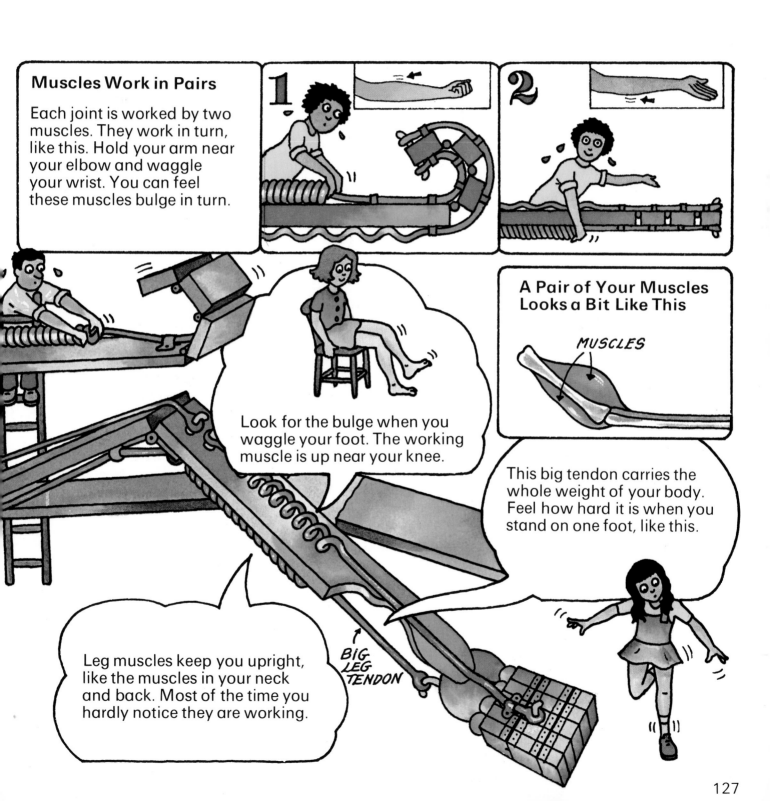

Muscles Work in Pairs

Each joint is worked by two muscles. They work in turn, like this. Hold your arm near your elbow and waggle your wrist. You can feel these muscles bulge in turn.

Look for the bulge when you waggle your foot. The working muscle is up near your knee.

A Pair of Your Muscles Looks a Bit Like This

MUSCLES

This big tendon carries the whole weight of your body. Feel how hard it is when you stand on one foot, like this.

Leg muscles keep you upright, like the muscles in your neck and back. Most of the time you hardly notice they are working.

BIG LEG TENDON

What Skin Does

All over your body is a coat of skin. You can only see the surface of it. On this page we have made a huge picture of a piece of skin to show what happens underneath.

The skin you see is a layer of dead bits. This layer is dry and tough and waterproof. It protects your body from germs and from drying up.

Just under it is a second layer where new skin is made. These bits are fed by blood vessels in the deep layer. They die as they get pushed up to the surface.

What Would Happen If You Had No Skin?

Your body is made mostly of water. There is even some water in your bones. If you had no skin, the sun and air would dry you up like a prune.

Skin is Waterproof

Your skin makes oil which helps to keep it waterproof. Water does not soak into your skin. You can rub it off with a towel.

Why Should You Wash?

Dirt and dust from the air stick to the oil made by your skin. You have to use soap and warm water to get the dirty oil off.

When it is Hot and Sunny

When you are hot, the sweat glands make more sweat. The sweat goes out through pores in your skin. As it dries, it cools down your skin.

Your blood takes heat from your body. When you are hot, more blood moves through the vessels near the surface of your skin. Then the air can cool it.

Sunlight makes the colour cells go darker. Some of the sun's rays are bad for you. Dark skin protects your body from the harmful rays.

When it is Cold

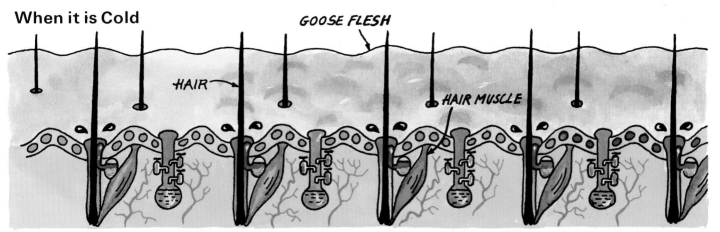

The air takes heat from your skin. When it is cold your blood vessels squeeze down in your skin to keep the warmth in. This makes you look paler.

Cold makes your hair muscles tighten. Then your hair stands up. On furry animals, hair traps a blanket of warm air. This helps to keep them warm.

When a hair muscle tightens, it gets short and fat. This squeezes out oil, makes your hair stand up, and makes goose flesh on your skin.

129

How Bodies Fight Germs

Your body is always being attacked by germs. But it is well defended, like the castle in this picture. Your skin is a strong wall — like a castle wall.

Germs cannot get through healthy skin. If skin is hurt, cells in the blood help to heal it and fight off the germs. They act like the warriors here.

Germs can get into your body through openings like your mouth and nose. But each of these is protected in some way. And there are ways you can help your body to defend itself. Look round and see.

> Tears kill germs. When you blink, tears wash your eyes.

> Your nose has sticky hairs that trap germs in the air you breathe.

> Spit washes germs down into your stomach. Stomach juices can kill most germs.

> Your mouth is an easy place for germs to get in. Be careful what you put in it.

SPIT

← *GERM ARMY*

What are Germs?

Germs are tiny creatures, too small to see. If they get into your body they make you ill. They make poisons. They become powerful armies.

Germs like warm, dark, dirty places. Sun and fresh air kill them. Soapy water kills them. Good food helps your body make weapons to fight them.

Why do You Get Injections?

Some germs have secret weapons. If a lot of them made a surprise attack you would be very ill. So the Doctor shoots some weak germs into you.

NEEDLE

Your ear hole has wax and hairs to trap germs.

Special white cells in your blood fight germs. Different kinds do different jobs. Some of them corner the germs and others kill them.

Your blood is always moving round your body. When germs attack, your blood carries messages for help. Then lots of fighting white cells come.

RED BLOOD CELLS

WHITE BLOOD CELL

EAR HOLE

CUT →

SWEAT PORES

Repair cells make a net and other cells bunch up behind it. Then blood cannot run out and germs cannot get in.

Your blood has special repair cells. When you are cut they make some gluey stuff that turns tiny bits in your blood into a net.

Tiny holes called pores let out sweat. Clean sweat kills germs. But old sweat traps dirt — so wash it off.

Your blood cells learn about the new weapons from the weak germs, and work out how to destroy them. Then you are prepared for an attack.

What is a Scab?

Part of your blood makes a net when you are cut. Your blood cells bunch up behind it. This makes a blood clot. Dried clotted blood becomes a scab.

The scab protects you while new skin is built. When the new skin is ready, the scab falls off.

Shopping-Trip Game

On the right are pictures of seven important kinds of food. You need a little of each kind at least every few days to stay really fit and healthy.

Play this game to practice choosing the right kinds of food.

The object of this game is to get some of each of the seven important kinds of food before you get Home. Make a score card like the one shown below. Mark it each time you land on a food square. The winner is the first player Home with a Seven-Up.

Sweets take up room needed for important things. If you score more than one of these, you must return to Start.

Rules
Each player needs a counter, a pencil and a score card. Throw a dice to see how many places you may move. Score your card every time you land on a food square. If you collect two sweet things cross out both and return to Start. If you get Home without a Seven-Up, return to Start. You may use your turn to swap places with another player. He does not lose his next turn.

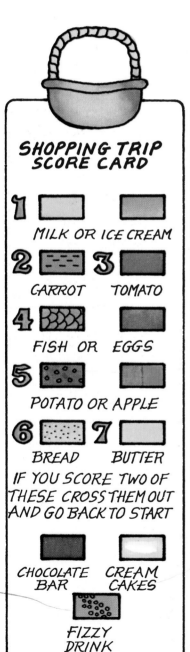

SHOPPING TRIP SCORE CARD

1 — MILK OR ICE CREAM

2 CARROT **3** TOMATO

4 FISH OR EGGS

5 POTATO OR APPLE

6 BREAD **7** BUTTER

IF YOU SCORE TWO OF THESE CROSS THEM OUT AND GO BACK TO START

CHOCOLATE BAR — CREAM CAKES

FIZZY DRINK

1 SCORE FISH

2 SCORE EGGS

3 SCORE BUTTER AND MILK

14 SCORE POTATOES

13 CHOCOLATE MELTS- CROSS OFF SCORE

12 SCORE FIZZY DRINK

15 SCORE BREAD

16 SCORE CREAM CAKES

17 POTATOES ARE BAD- CROSS OUT ONE POTATO SCORE

Food Groups

1
Milk and cheese for strong bones and healthy teeth.

2
Leafy green and yellow vegetables for shiny hair and good skin.

3
These help to fight germs — especially cold germs.

4
Meat, fish and eggs for good muscle.

5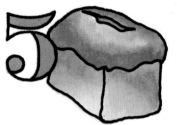
Brown bread and cereals for energy.

6
These vegetables and fruit help all round.

7
Butter for healthy skin and hair.

4 SCORE ICE CREAM

5 EGGS BROKEN. CROSS OUT ONE EGG SCORE.

6 ICE CREAM MELTS — CROSS OUT SCORE.

7 SCORE CHOCOLATE BAR

11 FISH LOST — CROSS OUT ONE FISH SCORE

10 SCORE TOMATOES

9 SCORE APPLES

8 SCORE CARROTS

18 DROP CREAM CAKES — CROSS OFF SCORE

19 APPLE HAS WORM CROSS OUT ONE APPLE SCORE

20 TOMATOES SQUASHED CROSS OUT ONE TOMATO SCORE

HOME

How a Baby Starts

A baby starts when two special cells meet – a sperm cell from a man's body and an egg cell from a woman's body. Joined inside the woman's body, these two cells grow into a whole new person.

Men and women each have special bits for making these cells and helping them join up. We made up these Mum and Dad machines to show how they work.

The Dad Machine

Sperm cells go out through the penis. It must get long and strong to reach inside the woman's body.

BRAIN

At special times, extra blood is pumped into the spongy walls of the penis. This makes it long and hard. The pictures below show this.

Sperm and waste water go out through the same pipe. A tiny gate shuts off waste water while sperm goes through.

BLOOD MACHINE

BLOOD VESSEL

PENIS

WASTE WATER TANK

SPERM TANK

The sperm tanks are called testicles. They make lots of sperm each day. They store it until all the machinery is ready to work.

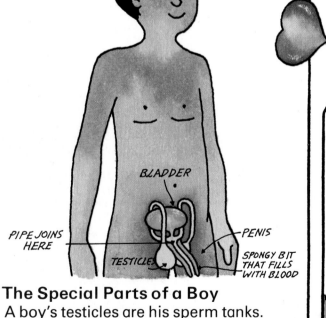

BLADDER

PIPE JOINS HERE

PENIS

TESTICLES

SPONGY BIT THAT FILLS WITH BLOOD

The Special Parts of a Boy
A boy's testicles are his sperm tanks. They start working usually between the ages of 10 and 18.
The sperm pipes join the pipe that takes waste water from his bladder.

How They Join Up
Extra blood pumped into the penis makes it stretch out.

The Mum Machine

This stretchy tunnel joins the uterus to the special opening in the woman's body.

Thousands of tiny egg cells are stored in here. Every four weeks, one egg slips down towards the uterus.

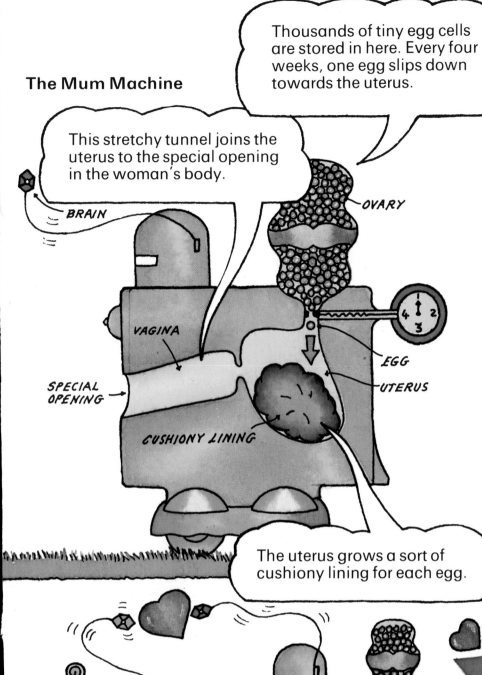

BRAIN

OVARY

VAGINA

SPECIAL OPENING

CUSHIONY LINING

EGG

UTERUS

The uterus grows a sort of cushiony lining for each egg.

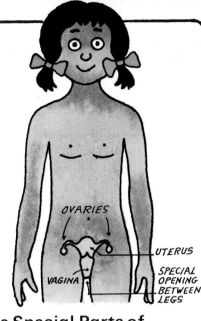

OVARIES

VAGINA

UTERUS

SPECIAL OPENING BETWEEN LEGS

The Special Parts of a Girl

A girl is born with thousands of tiny egg cells in her body. When she is between about 10 and 17 they start to travel one by one into her uterus. It makes a sort of cushion for each egg.

Unless a baby starts, the uterus clears everything out once a month to get ready for a new egg.

The vagina gets soft and stretchy. This makes it easy for the penis to fit in.

Special muscles squeeze the sperm pipe to shoot sperm far inside. They are on their way to meet the egg. Turn the page to see what happens next.

How a Baby is Born

These pictures show the main things that happen as a baby grows in its mother and as it is born.

The Mum's Story

NO ONE KNOWS YET THAT A BABY HAS STARTED.

THE BABY IS JUST A DOT INSIDE THE MUM.

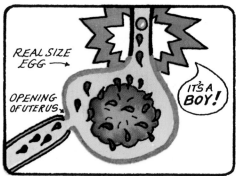

REAL SIZE EGG →

OPENING OF UTERUS →

IT'S A BOY!

The Baby's Story
First, sperms swim up to meet the egg. A sperm is much smaller than an egg. It has the message that decides whether a boy or girl is made.

AT THE BEGINNING...

The egg is joined by just one sperm. It grows by splitting into more cells which quickly grow and split again. The growing egg nestles down into the lining of the uterus.

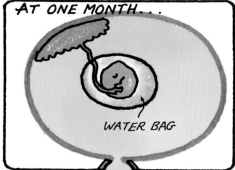

AT ONE MONTH...

WATER BAG

The cluster of cells is about the size of a small bean. It has grown a water bag around itself. The growing baby floats inside, warm and safe.

THE MUM'S BOSOM IS BIGGER NOW. IT IS GETTING READY TO MAKE MILK FOR THE BABY.

AT NINE MONTHS

The baby is ready to be born now. His head is down, like this. This will help when the muscles of the uterus start to push him out.

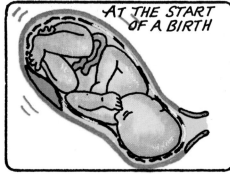

WHEN THE MUSCLES SQUEEZE, SHE KNOWS THE BABY WILL SOON BE BORN.

AT THE START OF A BIRTH

The muscles of the uterus begin to squeeze and stretch, to make the opening wide. The baby's water bag bursts – he does not need it any more.

THE MUSCLES SQUEEZE AND SQUEEZE. THIS IS HARD WORK.

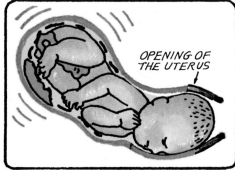

OPENING OF THE UTERUS →

The muscles have worked for hours now. See how wide the opening of the uterus is. The baby's head is pressing against it – this helps.

NOW THE MUM KNOWS A BABY HAS STARTED — HER UTERUS HAS KEPT ITS SPECIAL LINING.

BY THIS TIME SHE CAN FEEL A SMALL BUMP WHERE THE BABY IS GROWING.

SOMETIMES SHE CAN FEEL THE BABY KICK!

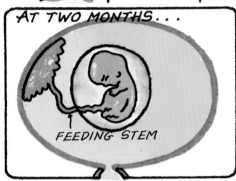

AT TWO MONTHS...

FEEDING STEM

Now the baby looks a bit like this. It grows on a sort of stem. Food and oxygen from the blood in the lining of the uterus go through the stem to the baby.

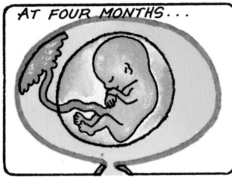

AT FOUR MONTHS...

The little buds on the bean shape have grown into arms and legs now. The cluster of cells is a complete baby. But he is still too weak to live in the outside world.

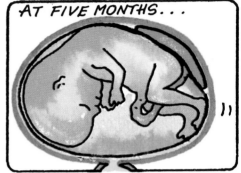

AT FIVE MONTHS...

The baby grows bigger and stronger every day. He can move about now — he even kicks sometimes. The doctor can hear his heart beating.

NOW THE MUM WORKS VERY HARD HELPING TO PUSH THE BABY DOWN AND OUT.

Now the muscles of the uterus begin to squeeze very hard. They push the baby's head right through the opening of the uterus.

Then the baby slides through the mother's vagina. This little tunnel can stretch very wide for the baby to go through.

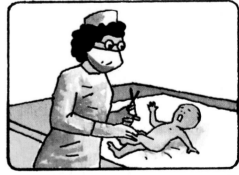

And the baby is born. His feeding stem is snipped and tied — his own lungs and eating machinery will do that work now. The knot becomes a tummy button, just like yours.

How Your Body Fits Together~1

These pictures show some of the main parts of your body. Trace the skeleton to see how your bones fit your breathing and eating machinery.

Pictures on the next pages show your main nerves and blood vessels. The skeleton fits these pictures too.

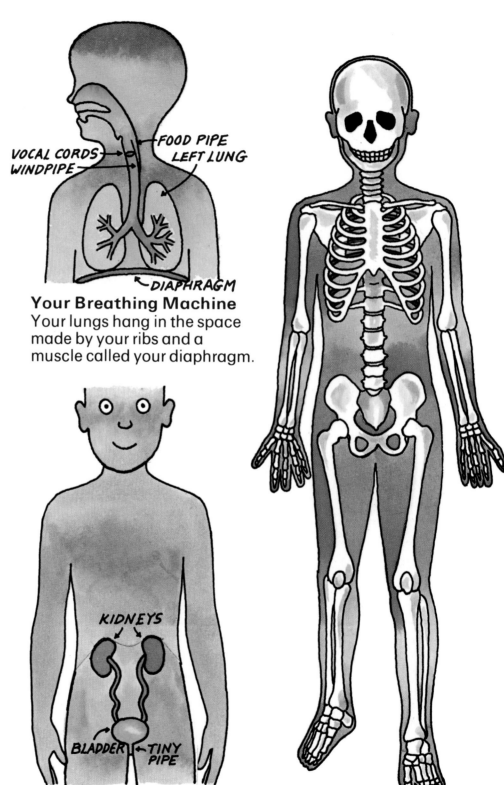

Your Breathing Machine
Your lungs hang in the space made by your ribs and a muscle called your diaphragm.

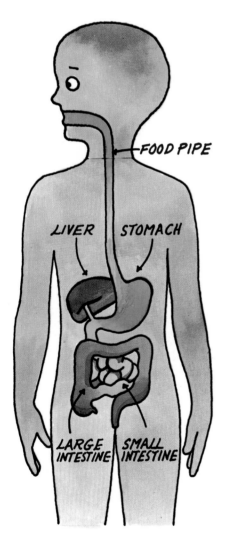

Your Eating Machine
Fine thready bits hold your intestines to your backbone. Stomach and back muscles help protect them.

How Waste Water Goes Out
Waste water stored in your bladder goes out through a tiny pipe. A boy's pipe is longer than a girl's.

Your Skeleton
There are more than 200 bones in your skeleton.

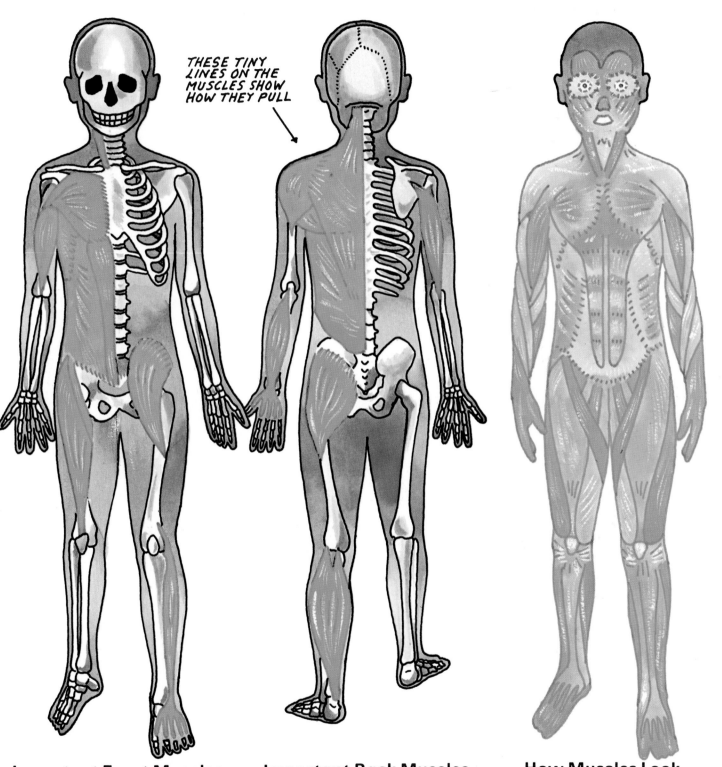

THESE TINY LINES ON THE MUSCLES SHOW HOW THEY PULL

Important Front Muscles
These are some of the main muscles that join the front of your skeleton.

Important Back Muscles
This picture shows some of the big muscles that join the back of your skeleton.

How Muscles Look
Hundreds of muscles weave together like this to make the fleshy cover of your body.

How Your Body Fits Together~2

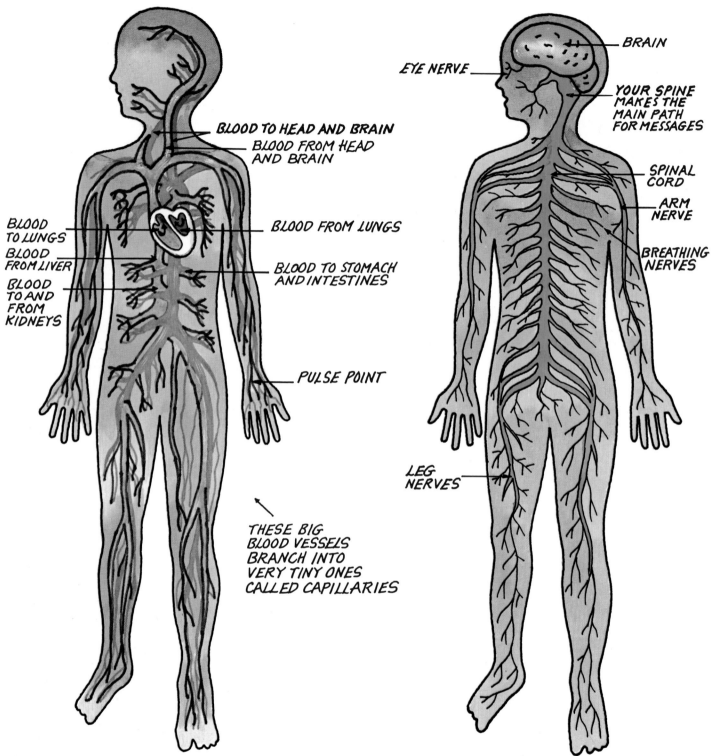

BLOOD TO HEAD AND BRAIN
BLOOD FROM HEAD AND BRAIN
BLOOD TO LUNGS
BLOOD FROM LIVER
BLOOD TO AND FROM KIDNEYS
BLOOD FROM LUNGS
BLOOD TO STOMACH AND INTESTINES
PULSE POINT
THESE BIG BLOOD VESSELS BRANCH INTO VERY TINY ONES CALLED CAPILLARIES

EYE NERVE
BRAIN
YOUR SPINE MAKES THE MAIN PATH FOR MESSAGES
SPINAL CORD
ARM NERVE
BREATHING NERVES
LEG NERVES

Your Main Blood Vessels
Here we have shown the heart a little bigger than it really is, so that you can see how the blood goes through it. The blood vessels leading out are called arteries. The ones leading in are called veins.

Your Main Nerves
The main path for messages to your brain goes right through the middle of your backbone. The main nerves connect to it like this. Hundreds of tiny nerves join these big ones.

What are Bodies Made Of?

Your body, like all living things, is made of very tiny bits called cells. You have many kinds of cell. Each does a different kind of work. Here are some of them.

Groups of the same kind of cell are called tissue. The different parts of your body are made of different kinds of body tissue.

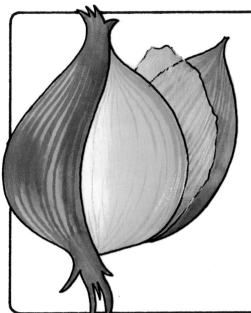

How Big is a Cell?

Most cells are so small that you would need a very strong microscope to see them. Try this to see how very small they are:

Peel off one of the layers of thick skin on an onion. Under it you will find a sort of thin tissue. This is just one cell thick. Feel it. It is so thin you can see through it.

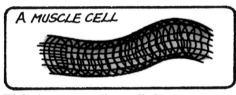

A MUSCLE CELL

This is a muscle cell. It can squeeze and stretch.

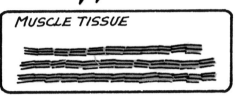

MUSCLE TISSUE

Muscle cells join into stringy bits called fibres. You can see them in meat. It is muscle tissue.

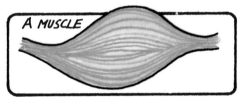

A MUSCLE

A muscle squeezes when all of its cells squeeze.

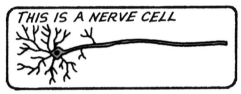

THIS IS A NERVE CELL

The long bits pick up and carry messages.

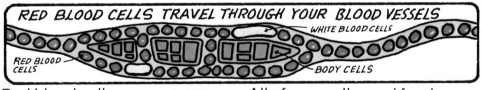

THIS IS A BUNDLE OF NERVE CELLS

Nerve cells join together into bundles, like wires in a telephone cable.

These bundles of nerves join the main cable in your spine that goes to your brain.

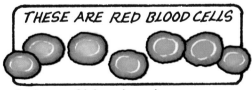

THESE ARE RED BLOOD CELLS

A drop of blood under a microscope shows cells like these floating in a colourless liquid.

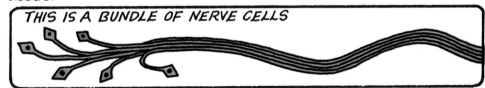

RED BLOOD CELLS TRAVEL THROUGH YOUR BLOOD VESSELS

WHITE BLOOD CELLS

RED BLOOD CELLS

BODY CELLS

Red blood cells carry oxygen to other body cells. The liquid part of your blood carries bits of food.

All of your cells need food and oxygen to stay alive and do their work.

THESE ARE SKIN CELLS

Only the bottom layer of cells is alive. It makes new cells and pushes them up.

A CELL GROWS LIKE THIS

This picture shows how a new cell is made. We have coloured the growing skin cell red.

See how the cell swells and stretches until it breaks into two cells.

Body Words

Eating Words

Oesophagus – the food pipe that goes to your stomach.
Epiglottis – a flap of gristle behind your tongue that stops food going down your windpipe.
Carbohydrates – foods such as bread and potatoes that give you energy.
Proteins – foods such as meat, eggs and cheese that make muscle.
Fats – foods such as butter and oil that give you energy.
Vitamins – important things in food that keep you healthy.
Abdomen – the part of your body under your chest where your stomach and intestines are.
Bladder – the bag that stores waste water.
Anus – the hole where solid waste goes out of your body.
Faeces – undigested food (solid waste) that goes out of your body through your anus.
Urine – a mixture of water and waste taken from your blood by your kidneys. It is stored in your bladder until it goes out of your body.

Breathing Words

Larynx – the part of your windpipe that holds your vocal cords.
Trachea – your windpipe.
Lungs – the two air bags in your chest you use for breathing.
Bronchial Tubes – the tubes that lead from your windpipe to your lungs.
Diaphragm – the sheet of muscle between your lungs and your stomach that helps you to breathe.

Blood and Heart Words

Blood Vessel – a tube that carries blood.
Vein – a blood vessel that carries blood to your heart.
Artery – a blood vessel that takes blood from your heart.
Capillary – a very tiny blood vessel that brings supplies to the cells and takes away waste.
Antibody – a special weapon made by the blood to fight germs.
Plasma – the watery liquid part of the blood.

Bone, Muscle and Skin Words

Spine – your backbone.
Vertebra – one of the bones that make up your backbone.
Cartilage – gristle, which is a bit like bendy bone.
Tendon – a tough, stringy bit that connects muscle to bone.
Joint – where two bones link up.

Baby-Making Words

Puberty – the time when the baby-making machinery starts working in a girl or boy.
Ovaries – the part of a girl's body that stores eggs.
Testicle – the part of a boy's body that makes and stores sperm.
Ovum – the egg cell in a girl's body that becomes a baby when it is fertilized.
Sperm – the special cells made by a boy's testicles that can fertilize egg cells.
Penis – the part of a boy that lets out urine and sperm.
Uterus – the part of a girl where an unborn baby grows.

Fertilization – the joining of an egg and a sperm to start making a baby.
Menstruation – the clearing out of the uterus each month if a baby does not start.
Placenta – the cushiony lining of the uterus that brings food to an unborn baby and takes away waste.
Umbilical cord – the tube that connects the placenta to the unborn baby.

General Words

Nerves – tiny threads that carry messages to and from your brain.
Cell – the very tiny bits all living things are made of.
Tissue – a group of cells that look and act the same, such as muscle tissue.
Organ – a group of cells that work together to do a special job. Your heart is an organ.
System – a group of organs that work together. Your heart and blood vessels together make up your blood system.

BODIES QUIZ

You will find the answers to all these questions somewhere in the "How Your Body Works" part of this book. When you have done the Quiz, check your answers with the list on page 239.

1. How is the food that we eat changed into tiny bits?
   a) By blood in the kidneys.
   b) By digestive juices.
   c) By the blood machine.

2. If all your blood vessels were joined end to end, they would stretch
   a) the length of a street.
   b) the length of three football pitches.
   c) More than twice around the world.

3. Here are the 5 senses:
   1) Hearing
   2) Sight
   3) Smell
   4) Taste
   5) Touch
   Which one would you use to tell the brain that:
   a) a cake is cooking in the kitchen next door.
   b) someone has started a motor cycle down the road.
   c) it is time to switch on the lights.
   d) a lemon is very sour.
   e) you have just sat on a drawing pin.

4. Which is the easiest place for germs to attack you?
   a) Your ears.
   b) Your nose.
   c) The pores of your skin.
   d) Your mouth.

5. Which of these does *not* help you to make words?
   a) The shape of your mouth.
   b) Your vocal cords.
   c) Lip reading.
   d) Air from your lungs.
   e) Your lips.

6. How can we tell if something is cold, hot, hard, soft, rough or smooth just by touching it?
   a) Your muscles can tell.
   b) There is too much pressure on your bones.
   c) Tiny nerves in the skin send messages to your brain.
   d) The cells in your blood feel the difference.

7. Which of these does *not* help your joints move?
   a) The skin.
   b) Ligaments.
   c) A special liquid to oil them.
   d) Covers to hold them together and keep liquid in.

8. How are freckles made?
   a) From oil squeezed out of the skin.
   b) Where colour cells are bunched up.
   c) Where pores are close together.
   d) From dry and dead skin.

9. Which two of these must meet for a baby to start?
   a) A sperm cell.
   b) Waste water.
   c) Bladder.
   d) Egg cell.
   e) The uterus.
   f) Blood vessels.

10. How old is the baby inside its mother when the doctor can hear its heart?
    a) One month.
    b) Two months.
    c) Four months.
    d) Five months.

11. How many bones are there in the skeleton?
    a) About 20.
    b) Over 50.
    c) More than 200.
    d) Over 550.
    e) More than 1000.

12. The main path for messages to your brain goes through your:
    a) chest?
    b) lungs?
    c) arms?
    d) backbone?
    e) heart?

13. How many new big teeth grow when your first teeth fall out?
    a) 24?
    b) 26?
    c) 32?
    d) 38?

14. Which of these things help to move your blood back to your heart?
    a) Your lungs?
    b) Your bones?
    c) Your muscles?
    d) Your brain?

15. As well as helping you to hear, your ears help you to:
    a) breathe?
    b) keep your balance?
    c) taste things?
    d) keep warm?

16. Most of your blood is a colourless liquid called:
    a) red cells?
    b) blood vessels?
    c) white cells?
    d) plasma?
    e) water?

PART 4
HOW
MACHINES
WORK

We wish to thank the following organizations for their help in checking the material in this part of the book.

Agricultural Press
Alfa-Laval
American Hoist and Derrick
Atlas Copco
Blackwood Hodge
British Aircraft Corp.
British Hovercraft Corp.
British Petroleum
British Rail
BSP International Foundations
Chubb Fire Security
Comex John Brown
Cunard-Trafalgar
ERF
GEC Machines
Hawker Siddeley Aviation
Hovercraft Development
Ing. Alfred Schmidt GMBH
Interconair
Lockheed Aircraft
Lola Cars
Massey Ferguson
Mining Magazine
Ministry of Defence
National Coal Board
Orenstein & Koppel
Plant Hire Magazine
Railway Gazette International
RNLI
Shipping World & Shipbuilder
Simon Engineering
Swiss National Tourist Office
Tarmac Construction
Vickers Oceanics
Westland Helicopters
Winget

Introduction to Part Four

This part of the book is a simple introduction to the world of machines and motors. It looks inside lots of exciting modern machines and answers the questions, "How do they work?" and "What do they do?".

Here are machines which help us to farm, such as the combine harvester, and mining machines, such as the bucket wheel excavator. You will see what happens on an oil rig and find out how a hovercraft floats on a cushion of air.

Join the Apollo astronauts as they circle high above the surface of the moon. Peep into the eerie world of a mini submarine deep underwater on the sea bed. It will help you to understand some of the most amazing machines in the world.

On pages 186 to 189 you will find lots of simple diagrams. They explain the motors which drive the machines in this book, from the simple steam engine to the powerful rocket motor.

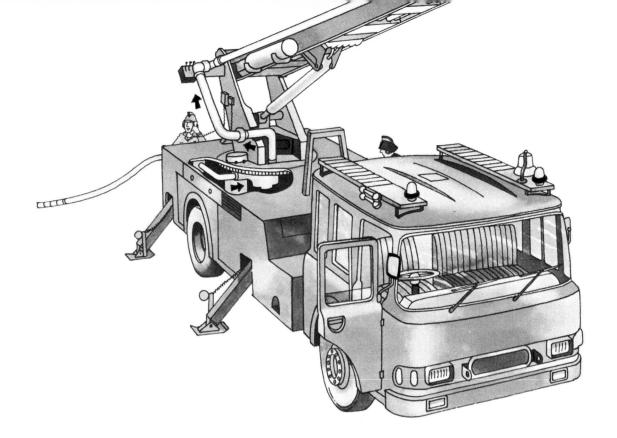

Written by Christopher Rawson

Illustrated by Colin King

Contents of Part Four

Space Machines

Rockets need very powerful motors to blast them into space. This is because they have to overcome the pull of gravity—the force that holds everything down on the earth. Rockets carry astronauts into space and launch unmanned satellites to explore other planets.

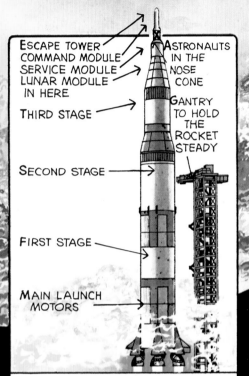

ESCAPE TOWER
COMMAND MODULE
SERVICE MODULE
LUNAR MODULE
IN HERE

ASTRONAUTS IN THE NOSE CONE

THIRD STAGE

GANTRY TO HOLD THE ROCKET STEADY

SECOND STAGE

FIRST STAGE

MAIN LAUNCH MOTORS

Saturn Blast-Off

The giant rocket fires its main engines. Astronauts in the nose cone set out for space from Cape Kennedy.

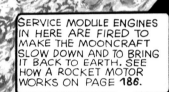

TANKS IN HERE CARRY ROCKET FUEL AND OXYGEN.

SERVICE MODULE

SERVICE MODULE ENGINES IN HERE ARE FIRED TO MAKE THE MOONCRAFT SLOW DOWN AND TO BRING IT BACK TO EARTH. SEE HOW A ROCKET MOTOR WORKS ON PAGE 186.

EXHAUST NOZZLE

THIS AERIAL PICKS UP RADIO SIGNALS FROM EARTH.

1 Viking

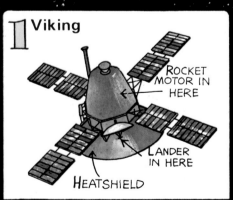

ROCKET MOTOR IN HERE

LANDER IN HERE

HEATSHIELD

This spacecraft was launched towards Mars in 1975. The journey took nearly a year. Inside the spacecraft, protected by the heat shield, was a fully automatic lander.

2

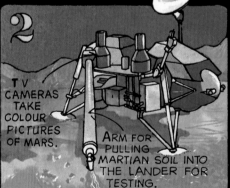

TV CAMERAS TAKE COLOUR PICTURES OF MARS.

ARM FOR PULLING MARTIAN SOIL INTO THE LANDER FOR TESTING.

The spacecraft released the lander while circling round Mars. The lander was fitted with cameras and many instruments to show scientists on earth what the surface of Mars is like.

Weather Satellite

This sort of satellite stays in orbit round the earth for many years. Cameras inside it take pictures of the earth's surface. They warn scientists of bad weather, such as cyclones and tornadoes.

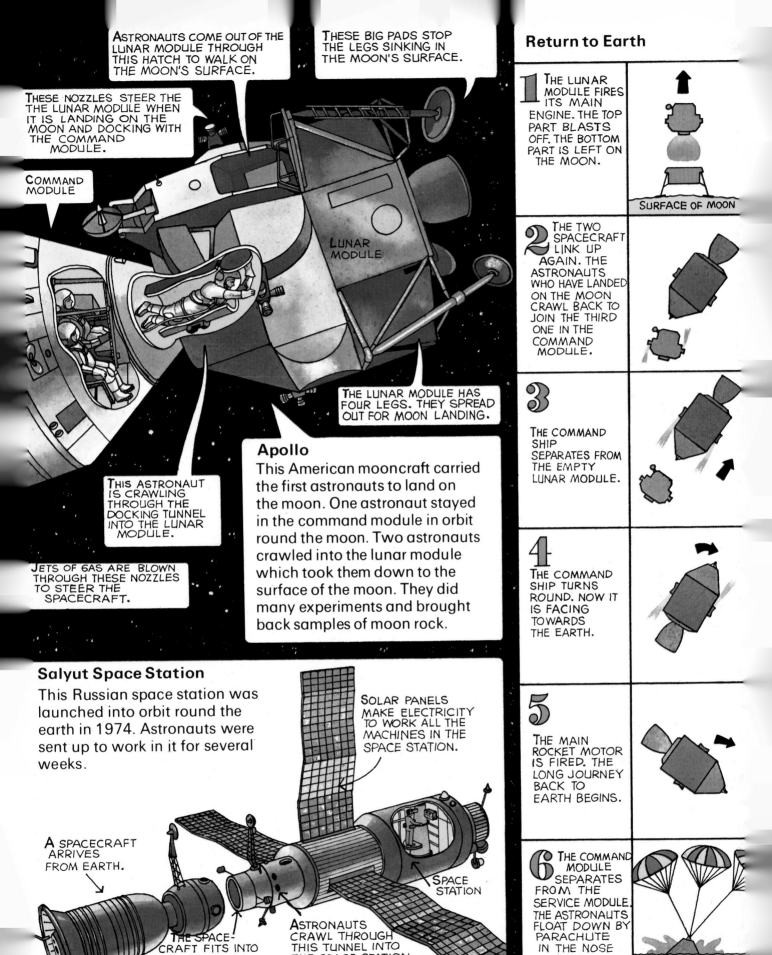

ASTRONAUTS COME OUT OF THE LUNAR MODULE THROUGH THIS HATCH TO WALK ON THE MOON'S SURFACE.

THESE BIG PADS STOP THE LEGS SINKING IN THE MOON'S SURFACE.

THESE NOZZLES STEER THE LUNAR MODULE WHEN IT IS LANDING ON THE MOON AND DOCKING WITH THE COMMAND MODULE.

COMMAND MODULE

LUNAR MODULE

THIS ASTRONAUT IS CRAWLING THROUGH THE DOCKING TUNNEL INTO THE LUNAR MODULE.

THE LUNAR MODULE HAS FOUR LEGS. THEY SPREAD OUT FOR MOON LANDING.

JETS OF GAS ARE BLOWN THROUGH THESE NOZZLES TO STEER THE SPACECRAFT.

Apollo

This American mooncraft carried the first astronauts to land on the moon. One astronaut stayed in the command module in orbit round the moon. Two astronauts crawled into the lunar module which took them down to the surface of the moon. They did many experiments and brought back samples of moon rock.

Salyut Space Station

This Russian space station was launched into orbit round the earth in 1974. Astronauts were sent up to work in it for several weeks.

SOLAR PANELS MAKE ELECTRICITY TO WORK ALL THE MACHINES IN THE SPACE STATION.

A SPACECRAFT ARRIVES FROM EARTH.

SPACE STATION

THE SPACE-CRAFT FITS INTO THE END OF THE SPACE STATION HERE.

ASTRONAUTS CRAWL THROUGH THIS TUNNEL INTO THE SPACE STATION.

Return to Earth

1 THE LUNAR MODULE FIRES ITS MAIN ENGINE. THE TOP PART BLASTS OFF. THE BOTTOM PART IS LEFT ON THE MOON.

SURFACE OF MOON

2 THE TWO SPACECRAFT LINK UP AGAIN. THE ASTRONAUTS WHO HAVE LANDED ON THE MOON CRAWL BACK TO JOIN THE THIRD ONE IN THE COMMAND MODULE.

3 THE COMMAND SHIP SEPARATES FROM THE EMPTY LUNAR MODULE.

4 THE COMMAND SHIP TURNS ROUND. NOW IT IS FACING TOWARDS THE EARTH.

5 THE MAIN ROCKET MOTOR IS FIRED. THE LONG JOURNEY BACK TO EARTH BEGINS.

6 THE COMMAND MODULE SEPARATES FROM THE SERVICE MODULE. THE ASTRONAUTS FLOAT DOWN BY PARACHUTE IN THE NOSE CONE.

Flying Machines

Aeroplanes fly through the air because their engines push them along and their wings keep them up in the air.

Aeroplanes can only leave the ground when air is rushing past their wings. They race down the runway to make this happen. Wings

are flat underneath and curved on top. This makes the air go faster over the top. The air underneath pushes up and helps the plane to rise.

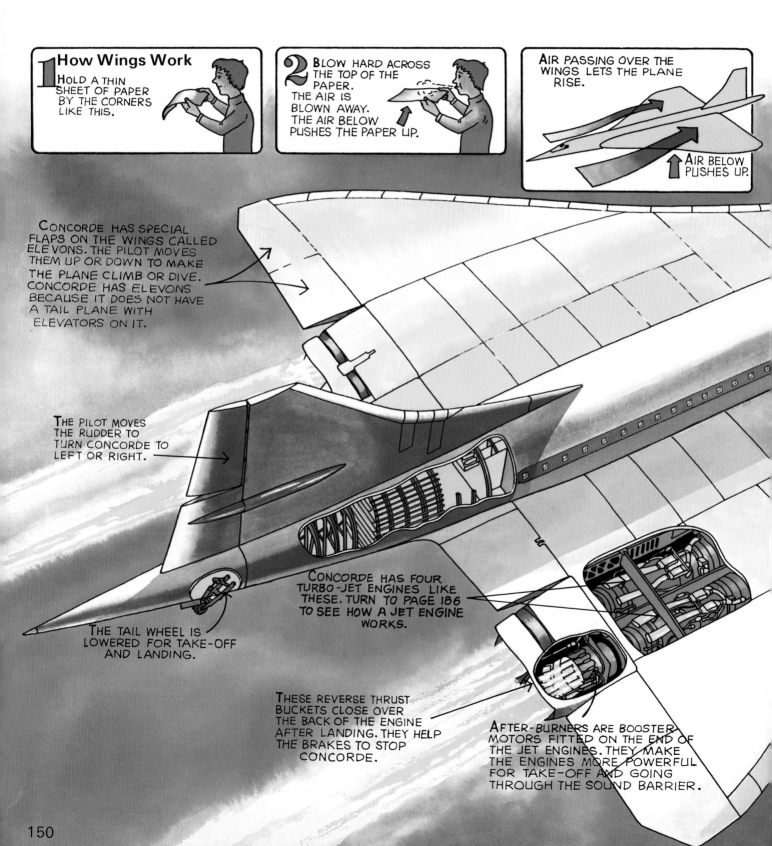

1 **How Wings Work**
HOLD A THIN SHEET OF PAPER BY THE CORNERS LIKE THIS.

2 BLOW HARD ACROSS THE TOP OF THE PAPER. THE AIR IS BLOWN AWAY. THE AIR BELOW PUSHES THE PAPER UP.

AIR PASSING OVER THE WINGS LETS THE PLANE RISE.

AIR BELOW PUSHES UP.

CONCORDE HAS SPECIAL FLAPS ON THE WINGS CALLED ELEVONS. THE PILOT MOVES THEM UP OR DOWN TO MAKE THE PLANE CLIMB OR DIVE. CONCORDE HAS ELEVONS BECAUSE IT DOES NOT HAVE A TAIL PLANE WITH ELEVATORS ON IT.

THE PILOT MOVES THE RUDDER TO TURN CONCORDE TO LEFT OR RIGHT.

THE TAIL WHEEL IS LOWERED FOR TAKE-OFF AND LANDING.

CONCORDE HAS FOUR TURBO-JET ENGINES LIKE THESE. TURN TO PAGE 186 TO SEE HOW A JET ENGINE WORKS.

THESE REVERSE THRUST BUCKETS CLOSE OVER THE BACK OF THE ENGINE AFTER LANDING. THEY HELP THE BRAKES TO STOP CONCORDE.

AFTER-BURNERS ARE BOOSTER MOTORS FITTED ON THE END OF THE JET ENGINES. THEY MAKE THE ENGINES MORE POWERFUL FOR TAKE-OFF AND GOING THROUGH THE SOUND BARRIER.

Concorde

This passenger plane cruises at supersonic speed—faster than the speed of sound (1,059 kph). It cruises about 17 km above the ground and can cross the Atlantic twice as fast as an ordinary passenger jet.

AIR IS PUMPED INTO CONCORDE'S BODY SO THAT PASSENGER'S CAN BREATHE EVEN WHEN THE PLANE IS FLYING VERY HIGH. THERE IS VERY LITTLE AIR HIGH ABOVE THE EARTH WHERE CONCORDE CRUISES.

Supersonic Flying

A special shield slides up to cover the windscreen. This makes the nose streamlined.

THE OUTSIDE SKIN GETS VERY HOT WHEN CONCORDE FLIES SUPERSONICALLY. SPECIAL MATERIAL INSIDE THE SKIN PROTECTS THE PASSENGERS AND CREW FROM THE HEAT AND THE NOISE.

CONCORDE HAS TWO PILOTS AND A FLIGHT ENGINEER.

FLIGHT DECK

RADAR IN THE NOSE WARNS THE PILOT OF BAD WEATHER AND OF OTHER PLANES.

GALLEY

SWEPT-BACK WINGS ALLOW CONCORDE TO FLY AT SUPERSONIC SPEED.

THE CABIN HAS SEATS FOR 108 PASSENGERS.

THIS STRIP HEATS UP TO STOP ICE FORMING ON THE WINGS WHEN CONCORDE IS CLIMBING AND COMING DOWN TO LAND.

FUEL IS STORED IN THE WINGS AND UNDER THE BODY. IT IS PUMPED INTO A SPECIAL TANK AT THE BACK WHILE THE PLANE IS IN THE AIR. THIS KEEPS IT BALANCED FOR SUPERSONIC FLIGHT.

The Droop Nose

Concorde has a movable nose. The pilot lowers it for take off. Then he raises it once the jet is in the air and for supersonic cruising. He lowers it again for landing so he can see the ground from the cockpit.

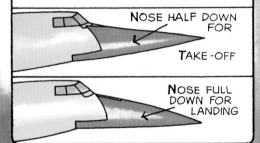

NOSE HALF DOWN FOR TAKE-OFF

NOSE FULL DOWN FOR LANDING

Steering an Aeroplane

NOSE GOES UP PLANE CLIMBS.

AIRFLOW

AIRFLOW

ELEVATORS ARE UP. AIRFLOW PUSHES AGAINST THEM. TAIL GOES DOWN.

NOSE GOES DOWN. PLANE DIVES.

AIRFLOW

AIRFLOW

ELEVATORS ARE DOWN. AIRFLOW PUSHES AGAINST THEM. TAIL GOES UP.

PLANE TURNS LEFT.

RIGHT AILERON IS DOWN AIR FLOW PUSHES RIGHT WING UP.

LEFT AILERON IS UP. AIRFLOW PUSHES LEFT WING DOWN.

RUDDER SWINGS LEFT. AIRFLOW PUSHES AGAINST IT SO TAIL PUSHED TO THE RIGHT.

TO TURN RIGHT EVERYTHING WORKS THE OPPOSITE WAY.

Climbing

The pilot raises flaps, called elevators, on the tail. They make the plane climb.

Diving

He lowers the elevators to make the plane dive.

Turning

The pilot moves the rudder on the tail to turn the plane. Flaps on the wings called ailerons make it bank.

Hovercraft

Hovercraft can travel over water, ice, mud and any flat land. They skim along, just above the surface, on a cushion of air.

This SRN4 hovercraft can carry 254 passengers and 30 cars. It goes at speeds of up to 130 kph. and rides over waves up to 3 metres high.

The propellers push the hovercraft along. The angles of the blades are changed to move it forwards slowly or very fast, or backwards.

The propellers can move round on their posts. They swing to the left to turn the hovercraft to the right. They swing right to turn it left.

How a Hovercraft Works

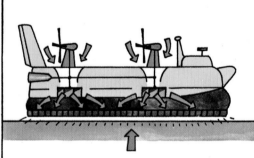

Fans suck in air at the top and blow it out underneath the skirt. The hovercraft rises up on the air trapped by the skirt.

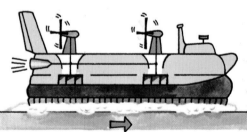

The propellers start to turn. When they grip the air, they push the hovercraft along.

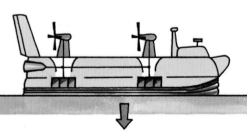

When the engines are switched off, the hovercraft stops. The fans stop pushing air down into the skirt and the hovercraft sinks slowly down to rest on its base.

CAPTAIN'S CABIN

INNER CABIN

ANCHOR

LIFEBOATS

The rubber skirt holds in the cushion of air. This cushion is about 2.5 metres deep.

The skirt bulges out at the top to stop the hovercraft from rolling from side to side.

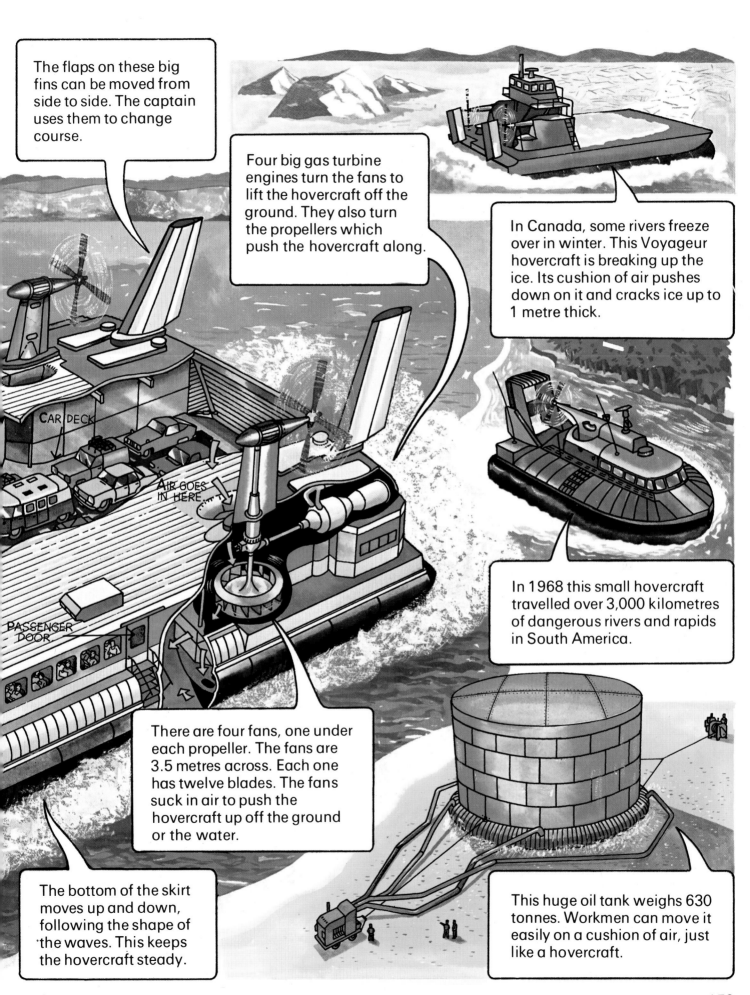

The flaps on these big fins can be moved from side to side. The captain uses them to change course.

Four big gas turbine engines turn the fans to lift the hovercraft off the ground. They also turn the propellers which push the hovercraft along.

In Canada, some rivers freeze over in winter. This Voyageur hovercraft is breaking up the ice. Its cushion of air pushes down on it and cracks ice up to 1 metre thick.

CAR DECK

AIR GOES IN HERE

PASSENGER DOOR

In 1968 this small hovercraft travelled over 3,000 kilometres of dangerous rivers and rapids in South America.

There are four fans, one under each propeller. The fans are 3.5 metres across. Each one has twelve blades. The fans suck in air to push the hovercraft up off the ground or the water.

The bottom of the skirt moves up and down, following the shape of the waves. This keeps the hovercraft steady.

This huge oil tank weighs 630 tonnes. Workmen can move it easily on a cushion of air, just like a hovercraft.

153

Hovering Machines

The two planes on these pages can fly along, up and down and hover in the air. The Harrier jet fighter can take off from small secret bases and from ships at sea.

Helicopters are useful for getting to places where there are no proper landing fields or roads.

Firing Missiles

The Harrier is firing one of its air-to-ground rockets. It can carry 2,270 kgs. of weapons under its body and wings.

Mid-air Refuelling

The Harrier pilot steers his probe into the funnel on the end of the fuel pipe. Jet fuel is then pumped from the tanker plane.

In the cockpit, a moving map on a screen tells the pilot about the ground below. A display on the windscreen helps him to fire his weapons accurately.

These flaps are for steering. Turn to page 150 to see how a pilot steers his aircraft.

The Harrier can fly at 1,186 kph. The jet engine sucks in air through a hole in each side. Turn to page 186 to see how different jet engines work.

Exhaust gases from the engine blow out through nozzles. When the nozzles point down the thrust of the engine lifts the plane up. When they point back, the plane goes forward.

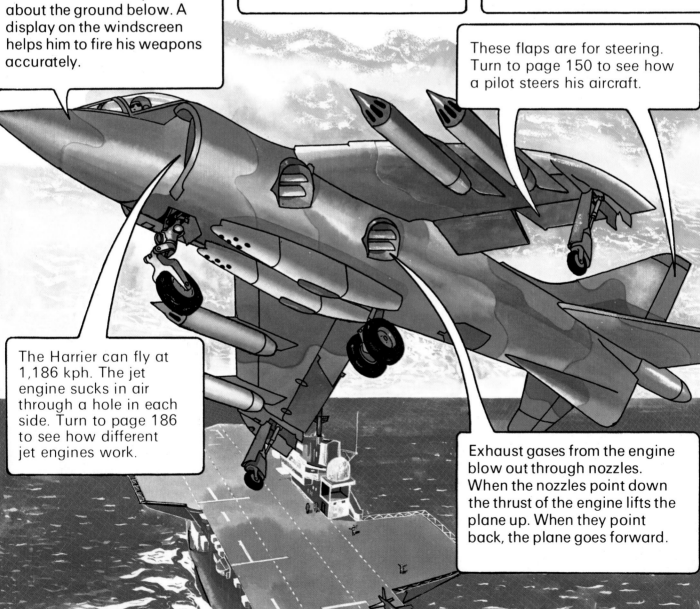

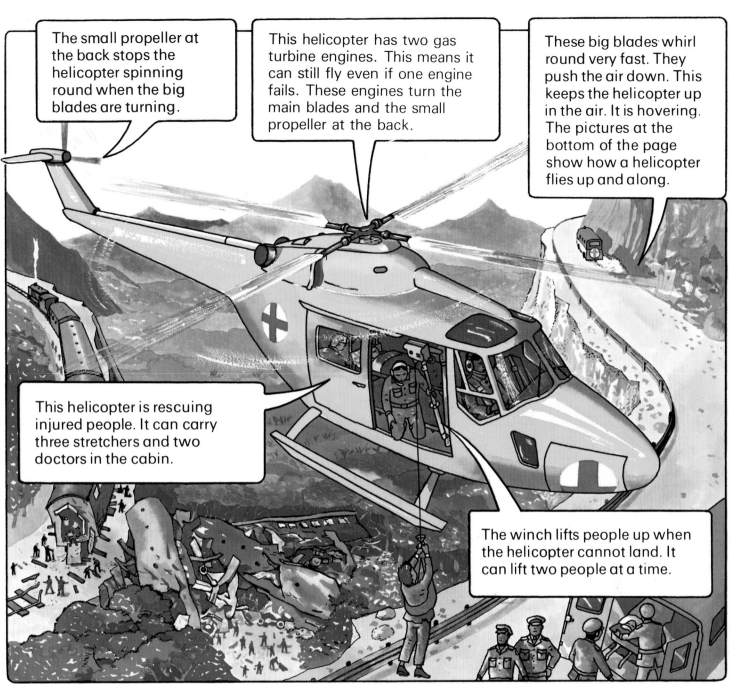

The small propeller at the back stops the helicopter spinning round when the big blades are turning.

This helicopter has two gas turbine engines. This means it can still fly even if one engine fails. These engines turn the main blades and the small propeller at the back.

These big blades whirl round very fast. They push the air down. This keeps the helicopter up in the air. It is hovering. The pictures at the bottom of the page show how a helicopter flies up and along.

This helicopter is rescuing injured people. It can carry three stretchers and two doctors in the cabin.

The winch lifts people up when the helicopter cannot land. It can lift two people at a time.

1 How a Helicopter Flies

BLADES FLAT. HELICOPTER STAYS ON THE GROUND.

The pilot starts the motor. The big blades spin round but the helicopter stays still on the ground.

2

BLADES TWISTED AT SPECIAL ANGLE.

AIR IS FORCED DOWN AND MAKES HELICOPTER RISE.

When the pilot makes the big blades twist at an angle, they grip the air. Then the helicopter rises off the ground.

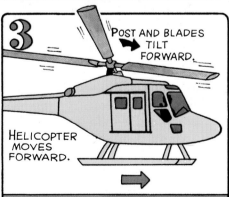

3

POST AND BLADES TILT FORWARD.

HELICOPTER MOVES FORWARD.

Then the pilot tilts the blades forward. The helicopter stops rising and moves along.

Floating Machines

These pictures show some of the different things that ships are used for at sea. Ships cannot travel as fast as aeroplanes or many vehicles on land, but they can carry very large and heavy cargoes over long distances.

EXHAUST GASES FROM THE DIESEL ENGINES ARE BLOWN OUT THROUGH THE FUNNEL.

Steering a Ship

Ships have propellers to push them along. They are steered by turning the rudder at the end of the ship to one side or the other.

SHIP SAILS STRAIGHT AHEAD.
RUDDER IS STRAIGHT.

SHIP TURNS LEFT.
RUDDER IS MOVED TO THE LEFT.

SHIP TURNS RIGHT.
RUDDER IS TURNED TO THE RIGHT.

Some ships have two engines and two propellers. These ships can be turned sharply by keeping one propeller going forwards, putting the other into reverse, and changing the angle of the rudder.

SHIP SAILS STRAIGHT AHEAD.
BOTH PROPELLERS GOING AHEAD.

SHIP TURNS LEFT.
LEFT PROPELLER REVERSES.
RIGHT PROPELLER GOES AHEAD.

SHIP TURNS RIGHT.
RIGHT PROPELLER REVERSES.
LEFT PROPELLER GOES AHEAD.

ALL BIG SHIPS CARRY LIFE BOATS. PASSENGERS AND CREW USE THEM TO ESCAPE IN EMERGENCY.

THE BACK OF A SHIP IS CALLED THE STERN

THE ENGINE ROOM IS JUST BELOW THE WATER LINE. THIS SHIP HAS TWO DIESEL ENGINES. SEE HOW DIESEL ENGINES WORK ON PAGE 45.

RUDDER

THE PROPELLERS ARE JOINED TO THE ENGINES BY LONG SHAFTS. AS THE PROPELLERS SPIN ROUND THEY TRY TO PUSH THE WATER BACKWARDS. THIS MOVES THE SHIP FORWARDS.

THE BOTTOM OF A SHIP IS CALLED THE KEEL. THIS KEEL IS 5·5 METRES BELOW THE WATER LINE. SOME SHIPS LIKE GIANT OIL TANKERS HAVE KEELS 60 METRES BELOW THE WATER LINE.

Dumping Log Carrier

This ship carries logs to a paper mill. Big water tanks inside the ship hold it steady when the logs slide off into the water.

1 CRANES ON THE SHIP LOAD THE LOGS.

2 THE SHIP CARRIES ITS LOAD. THE EXTRA WEIGHT PUSHES IT LOWER IN THE WATER.

3 TO UNLOAD, THE WATER IS PUMPED TO ONE SIDE. THE SHIP TILTS UNTIL THE LOGS FALL OFF.

4 WHEN THE LOGS FALL OFF, SOME OF THE WATER FLOWS BACK TO THE OTHER SIDE. THE SHIP RIGHTS ITSELF.

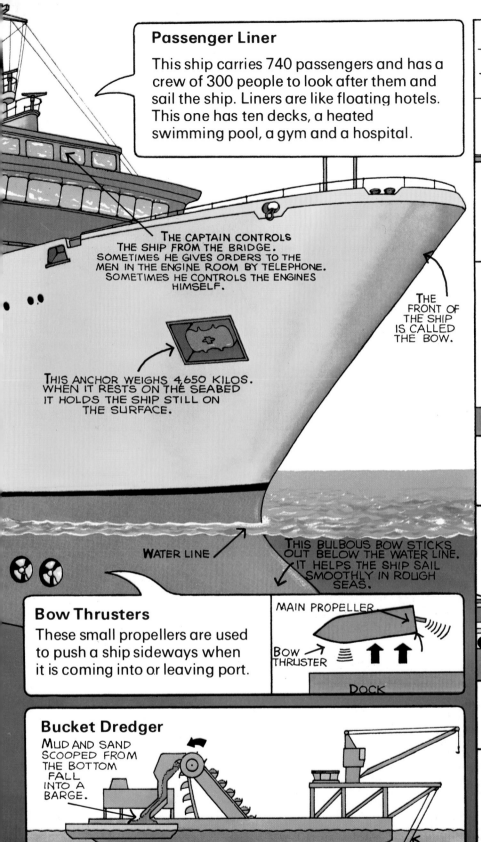

Passenger Liner

This ship carries 740 passengers and has a crew of 300 people to look after them and sail the ship. Liners are like floating hotels. This one has ten decks, a heated swimming pool, a gym and a hospital.

THE CAPTAIN CONTROLS THE SHIP FROM THE BRIDGE. SOMETIMES HE GIVES ORDERS TO THE MEN IN THE ENGINE ROOM BY TELEPHONE. SOMETIMES HE CONTROLS THE ENGINES HIMSELF.

THE FRONT OF THE SHIP IS CALLED THE BOW.

THIS ANCHOR WEIGHS 4,650 KILOS. WHEN IT RESTS ON THE SEABED IT HOLDS THE SHIP STILL ON THE SURFACE.

WATER LINE

THIS BULBOUS BOW STICKS OUT BELOW THE WATER LINE. IT HELPS THE SHIP SAIL SMOOTHLY IN ROUGH SEAS.

Bow Thrusters

These small propellers are used to push a ship sideways when it is coming into or leaving port.

MAIN PROPELLER

BOW THRUSTER

DOCK

Bucket Dredger

MUD AND SAND SCOOPED FROM THE BOTTOM FALL INTO A BARGE.

EMPTY BUCKETS

FULL BUCKETS

THESE WIRES HOLD UP THE BUCKET CHAIN.

MUD AND SAND

Banks of mud and sand often build up in ports and harbours. Dredgers scoop them up to keep the water deep enough for ships.

Loading a Container Ship

1

Containers are large metal boxes used to carry many different sorts of goods. They come from factories to the docks by road and by train.

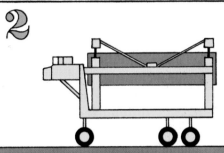

2

These machines, called straddle carriers, are moved round a dock to pick up containers.

3

They dump the containers near big cranes which ride on rails along the edge of the dock.

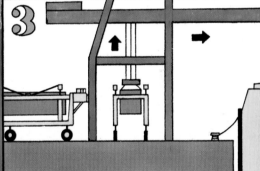

4

The cranes load the containers on to ships, slotting them into holds or stacking them on deck.

Machines on Rails

Trains are used all over the world to carry goods and passengers. Modern electric and diesel engines are easier to run for long distances than the old steam engines. Turn to pages 186–189 to see how they all work.

Steam Engine

Steam engines need coal for the fire and water to fill the boiler. Together they make steam to turn the wheels.

How Wheels Fit the Rails

A ridge on the inside edge keeps the wheel from slipping off the rail.

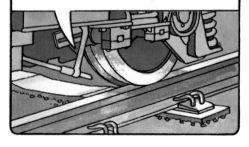

Underground Train

Some big cities, such as Paris, London and New York, have underground passenger railways. The engines are driven by electricity which is picked up from a third rail beside the track. The doors slide open sideways automatically to let the passengers off and on.

THIS CABLE CARRIES ELECTRICITY. IT IS HELD UP BY STEEL POSTS BESIDE THE TRACK.

THE CABLE HANGS FROM SPECIAL PIECES OF CHINA CALLED INSULATORS. THEY STOP THE ELECTRICITY GETTING INTO THE POSTS.

THE DRIVER CONTROLS THE ENGINE FROM HIS CAB. LOTS OF DIFFERENT DIALS SHOW HIM THAT ALL THE PARTS ARE WORKING PROPERLY.

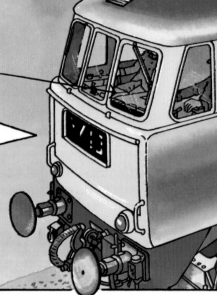

Electric Train

This engine has four electric motors. It can get up speed very quickly, even when pulling a long, heavy train. The electricity which drives the motors is made at power stations and is carried by overhead cables.

Laying a New Line

When rails and sleepers are worn out, they are taken up and new ones laid in their place. First the new rail (red) is laid beside the old one (blue). Now follow the numbers in the picture to see how this machine picks up the old rails and lays down the new ones.

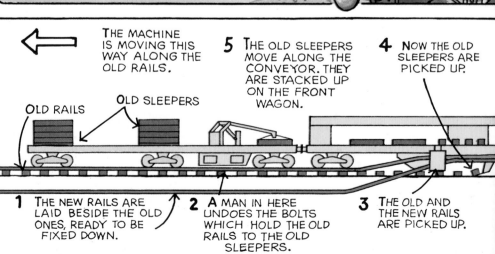

THE MACHINE IS MOVING THIS WAY ALONG THE OLD RAILS.

OLD RAILS

OLD SLEEPERS

5 THE OLD SLEEPERS MOVE ALONG THE CONVEYOR. THEY ARE STACKED UP ON THE FRONT WAGON.

4 NOW THE OLD SLEEPERS ARE PICKED UP.

1 THE NEW RAILS ARE LAID BESIDE THE OLD ONES, READY TO BE FIXED DOWN.

2 A MAN IN HERE UNDOES THE BOLTS WHICH HOLD THE OLD RAILS TO THE OLD SLEEPERS.

3 THE OLD AND THE NEW RAILS ARE PICKED UP.

Rack Railway

Only special trains can climb steep mountains. On this train a cog wheel under the engine fits into the notches in a centre rail. If the brakes failed, this would stop the train from crashing down the slope.

Heavy Goods Train

This train has 105 wagons. The load is so heavy it needs four diesel engines to pull it. All the engines are controlled by the driver in the front cab.

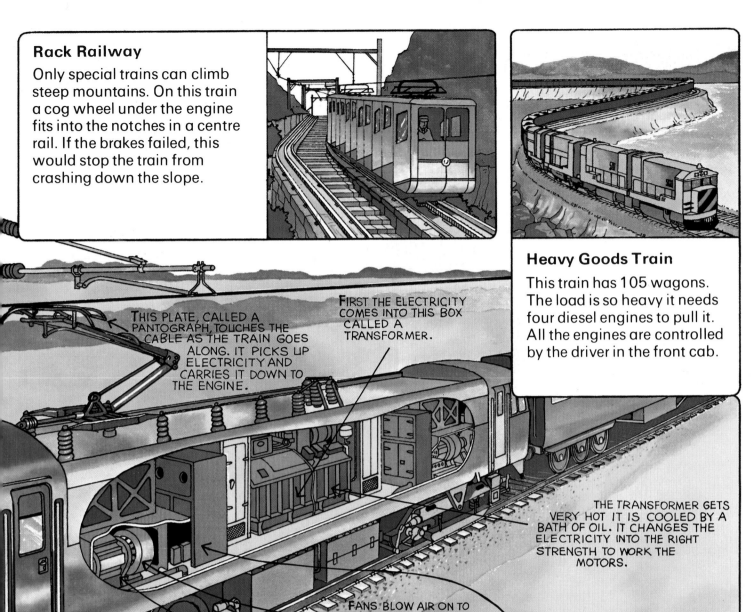

FIRST THE ELECTRICITY COMES INTO THIS BOX CALLED A TRANSFORMER.

THIS PLATE, CALLED A PANTOGRAPH, TOUCHES THE CABLE AS THE TRAIN GOES ALONG. IT PICKS UP ELECTRICITY AND CARRIES IT DOWN TO THE ENGINE.

THE TRANSFORMER GETS VERY HOT. IT IS COOLED BY A BATH OF OIL. IT CHANGES THE ELECTRICITY INTO THE RIGHT STRENGTH TO WORK THE MOTORS.

FANS BLOW AIR ON TO THE MOTORS TO COOL THEM.

THE ELECTRICITY FROM THE TRANSFORMER POWERS THE MOTORS. EACH ONE TURNS AN AXLE. THE WHEELS ARE FIXED TO THE ENDS OF THE AXLES.

GEARS, IN A GEAR BOX BESIDE EACH MOTOR MAKE IT EASIER FOR THE MOTOR TO DRIVE THE AXLES. THE DRIVER MOVES A LEVER TO MAKE THE TRANSFORMER SUPPLY MORE ELECTRICITY TO THE MOTORS. THIS MAKES THE TRAIN GO FASTER.

STRONG SPRINGS KEEP THE WEIGHT OF THE ENGINES RESTING GENTLY ON THE AXLES.

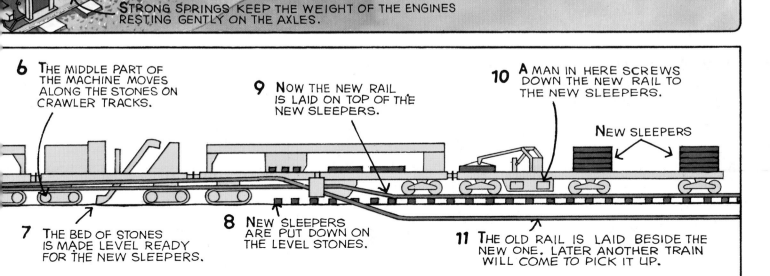

6 THE MIDDLE PART OF THE MACHINE MOVES ALONG THE STONES ON CRAWLER TRACKS.

9 NOW THE NEW RAIL IS LAID ON TOP OF THE NEW SLEEPERS.

10 A MAN IN HERE SCREWS DOWN THE NEW RAIL TO THE NEW SLEEPERS.

NEW SLEEPERS

7 THE BED OF STONES IS MADE LEVEL READY FOR THE NEW SLEEPERS.

8 NEW SLEEPERS ARE PUT DOWN ON THE LEVEL STONES.

11 THE OLD RAIL IS LAID BESIDE THE NEW ONE. LATER ANOTHER TRAIN WILL COME TO PICK IT UP.

Racing Machines

All these machines are specially made for sport racing. Most of them are very light and have a powerful engine to push them along the ground or over water as fast as possible. All the ones which race on land also need very safe brakes to make them stop.

Rally Car

This ordinary car has been made extra strong and fast for long-distance races. Metal studs in the tyres stop it skidding on ice.

Racing Car

This picture shows some of the special parts which make a racing car different from an ordinary car. The body is pointed at the front so it cuts easily through the air. When the car is being raced, the petrol engine behind the driver uses a litre of petrol every 2.5 kilometres.

THIS RACING CAR HAS A PETROL ENGINE WITH EIGHT CYLINDERS. SEE WHAT HAPPENS INSIDE A PETROL ENGINE ON PAGE 44.

GEARS IN THE GEAR BOX MAKE THE ENGINE DRIVE THE BACK WHEELS FASTER OR SLOWER.

AIR BLOWS INTO THIS SCOOP. IT IS MIXED WITH THE PETROL IN THE ENGINE.

AS THE CAR RACES ALONG, THE AIR PUSHES AGAINST THIS WING. THIS PRESSES THE BACK WHEELS DOWN ON THE TRACK.

EXHAUST GASES FROM THE ENGINE ARE BLOWN OUT HERE.

THE BACK TYRES ARE VERY BIG AND SMOOTH SO THAT AS MUCH POWER AS POSSIBLE PUSHES AGAINST THE ROAD. THIS MAKES THE CAR GO FASTER.

OIL IN HERE IS PUMPED INTO THE MOTOR TO KEEP ALL THE DIFFERENT PARTS MOVING EASILY.

SPECIAL RUBBER BAGS IN THE SIDES OF THE CAR CONTAIN 118 LITRES OF PETROL. THE PETROL IS PUMPED FROM BOTH SIDES AT ONCE TO KEEP THE CAR BALANCED.

Changing Tyres in the Pits

When it rains during a race, mechanics fit special tyres with grooves to the cars to stop them skidding. All four tyres can be changed in 30 seconds.

Dragster

These cars race on short, straight tracks at speeds up to 380 kph. They go so fast that they have parachutes to help them stop at the end of a race.

Motor Cycle

These motor cycles race on roads or specially-curved tracks at up to 280 kph. Expert riders lean right over with their machines to go very fast round corners.

Power Boat

Racing boats are specially-shaped to skim over the water. When a boat is racing at full speed, it lifts up at the front until most of it is out of the water.

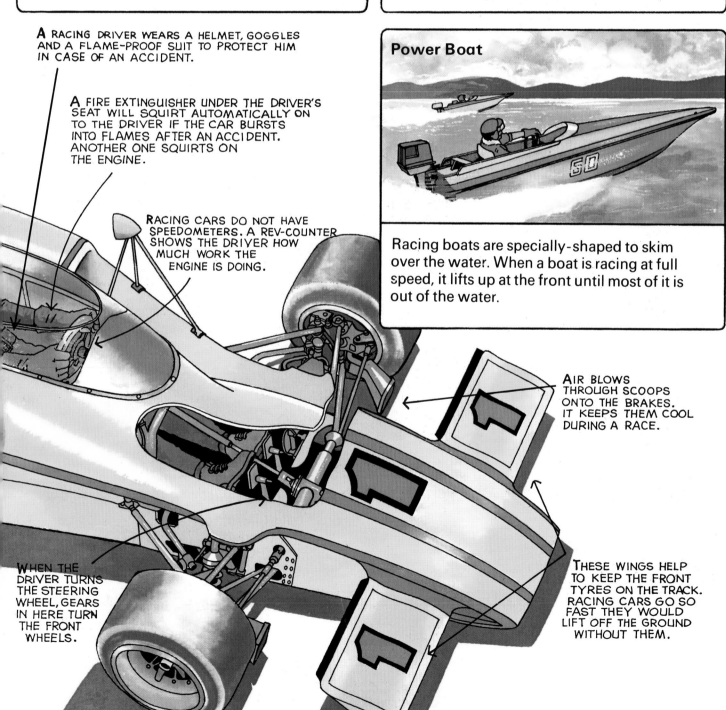

A RACING DRIVER WEARS A HELMET, GOGGLES AND A FLAME-PROOF SUIT TO PROTECT HIM IN CASE OF AN ACCIDENT.

A FIRE EXTINGUISHER UNDER THE DRIVER'S SEAT WILL SQUIRT AUTOMATICALLY ON TO THE DRIVER IF THE CAR BURSTS INTO FLAMES AFTER AN ACCIDENT. ANOTHER ONE SQUIRTS ON THE ENGINE.

RACING CARS DO NOT HAVE SPEEDOMETERS. A REV-COUNTER SHOWS THE DRIVER HOW MUCH WORK THE ENGINE IS DOING.

AIR BLOWS THROUGH SCOOPS ONTO THE BRAKES. IT KEEPS THEM COOL DURING A RACE.

WHEN THE DRIVER TURNS THE STEERING WHEEL, GEARS IN HERE TURN THE FRONT WHEELS.

THESE WINGS HELP TO KEEP THE FRONT TYRES ON THE TRACK. RACING CARS GO SO FAST THEY WOULD LIFT OFF THE GROUND WITHOUT THEM.

Finding a Lost Torpedo

1

THE MOTHER SHIP CARRIES SPECIAL EQUIPMENT TO TRACK THE SUBMARINE.

A midget submarine arrives in the search area on the deck of its mother ship.

2

THE SUBMARINE DIVES.

The crew climb on board. A crane lifts the submarine from the deck into the sea.

3

THE SONAR SENDS OUT PULSES OF SOUND. THEY BOUNCE OFF THINGS ON THE BOTTOM.

When the submarine reaches the bottom a machine, called a sonar, searches the sea bed.

4

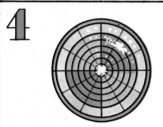

The flash on the screen shows the pilot that the sonar has found something.

5

THE CLAW AT THE FRONT GRABS THE TORPEDO

The submarine finds the torpedo. Now it takes it back to the ship on the surface.

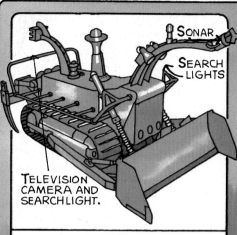

SONAR

SEARCH LIGHTS

TELEVISION CAMERA AND SEARCHLIGHT.

Underwater Bulldozer

This machine works on the sea bed without a driver. A man on the surface controls it and watches it with a television camera.

Deep-Sea Diving Suit

A diver inside this armoured suit can work or use a camera 300 metres underwater. A telephone line links him to people on the surface.

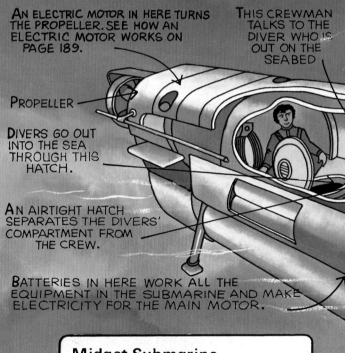

AN ELECTRIC MOTOR IN HERE TURNS THE PROPELLER. SEE HOW AN ELECTRIC MOTOR WORKS ON PAGE 189.

PROPELLER

DIVERS GO OUT INTO THE SEA THROUGH THIS HATCH.

AN AIRTIGHT HATCH SEPARATES THE DIVERS' COMPARTMENT FROM THE CREW.

BATTERIES IN HERE WORK ALL THE EQUIPMENT IN THE SUBMARINE AND MAKE ELECTRICITY FOR THE MAIN MOTOR.

THIS CREWMAN TALKS TO THE DIVER WHO IS OUT ON THE SEABED

THIS GAUGE SHOWS HOW DEEP THE SUBMARINE IS.

THE PILOT CHANGES THE ANGLE OF THESE FINS TO HELP THE SUBMARINE CLIMB OR DIVE.

Midget Submarine

This machine does all sorts of underwater jobs. It carries three crew and two divers. Tanks inside are flooded with water to make it heavy. This makes it sink. The water is blown out of the tanks to make it rise up to the surface again.

Underwater Machines

Many different machines are used to explore the sea bed and work underwater. The ones that dive very deep have to be a special shape and extra strong. This is to stop them being squashed by the huge weight of water pressing down on them.

Underwater Sports

DIVERS USE WATERPROOF CAMERAS AND LIGHTS TO TAKE PHOTOGRAPHS OF STRANGE CREATURES AND PLANTS.

THIS SEA SCOOTER TOWS A DIVER FOR ABOUT A KILOMETER ALONG THE SEA BED.

MOTOR

PROPELLERS

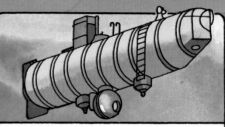

The Deepest Dive
In 1960 this underwater machine, called a bathyscape, dived 10,900 metres below the surface of the sea near Japan.

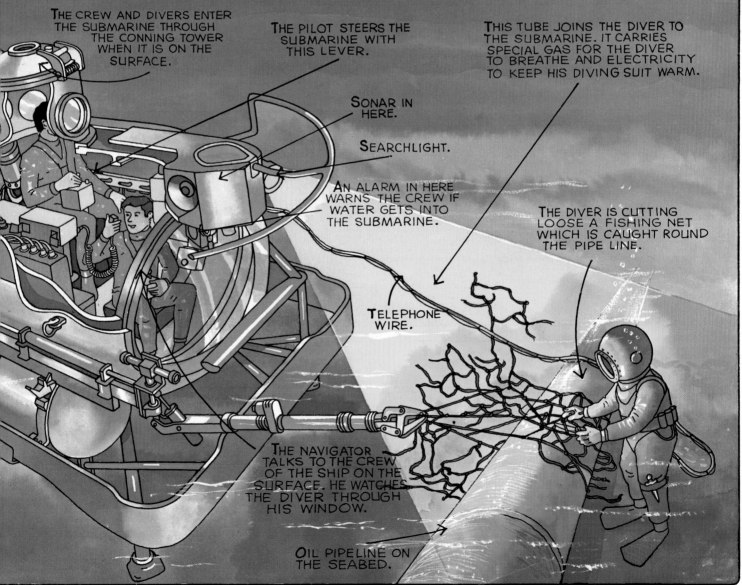

THE CREW AND DIVERS ENTER THE SUBMARINE THROUGH THE CONNING TOWER WHEN IT IS ON THE SURFACE.

THE PILOT STEERS THE SUBMARINE WITH THIS LEVER.

THIS TUBE JOINS THE DIVER TO THE SUBMARINE. IT CARRIES SPECIAL GAS FOR THE DIVER TO BREATHE AND ELECTRICITY TO KEEP HIS DIVING SUIT WARM.

SONAR IN HERE.

SEARCHLIGHT.

AN ALARM IN HERE WARNS THE CREW IF WATER GETS INTO THE SUBMARINE.

THE DIVER IS CUTTING LOOSE A FISHING NET WHICH IS CAUGHT ROUND THE PIPE LINE.

TELEPHONE WIRE.

THE NAVIGATOR TALKS TO THE CREW OF THE SHIP ON THE SURFACE. HE WATCHES THE DIVER THROUGH HIS WINDOW.

OIL PIPELINE ON THE SEABED.

Fighting Machines on Land

Modern armies use tanks and armoured cars like the ones on these pages to fight battles on land.

They are made of thick steel plates to protect the soldiers inside from enemy bullets and mines.

The tank is painted in different colours to make it difficult to see. This is called camouflage.

Battle Tank

This fighting machine has a crew of four—a commander, a gunner, a driver and a radio operator. It has two diesel engines at the back. The main one turns the wheels which drive the crawler tracks round. The small one helps the main engine to start.

RADIO AERIAL

TANK COMMANDER

TANK COMMANDER'S MACHINE GUN

THIS SEARCHLIGHT SHINES SPECIAL RAYS, CALLED INFRA-RED RAYS, AT ENEMY TARGETS AT NIGHT. NO ONE CAN SEE THE RAYS. THE TARGET SHOWS UP ON A SCREEN INSIDE.

SMOKE GRENADES ARE FIRED FROM HERE.

THE WHOLE TURRET TURNS RIGHT ROUND SO THAT THE GUN CAN FIRE IN ALL DIRECTIONS.

SPARE AMMUNITION FOR THE MAIN GUN IS STORED IN SPECIAL BINS OF WATER INSIDE THE TANK TO PREVENT EXPLOSIONS.

ALL THE HATCHES, LIKE THIS ONE, MUST FIT VERY TIGHTLY TO STOP WATER AND FLAMES GETTING INTO THE TANK.

THE DRIVER SITS LOW AT THE FRONT. HE STEERS THE TANK BY MAKING THE WHEELS ON ONE SIDE GO FASTER THAN THE OTHER.

THE BOTTOM OF THE TANK IS ROUNDED TO MAKE IT EXTRA STRONG IN CASE A MINE EXPLODES UNDER IT.

1 What a Tank Can Do

TANKS ARE WATERTIGHT AND CAN CROSS RIVERS. THE COMMANDER GIVES ORDERS TO THE CREW FROM THE TOP OF THE TOWER.

COMMANDER'S WATERTIGHT TOWER

2

THE GROOVES IN THE STEEL TRACKS GRAB A STEEP BANK. THE TANK'S POWERFUL MOTOR PUSHES IT UP.

3

TANKS MAKE SMOKE SCREENS DURING A BATTLE TO HIDE THEIR EXACT POSITION FROM THE ENEMY.

Guided Missile

This weapon is fired from an armoured car. It trails very thin wires behind it as it flies through the air. The soldier in the armoured car guides it on to the target by steering it with the wires.

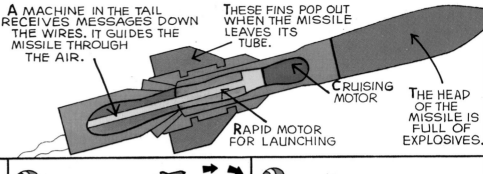

A MACHINE IN THE TAIL RECEIVES MESSAGES DOWN THE WIRES. IT GUIDES THE MISSILE THROUGH THE AIR.

THESE FINS POP OUT WHEN THE MISSILE LEAVES ITS TUBE.

CRUISING MOTOR

THE HEAD OF THE MISSILE IS FULL OF EXPLOSIVES.

RAPID MOTOR FOR LAUNCHING

1 THE MISSILE IS READY IN ITS TUBE.

The commander of the armoured car sights an enemy tank. The missile is in its tube.

2 FINS POP OUT.

WIRES TRAIL BEHIND.

He fires. The missile flies towards its target at 260 metres a second.

3

He scores a direct hit. The explosives in the nose of the missile blow up the tank.

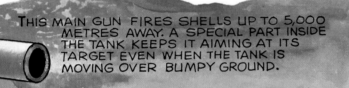

THIS MAIN GUN FIRES SHELLS UP TO 5,000 METRES AWAY. A SPECIAL PART INSIDE THE TANK KEEPS IT AIMING AT ITS TARGET EVEN WHEN THE TANK IS MOVING OVER BUMPY GROUND.

Armoured Troop Carrier

This machine carries 12 soldiers into battle. It can travel at 80 kph on roads. It is watertight and can go over water. Sometimes the carrier is used as an ambulance —it has room for seven wounded soldiers and two doctors.

SOLDIERS INSIDE FIRE THEIR WEAPONS THROUGH SMALL WINDOWS AND SLITS IN THE BACK AND SIDES.

THE TYRES HAVE SPECIAL TUBES WHICH CANNOT BE PUNCTURED

ALL THE WINDOWS ARE MADE OF VERY STRONG GLASS. THEY WILL NOT BREAK EVEN WHEN BULLETS HIT THEM.

THE BOTTOM IS HIGH OFF THE GROUND SO THE CARRIER CAN TRAVEL OVER VERY BUMPY GROUND.

STEEL TRACKS COVER THE WHEELS.

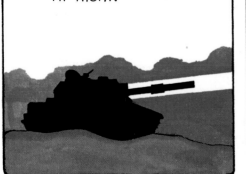

4 POWERFUL SEARCHLIGHTS ALLOW TANKS TO MOVE AND FIRE AT ENEMY TARGETS AT NIGHT.

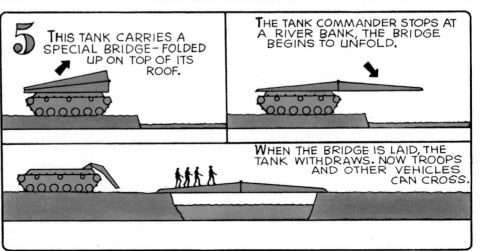

5 THIS TANK CARRIES A SPECIAL BRIDGE-FOLDED UP ON TOP OF ITS ROOF.

THE TANK COMMANDER STOPS AT A RIVER BANK, THE BRIDGE BEGINS TO UNFOLD.

WHEN THE BRIDGE IS LAID, THE TANK WITHDRAWS. NOW TROOPS AND OTHER VEHICLES CAN CROSS.

Fighting Machines in the Air

Fighting aeroplanes do many different jobs. Reconnaissance planes fly very high and fast to avoid enemy guns and missiles. Fighters are ready to attack enemy planes in the air, and transport planes carry troops and heavy weapons.

F.16 Fighter

This plane flies at over twice the speed of sound. It is very light and can turn quickly to dodge enemy planes during an air battle.

RADAR IN THE NOSE TRACKS ENEMY PLANES.

A RADAR SCREEN IN THE COCKPIT SHOWS THE PILOT WHICH WAY TO FLY.

COCKPIT COVER

AMMUNITION STORED HERE.

THIS BELT TAKES AMMUNITION TO THE GUN.

FLYING CONTROLS IN HERE.

GUN

THE PILOT PRESSES THIS PEDAL TO MOVE THE RUDDER.

THE ENGINE SUCKS IN AIR HERE.

FRONT LANDING WHEEL

AIR TUNNEL TO ENGINE.

SR.71A Blackbird

This reconnaissance plane cruises at 24,000 metres up, at three times the speed of sound. Special cameras, which can see through clouds, take photographs of the ground.

HATCH FOR MID-AIR REFUELLING.

THE TWO-MAN CREW WEAR SPACE SUITS TO PROTECT THEM IN CASE THEY HAVE TO EJECT AT GREAT HEIGHT.

MRCA Fighter

This plane has movable wings. The parts near the fuselage are fixed but the ends can swing backwards or forwards. When the wings are forward, the plane can take off and land slowly. When they are back, it cuts through the air more easily and can fly faster.

WINGS FORWARD FOR TAKING OFF AND LANDING.

WINGS BACK FOR SPEED.

ENGINE SUCKS IN AIR HERE.

NOSE LANDING WHEEL

166

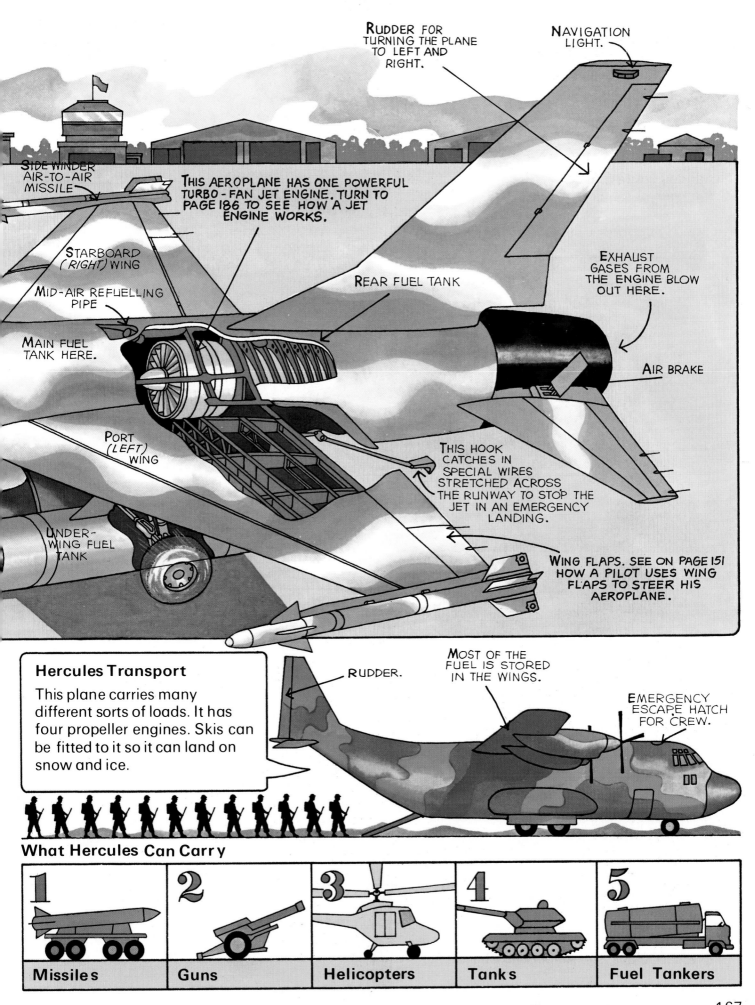

RUDDER FOR TURNING THE PLANE TO LEFT AND RIGHT.

NAVIGATION LIGHT.

SIDE WINDER AIR-TO-AIR MISSILE

THIS AEROPLANE HAS ONE POWERFUL TURBO-FAN JET ENGINE. TURN TO PAGE 186 TO SEE HOW A JET ENGINE WORKS.

STARBOARD (RIGHT) WING

MID-AIR REFUELLING PIPE

REAR FUEL TANK

EXHAUST GASES FROM THE ENGINE BLOW OUT HERE.

MAIN FUEL TANK HERE.

AIR BRAKE

PORT (LEFT) WING

THIS HOOK CATCHES IN SPECIAL WIRES STRETCHED ACROSS THE RUNWAY TO STOP THE JET IN AN EMERGENCY LANDING.

UNDER-WING FUEL TANK

WING FLAPS. SEE ON PAGE 151 HOW A PILOT USES WING FLAPS TO STEER HIS AEROPLANE.

Hercules Transport

This plane carries many different sorts of loads. It has four propeller engines. Skis can be fitted to it so it can land on snow and ice.

MOST OF THE FUEL IS STORED IN THE WINGS.

RUDDER.

EMERGENCY ESCAPE HATCH FOR CREW.

What Hercules Can Carry

1	2	3	4	5
Missiles	Guns	Helicopters	Tanks	Fuel Tankers

Guided Missile Launcher
Sailors below deck fire the missiles and guide them on to targets by radio signals.

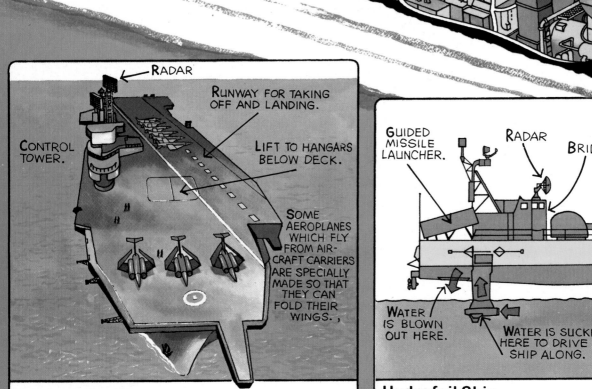

THE HELICOPTER IS COMING INTO LAND ON THE FLIGHT DECK. IT HAS BEEN SEARCHING FOR NEAR-BY ENEMY SHIPS AND SUBMARINES.

THIS AERIAL SENDS OUT AND PICKS UP RADIO MESSAGES. IT CAN INTERCEPT MESSAGES BETWEEN ENEMY SHIPS AND SHORE BASES.

THIS RADAR AERIAL ON THE MAIN MAST BEAMS OUT RADIO WAVES. WHEN THEY HIT A METAL OBJECT, SUCH AS ANOTHER SHIP, THEY BOUNCE BACK TO A RECEIVER. THE OBJECT SHOWS UP ON A SCREEN IN THE OPERATIONS ROOM.

THIS MACHINE TRACKS MISSILES AFTER THEY ARE LAUNCHED. SEAMEN IN THE OPERATING ROOM GUIDE THEM ON TO THEIR TARGET.

HELICOPTER LANDING DECK

HELICOPTER HANGAR

THIS SHIP HAS FOUR GAS TURBINE ENGINES—TWO BIG ONES FOR HIGH SPEED AND TWO SMALLER ONES FOR CRUISING.

RADAR

RUNWAY FOR TAKING OFF AND LANDING.

CONTROL TOWER.

LIFT TO HANGARS BELOW DECK.

SOME AEROPLANES WHICH FLY FROM AIR-CRAFT CARRIERS ARE SPECIALLY MADE SO THAT THEY CAN FOLD THEIR WINGS.

Aircraft Carrier
This giant ship is like a floating airport. Jets and helicopters are stored inside and brought up on to deck by lift. Ships like this have a crew of over 2,000 officers, sailors and pilots.

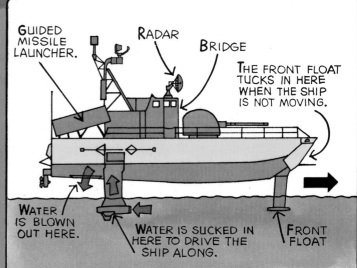

GUIDED MISSILE LAUNCHER.

RADAR

BRIDGE

THE FRONT FLOAT TUCKS IN HERE WHEN THE SHIP IS NOT MOVING.

WATER IS BLOWN OUT HERE.

WATER IS SUCKED IN HERE TO DRIVE THE SHIP ALONG.

FRONT FLOAT

Hydrofoil Ship
This ship has wings, called foils, which are just below the surface. When it is not moving, it sits on the water like an ordinary ship. As it gets up speed it skims along on the foils at up to 90 kph.

Fighting Machines at Sea

Frigate
This fast warship is used to defend slower ships from attack by enemy ships, aircraft and submarines.

The ships sailed by the world's navies have to be ready for action at any time. In a war, they help to defend their country from attack and carry troops and weapons to other countries.

They also protect convoys of cargo ships from enemy ships and submarines. In peace time, the ships have many important jobs, such as mapping the sea bed and rescuing people from accidents at sea.

THE SHIP IS STEERED FROM THE BRIDGE. A MACHINE CALLED AN AUTOPILOT KEEPS IT SAILING IN THE RIGHT DIRECTION, EVEN IN VERY ROUGH WEATHER.

THIS IS THE MAIN GUN. IT FIRES SHELLS UP TO 11 KILOMETRES AWAY. SAILORS BELOW DECK LOAD SHELLS ON TO A CONVEYOR WHICH FEEDS THE GUN. WHEN ELECTRONIC EQUIPMENT HAS WORKED OUT WHERE THE TARGET IS, THE GUN AIMS AND FIRES AUTOMATICALLY.

THE OPERATIONS ROOM IS BELOW THE BRIDGE. DURING A BATTLE THE CAPTAIN CONTROLS THE SHIP FROM HERE.

Nuclear Submarine
This submarine carries enough food and air to go all round the world without coming to the surface. It has a crew of 143. Its 16 missiles can be fired from under the water at targets up to 4,000 kilometres away.

Rescue Machines

These machines have all been specially made to rescue people trapped by fires, in snow, in crashed planes and cars, or from sinking ships. They are always ready for action.

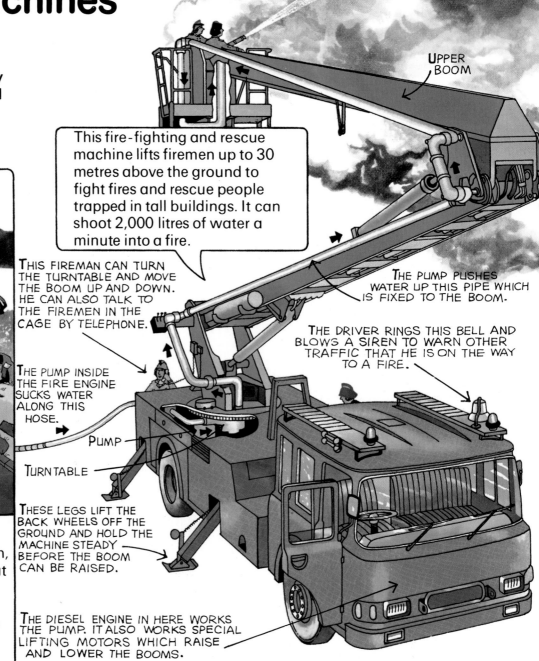

UPPER BOOM

This fire-fighting and rescue machine lifts firemen up to 30 metres above the ground to fight fires and rescue people trapped in tall buildings. It can shoot 2,000 litres of water a minute into a fire.

THIS FIREMAN CAN TURN THE TURNTABLE AND MOVE THE BOOM UP AND DOWN. HE CAN ALSO TALK TO THE FIREMEN IN THE CAGE BY TELEPHONE.

THE PUMP PUSHES WATER UP THIS PIPE WHICH IS FIXED TO THE BOOM.

THE DRIVER RINGS THIS BELL AND BLOWS A SIREN TO WARN OTHER TRAFFIC THAT HE IS ON THE WAY TO A FIRE.

THE PUMP INSIDE THE FIRE ENGINE SUCKS WATER ALONG THIS HOSE.

PUMP

TURNTABLE

THESE LEGS LIFT THE BACK WHEELS OFF THE GROUND AND HOLD THE MACHINE STEADY BEFORE THE BOOM CAN BE RAISED.

THE DIESEL ENGINE IN HERE WORKS THE PUMP. IT ALSO WORKS SPECIAL LIFTING MOTORS WHICH RAISE AND LOWER THE BOOMS.

Motorway Fire Fighter

If there is a bad road crash, a truck like this races to put out the fire. It can shoot out more than 13,000 litres of foam in less than a minute.

Airport Crash Lorry

Firemen use this sort of machine to fight fires in crashed aeroplanes. The machine is full of water and foam. The pump on top shoots foam on to a blazing aeroplane up to 100 metres away. The foam spreads over the flames and smothers them. Small pumps shoot foam round the lorry.

Launching a Lifeboat

Some lifeboats are kept in sheds on the seashore. They are launched down a slipway into the sea.

Lifeboat

Specially-trained seamen go out in lifeboats like this to rescue people at sea. Lifeboats are made to stay afloat in even the worst storms. This one has two diesel engines which turn two propellers to drive the boat through the water. See how diesel engines work on page 189.

MASTHEAD LIGHT

RADAR SCANNER

THE MAN IN COMMAND IS CALLED THE COXSWAIN. HE STEERS THE BOAT FROM THE WHEELHOUSE.

THE BACK AIRTIGHT COMPARTMENT CARRIES STRETCHERS AND FIRST AID EQUIPMENT FOR INJURED SURVIVORS.

FRONT AIRTIGHT COMPARTMENT IN HERE.

THE HULL OF THIS LIFE BOAT IS MADE OF STEEL. SOME ARE MADE OF WOOD OR GLASSFIBRE.

What Happens if a Lifeboat Capsizes

1 THE TOP PART IS AIRTIGHT

THE HULL IS HEAVY

A giant wave hits the side of the boat.

2 NOW THE HEAVY HULL IS ON THE SURFACE

THE AIRTIGHT PART IS UNDER WATER

The boat rolls over. Now it is top heavy.

3 THE HEAVY HULL PUSHES DOWN

THE AIRTIGHT PART PUSHES UP

It begins to turn the right way up again.

4 THE AIRTIGHT PART IS ABOVE THE WATER AGAIN

THE HEAVY HULL HOLDS THE BOAT DOWN IN THE WATER.

Now the boat is upright again.

Snow Blower

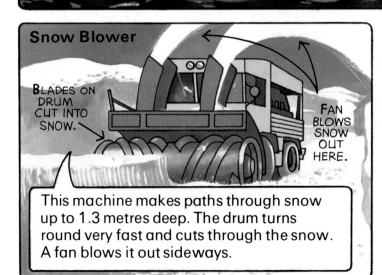

BLADES ON DRUM CUT INTO SNOW.

FAN BLOWS SNOW OUT HERE.

This machine makes paths through snow up to 1.3 metres deep. The drum turns round very fast and cuts through the snow. A fan blows it out sideways.

Mountain Rescue Aeroplane

Small aeroplanes with skis can land on the snow on high mountains. They rescue injured climbers and people trapped by storms and avalanches.

Building Machines

Tall buildings need strong foundations deep in the ground for them to stand on. The crane and drilling machine on this building site are boring holes for the concrete foundations.

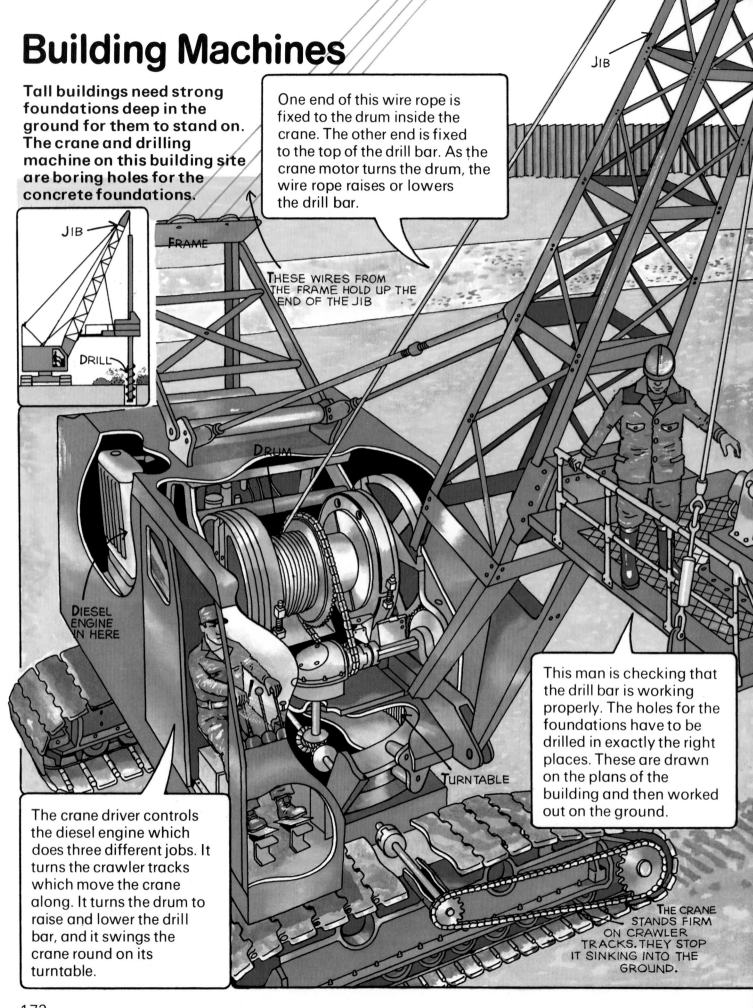

JIB

DRILL

JIB

One end of this wire rope is fixed to the drum inside the crane. The other end is fixed to the top of the drill bar. As the crane motor turns the drum, the wire rope raises or lowers the drill bar.

FRAME

THESE WIRES FROM THE FRAME HOLD UP THE END OF THE JIB

DRUM

DIESEL ENGINE IN HERE

TURNTABLE

This man is checking that the drill bar is working properly. The holes for the foundations have to be drilled in exactly the right places. These are drawn on the plans of the building and then worked out on the ground.

The crane driver controls the diesel engine which does three different jobs. It turns the crawler tracks which move the crane along. It turns the drum to raise and lower the drill bar, and it swings the crane round on its turntable.

THE CRANE STANDS FIRM ON CRAWLER TRACKS. THEY STOP IT SINKING INTO THE GROUND.

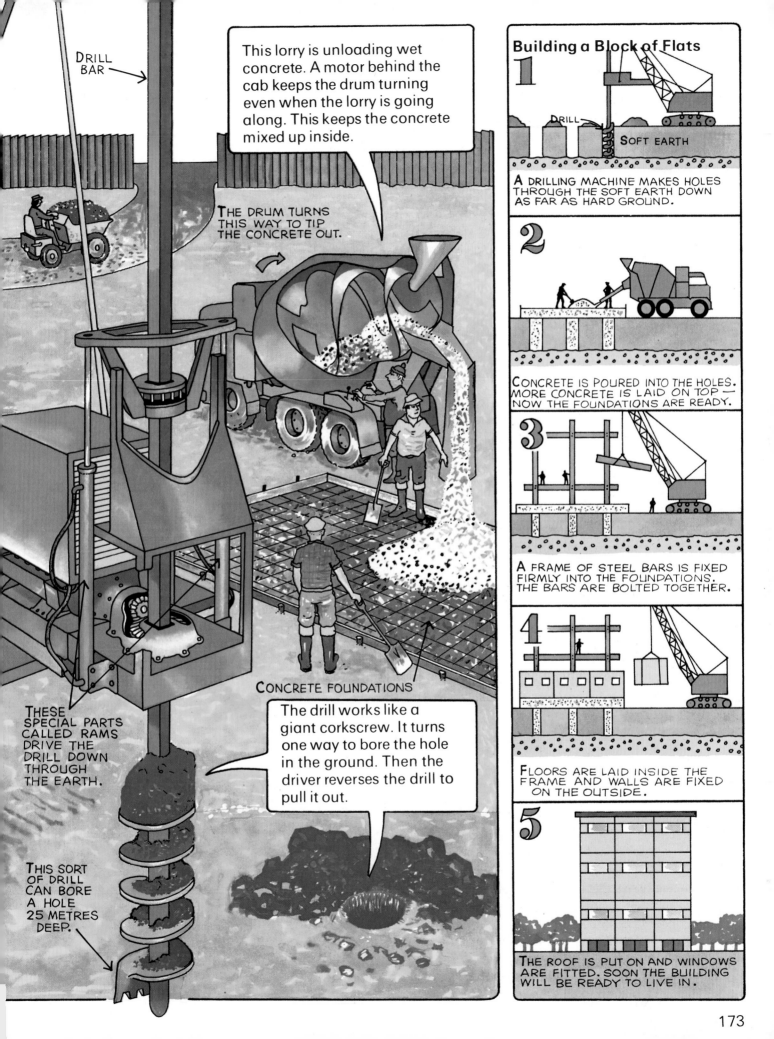

DRILL BAR

This lorry is unloading wet concrete. A motor behind the cab keeps the drum turning even when the lorry is going along. This keeps the concrete mixed up inside.

THE DRUM TURNS THIS WAY TO TIP THE CONCRETE OUT.

THESE SPECIAL PARTS CALLED RAMS DRIVE THE DRILL DOWN THROUGH THE EARTH.

THIS SORT OF DRILL CAN BORE A HOLE 25 METRES DEEP.

CONCRETE FOUNDATIONS

The drill works like a giant corkscrew. It turns one way to bore the hole in the ground. Then the driver reverses the drill to pull it out.

Building a Block of Flats

1 DRILL · SOFT EARTH

A DRILLING MACHINE MAKES HOLES THROUGH THE SOFT EARTH DOWN AS FAR AS HARD GROUND.

2

CONCRETE IS POURED INTO THE HOLES. MORE CONCRETE IS LAID ON TOP — NOW THE FOUNDATIONS ARE READY.

3

A FRAME OF STEEL BARS IS FIXED FIRMLY INTO THE FOUNDATIONS. THE BARS ARE BOLTED TOGETHER.

4

FLOORS ARE LAID INSIDE THE FRAME AND WALLS ARE FIXED ON THE OUTSIDE.

5

THE ROOF IS PUT ON AND WINDOWS ARE FITTED. SOON THE BUILDING WILL BE READY TO LIVE IN.

173

Road Making

Motorways are specially built so that cars and very heavy lorries can speed safely along them. They have to be level with strong foundations.

Follow the numbers at the bottom of the page. They show how the different machines are used to carve out a new road. First they prepare the ground. Then they build up a motorway on the top.

The blade underneath this grader smooths out the ground. It is slightly tilted so the road will slope from the middle to the sides.

This asphalt machine is pushing the lorry slowly in front of it. As the hot asphalt tips out, the machine spreads it on while it is soft.

ARMS

DIESEL ENGINE

HOOKS LIKE THIS AT THE BACK ARE USED TO DRAG OUT TREE ROOTS OR BIG BOULDERS.

The bulldozer driver uses the big blade at the front to push earth and rocks out of the way. The blade is worked by long arms which move it up and down and tip it forwards and backwards.

Bulldozers have crawler tracks like tanks. The tracks are made of steel and fit over the wheels. They stop bulldozers sinking and help them to push heavy loads when the ground is very soft or muddy.

1 Bulldozing	**2 Scraping**	**3 Grading**	**4 Rolling**
After the path of a new road has been worked out, bulldozers are the first machines used. They clear the path.	Scrapers level out the road bed. They pile up the earth into banks beside the road or take it away and dump it.	Graders work like snowploughs. A heavy steel blade sweeps aside loose earth, levels bumps and fills in holes.	Heavy rollers pack down the earth until the road bed is hard and flat. Now the road can be built on top.

EARTH IS PILED UP BESIDE THE TRENCH. IT WILL BE PUT BACK AFTER THE DRAINS HAVE BEEN PUT IN.

An excavator is digging a trench for drains. Roads slope down from the middle so rain water will run off at each side.

This giant scraper levels out the ground. It scoops up huge loads of earth, takes them away and dumps them. A diesel engine drives the scraper along, turns the paddles round and raises and lowers the blade. See how a diesel engine works on page 189.

THE PADDLES WORK LIKE A MOVING STAIRCASE. THEY PICK UP THE EARTH AND DROP IT INTO THE BOWL.

BOWL

PADDLES

BLADE

DIESEL ENGINE

The blade is fixed across the front of the bowl. When the driver lowers the bowl, the blade slices off the top layer of earth as the scraper goes along.

Deep grooves in the tyres help the scraper to grip when it is carrying a heavy load.

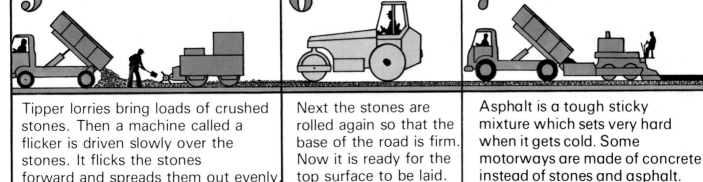

5 Laying Stones

Tipper lorries bring loads of crushed stones. Then a machine called a flicker is driven slowly over the stones. It flicks the stones forward and spreads them out evenly.

6 Rolling

Next the stones are rolled again so that the base of the road is firm. Now it is ready for the top surface to be laid.

7 Laying Asphalt

Asphalt is a tough sticky mixture which sets very hard when it gets cold. Some motorways are made of concrete instead of stones and asphalt.

Mining and Excavating

Lots of valuable metals and minerals, such as gold, copper, coal and diamonds, lie buried in the ground. Some are only a few metres down. Giant shovels and excavators dig them out at open surface mines.

Some things are found thousands of metres under the ground. Miners dig deep shafts down to reach them. Underground mining is dangerous because tunnels can cave in and gases in mines cause explosions.

Bucket Wheel Excavator

This giant machine digs on the surface. It has 26 electric motors to make all the parts work. It uses as much electricity as a small town and needs 13 men to work it. See how electric motors work on page 189.

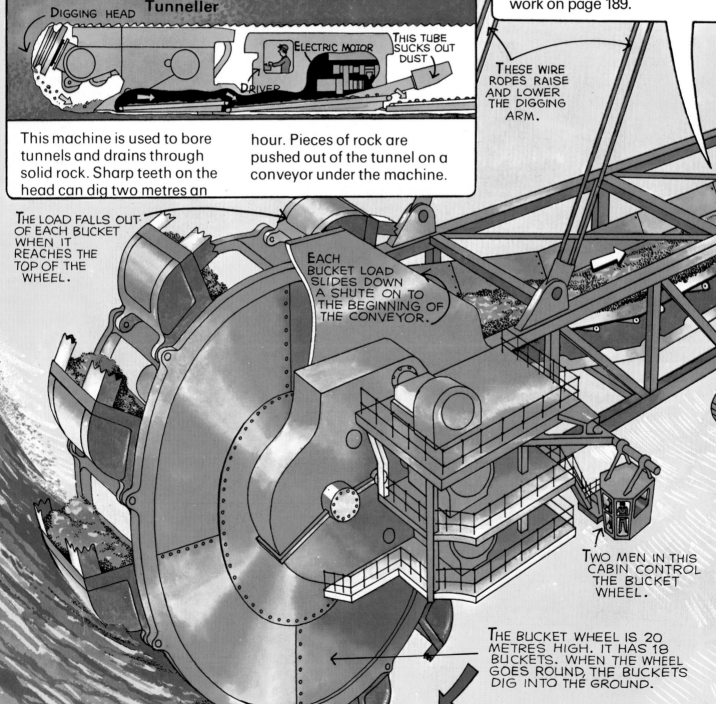

Tunneller

DIGGING HEAD

ELECTRIC MOTOR

THIS TUBE SUCKS OUT DUST

DRIVER

This machine is used to bore tunnels and drains through solid rock. Sharp teeth on the head can dig two metres an hour. Pieces of rock are pushed out of the tunnel on a conveyor under the machine.

THESE WIRE ROPES RAISE AND LOWER THE DIGGING ARM.

THE LOAD FALLS OUT OF EACH BUCKET WHEN IT REACHES THE TOP OF THE WHEEL.

EACH BUCKET LOAD SLIDES DOWN A SHUTE ON TO THE BEGINNING OF THE CONVEYOR.

TWO MEN IN THIS CABIN CONTROL THE BUCKET WHEEL.

THE BUCKET WHEEL IS 20 METRES HIGH. IT HAS 18 BUCKETS. WHEN THE WHEEL GOES ROUND, THE BUCKETS DIG INTO THE GROUND.

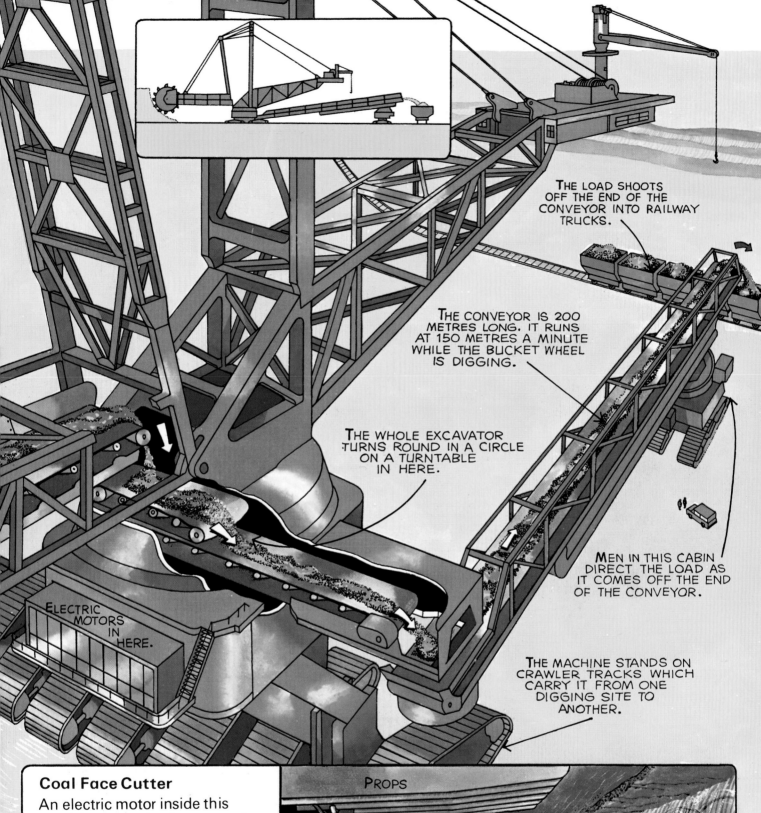

THE LOAD SHOOTS OFF THE END OF THE CONVEYOR INTO RAILWAY TRUCKS.

THE CONVEYOR IS 200 METRES LONG. IT RUNS AT 150 METRES A MINUTE WHILE THE BUCKET WHEEL IS DIGGING.

THE WHOLE EXCAVATOR TURNS ROUND IN A CIRCLE ON A TURNTABLE IN HERE.

MEN IN THIS CABIN DIRECT THE LOAD AS IT COMES OFF THE END OF THE CONVEYOR.

ELECTRIC MOTORS IN HERE.

THE MACHINE STANDS ON CRAWLER TRACKS WHICH CARRY IT FROM ONE DIGGING SITE TO ANOTHER.

Coal Face Cutter

An electric motor inside this machine turns the drum round very fast. Teeth on the drum tear out the coal from the coal face. The machine pulls itself along the chain beside the rails. Miners work the levers which push the props forward and hold up the roof after the machine goes past.

PROPS

TEETH

COAL FACE

MOTOR

DRUM

CHAIN

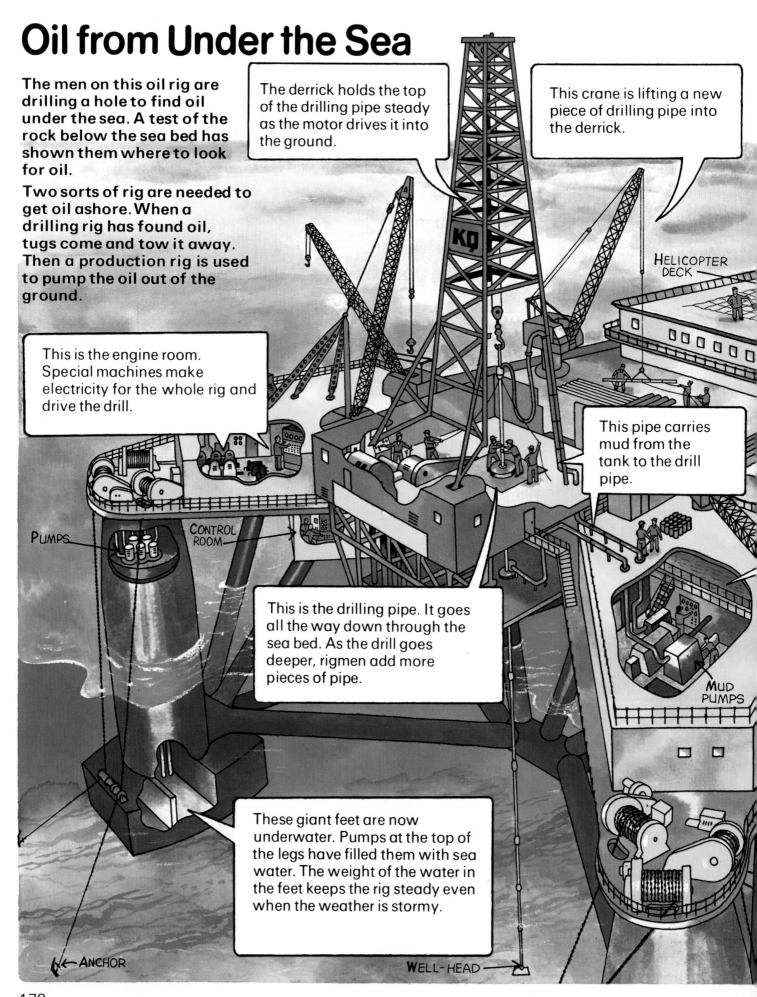

Oil from Under the Sea

The men on this oil rig are drilling a hole to find oil under the sea. A test of the rock below the sea bed has shown them where to look for oil.

Two sorts of rig are needed to get oil ashore. When a drilling rig has found oil, tugs come and tow it away. Then a production rig is used to pump the oil out of the ground.

The derrick holds the top of the drilling pipe steady as the motor drives it into the ground.

This crane is lifting a new piece of drilling pipe into the derrick.

HELICOPTER DECK

This is the engine room. Special machines make electricity for the whole rig and drive the drill.

This pipe carries mud from the tank to the drill pipe.

PUMPS

CONTROL ROOM

This is the drilling pipe. It goes all the way down through the sea bed. As the drill goes deeper, rigmen add more pieces of pipe.

MUD PUMPS

These giant feet are now underwater. Pumps at the top of the legs have filled them with sea water. The weight of the water in the feet keeps the rig steady even when the weather is stormy.

ANCHOR

WELL-HEAD

A helicopter is bringing fresh crewmen out to the rig. This drilling rig needs a crew of 70 to keep it working day and night.

The men in the radio room are in touch with near-by ships and other oil rigs. Local weather stations warn them of storms.

BEDROOMS

To find out if there is oil, special mud is pumped down the drill pipe. It is sucked back up with bits of rock from the bottom. If oil is there, traces will be found on the rocks.

A supply boat is bringing water and stores for the crewmen from the nearest port.

Deep-sea divers are going down to check the anchors. If the anchors slipped, the waves would move the rig from its place above the well-head.

Striking Oil

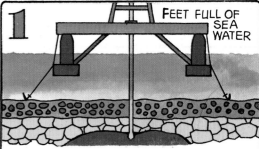

1 FEET FULL OF SEA WATER

The rig is low in the water for drilling. It has found a pocket of oil under the sea.

2 TUGS TOW DRILLING RIG TO ANOTHER SITE.

The drilling rig has done its job. The water is pumped out of its feet. It floats to the surface.

3 PRODUCTION RIG STANDS ON SEA BED.

Now the production rig is towed into place. It will pump the oil out of the ground.

4 PIPE-LAYING BARGE   OIL PIPE

A pipeline is laid on the seabed. The oil is pumped along it from the rig to an oil refinery.

Farming Machines

Farmers use lots of machines to prepare their land, sow seeds and harvest the crops.

Follow the numbers at the bottom of the page to see how a farmer grows a crop of wheat.

Tractors and combine harvesters have diesel engines. See how they work on page 189.

Combine Harvester

This machine can harvest many different crops, such as wheat, rice and maize. It cuts the crop, then it separates the seeds from the stalks. The diesel engine beside the driver works all the different parts and drives the machine along.

THE TABLE IS FIVE METRES WIDE. THE FARMER TAKES IT OFF TO DRIVE ALONG THE ROAD. HE PULLS IT ON A TRAILER BEHIND THE COMBINE HARVESTER.

DIESEL ENGINE

5 THE ELEVATOR PUSHES THE CROP UP TO THE CYLINDER.

1 THE REEL SPINS AS THE COMBINE HARVESTER DRIVES THROUGH THE CROP. IT COMBS THE WHEAT TOWARDS THE CUTTER BAR.

2 THE KNIFE IN THE CUTTER BAR MOVES FROM SIDE TO SIDE VERY QUICKLY TO CUT THE STALKS.

1 Ploughing

In winter and spring, farmers use ploughs to break up the soil. Blades cut into the ground and turn it over in furrows

2 Tilling

Clods of earth left by the plough are broken up into small pieces. Now the soil is level and ready for the seeds.

3 Sowing

This long box is full of seeds and fertilizer. As the tractor pulls the drill along, each tube sows a row of seeds.

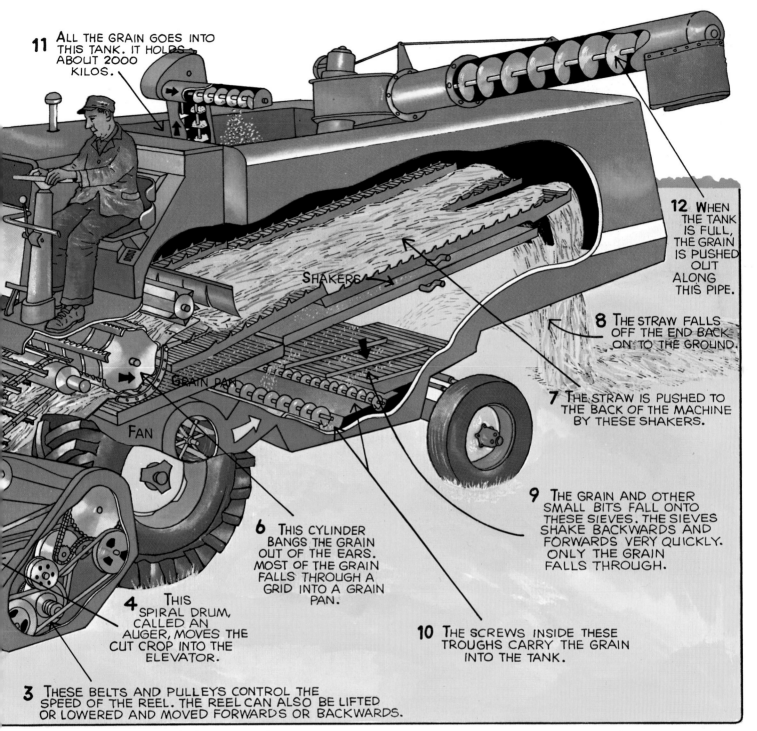

11 ALL THE GRAIN GOES INTO THIS TANK. IT HOLDS ABOUT 2000 KILOS.

12 WHEN THE TANK IS FULL, THE GRAIN IS PUSHED OUT ALONG THIS PIPE.

SHAKERS

8 THE STRAW FALLS OFF THE END BACK ON TO THE GROUND.

7 THE STRAW IS PUSHED TO THE BACK OF THE MACHINE BY THESE SHAKERS.

GRAIN PAN

FAN

9 THE GRAIN AND OTHER SMALL BITS FALL ONTO THESE SIEVES. THE SIEVES SHAKE BACKWARDS AND FORWARDS VERY QUICKLY. ONLY THE GRAIN FALLS THROUGH.

6 THIS CYLINDER BANGS THE GRAIN OUT OF THE EARS. MOST OF THE GRAIN FALLS THROUGH A GRID INTO A GRAIN PAN.

4 THIS SPIRAL DRUM, CALLED AN AUGER, MOVES THE CUT CROP INTO THE ELEVATOR.

10 THE SCREWS INSIDE THESE TROUGHS CARRY THE GRAIN INTO THE TANK.

3 THESE BELTS AND PULLEYS CONTROL THE SPEED OF THE REEL. THE REEL CAN ALSO BE LIFTED OR LOWERED AND MOVED FORWARDS OR BACKWARDS.

4 Spraying

Farmers spray the small plants to kill insects and weeds. A pump squirts out liquid through nozzles on to the wheat.

5 Baling

After the grain has been harvested, this machine gathers up the straw. It squeezes it into bales and ties them up.

6 Drying

DAMP GRAIN GOES IN HERE.

DRY GRAIN

HOT AIR

FAN

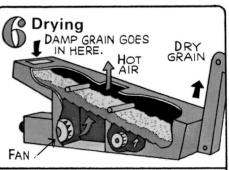

Damp grain from the combine harvester is fed into this machine. A fan blows hot air over the grain to dry it.

Dairy Machines

This modern milking machine helps farmers to milk their cows quickly and easily. An electric motor turns the whole machine slowly round with the cows standing on it. Follow the numbers to see how all the different parts work. Turn to page 189 to see how an electric motor works.

WHEN THE COWS HAVE NO MORE MILK TO GIVE, THE FARMER TAKES OFF THE PIPES.

← COWS GO OUT THIS WAY

COWS STEP OFF THE MACHINE HERE.

COWS COME IN HERE.

A SPECIAL GATE LETS THEM IN ONE AT A TIME

EACH COW STEPS ON TO THE SLOWLY MOVING TURNTABLE HERE.

THIS COW IS WALKING IN TO THE FIRST EMPTY MANGER.

THIS COW IS BEGINNING TO EAT FROM A MANGER. THE FARMER HAS FITTED THE PIPES TO ITS UDDERS.

1 Working the Machine

CONTROL PANELS

The farmer stands in the middle of the machine. He makes it start and stop. He dials the right amount of food for each cow.

2 Feeding

PELLETS OF SPECIAL FOOD FALL DOWN A SHUTE FROM THE LOFT INTO EACH MANGER.

Cows eat grass in the summer and hay in the winter. Farmers also give them some special food each day to help them make extra milk.

3 Neck Yokes

THIS GAP IS READY FOR THE COW TO PUSH ITS HEAD THROUGH.

WHEN THE COW COMES TO THE MANGER IT MUST PUSH ITS HEAD THROUGH THE BARS TO REACH THE FOOD.

AS IT LOWERS ITS HEAD IT PUSHES THE BOTTOM OF THE BAR OUT SO THAT THE TOP SWINGS IN TO HOLD ITS NECK.

Cows give more milk if they stand quietly while they are being milked. These yokes hold them firmly by the neck when they lower their heads to feed.

MILK FROM EACH BOTTLE IS PUMPED ALONG THIS PIPE TO THE STORAGE TANK.

AS THE COWS MOVE ROUND ON THE TURNTABLE, THE MILKING MACHINE SUCKS THE MILK FROM THEIR UDDERS INTO THE GLASS JARS.

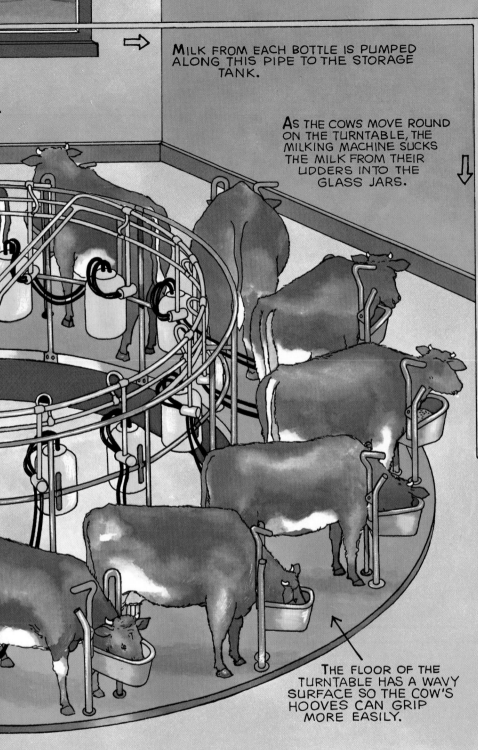

THE FLOOR OF THE TURNTABLE HAS A WAVY SURFACE SO THE COW'S HOOVES CAN GRIP MORE EASILY.

THE MACHINE RESTS ON SMOOTH RUNNING ROLLERS.

How the Machine Works

An electric motor under the floor turns a wheel with teeth on it. The teeth fit into notches round the bottom of the floor. As the wheel is turned, it pushes the whole milking machine round.

5 COOLER TANKER LORRY TANK

Where Milk Goes To

The milk is cooled and stored in a large cold tank. This stops it going sour. A lorry comes to collect it from the farm. The milk either goes to a factory to be bottled or to be made into butter, cheese or yoghurt.

4 **Milking**

The farmer cleans the cow's udders. Then he fits rubber tubes which are joined to a pump. This sucks out the milk into a bottle beside each cow.

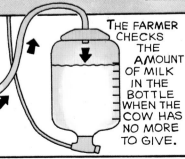

THE FARMER CHECKS THE AMOUNT OF MILK IN THE BOTTLE WHEN THE COW HAS NO MORE TO GIVE.

Each bottle has marks on it so the farmer can see how much milk each cow gives.

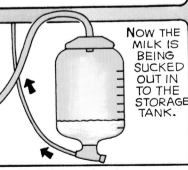

NOW THE MILK IS BEING SUCKED OUT INTO THE STORAGE TANK.

If a cow only gives a little milk, the farmer knows it is not well.

183

Home Machines

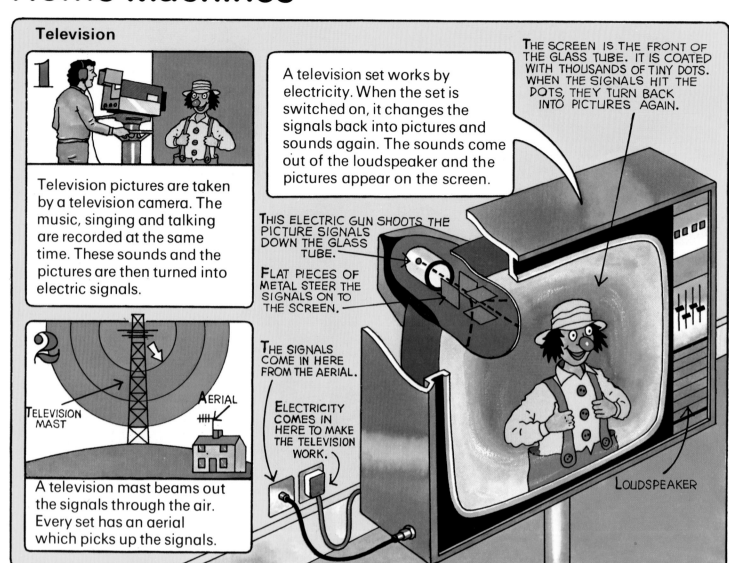

Television

1

Television pictures are taken by a television camera. The music, singing and talking are recorded at the same time. These sounds and the pictures are then turned into electric signals.

2

A television mast beams out the signals through the air. Every set has an aerial which picks up the signals.

TELEVISION MAST

AERIAL

A television set works by electricity. When the set is switched on, it changes the signals back into pictures and sounds again. The sounds come out of the loudspeaker and the pictures appear on the screen.

THE SCREEN IS THE FRONT OF THE GLASS TUBE. IT IS COATED WITH THOUSANDS OF TINY DOTS. WHEN THE SIGNALS HIT THE DOTS, THEY TURN BACK INTO PICTURES AGAIN.

THIS ELECTRIC GUN SHOOTS THE PICTURE SIGNALS DOWN THE GLASS TUBE.

FLAT PIECES OF METAL STEER THE SIGNALS ON TO THE SCREEN.

THE SIGNALS COME IN HERE FROM THE AERIAL.

ELECTRICITY COMES IN HERE TO MAKE THE TELEVISION WORK.

LOUDSPEAKER

Telephone

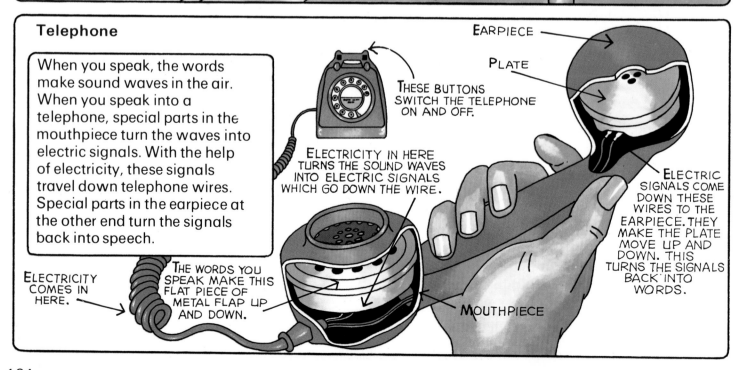

When you speak, the words make sound waves in the air. When you speak into a telephone, special parts in the mouthpiece turn the waves into electric signals. With the help of electricity, these signals travel down telephone wires. Special parts in the earpiece at the other end turn the signals back into speech.

ELECTRICITY COMES IN HERE.

THE WORDS YOU SPEAK MAKE THIS FLAT PIECE OF METAL FLAP UP AND DOWN.

THESE BUTTONS SWITCH THE TELEPHONE ON AND OFF.

ELECTRICITY IN HERE TURNS THE SOUND WAVES INTO ELECTRIC SIGNALS WHICH GO DOWN THE WIRE.

EARPIECE

PLATE

ELECTRIC SIGNALS COME DOWN THESE WIRES TO THE EARPIECE. THEY MAKE THE PLATE MOVE UP AND DOWN. THIS TURNS THE SIGNALS BACK INTO WORDS.

MOUTHPIECE

Refrigerator

A refrigerator is very cold inside because all the warmth is taken out of the air in it. This is done by a special liquid which is pumped through a pipe at the back. Follow the numbers to see how the liquid changes as it goes round inside the pipe.

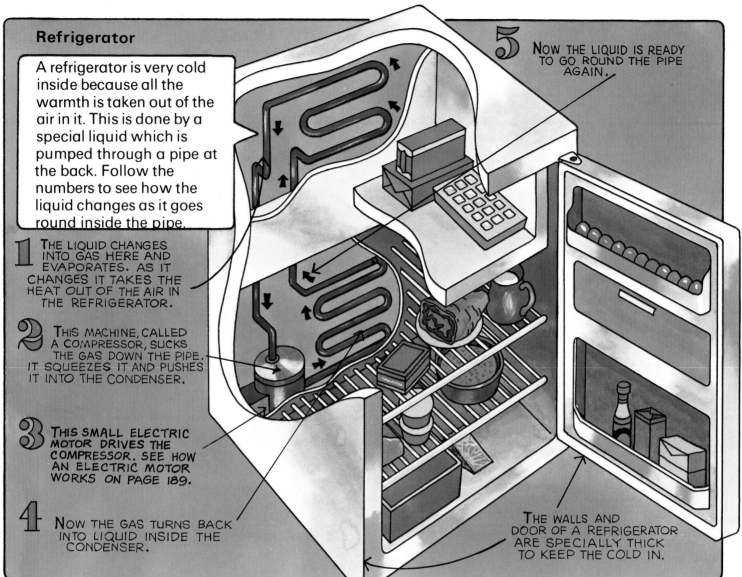

1 THE LIQUID CHANGES INTO GAS HERE AND EVAPORATES. AS IT CHANGES IT TAKES THE HEAT OUT OF THE AIR IN THE REFRIGERATOR.

2 THIS MACHINE, CALLED A COMPRESSOR, SUCKS THE GAS DOWN THE PIPE. IT SQUEEZES IT AND PUSHES IT INTO THE CONDENSER.

3 THIS SMALL ELECTRIC MOTOR DRIVES THE COMPRESSOR. SEE HOW AN ELECTRIC MOTOR WORKS ON PAGE 189.

4 NOW THE GAS TURNS BACK INTO LIQUID INSIDE THE CONDENSER.

5 NOW THE LIQUID IS READY TO GO ROUND THE PIPE AGAIN.

THE WALLS AND DOOR OF A REFRIGERATOR ARE SPECIALLY THICK TO KEEP THE COLD IN.

Lavatory

The water tank above a lavatory is called a cistern. This one is full of water because the handle is up.

Now the handle is down. It has pulled up the plunger and forced the water through the pipe to the bowl.

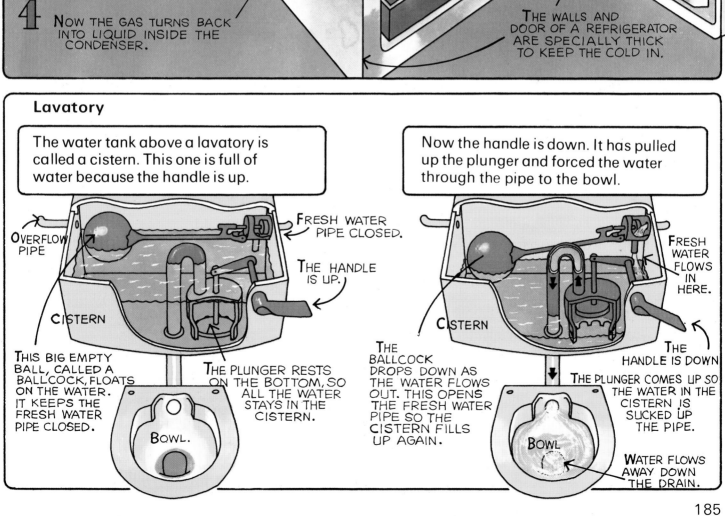

OVERFLOW PIPE

FRESH WATER PIPE CLOSED.

THE HANDLE IS UP.

CISTERN

THIS BIG EMPTY BALL, CALLED A BALLCOCK, FLOATS ON THE WATER. IT KEEPS THE FRESH WATER PIPE CLOSED.

THE PLUNGER RESTS ON THE BOTTOM, SO ALL THE WATER STAYS IN THE CISTERN.

BOWL.

CISTERN

THE BALLCOCK DROPS DOWN AS THE WATER FLOWS OUT. THIS OPENS THE FRESH WATER PIPE SO THE CISTERN FILLS UP AGAIN.

FRESH WATER FLOWS IN HERE.

THE HANDLE IS DOWN

THE PLUNGER COMES UP SO THE WATER IN THE CISTERN IS SUCKED UP THE PIPE.

BOWL

WATER FLOWS AWAY DOWN THE DRAIN.

How Motors Work

Jet Engines

Most jet aircraft have gas turbine engines. They burn special fuel called kerosene in a combustion chamber. As the kerosene burns, it makes hot gases which are blown out of the back of the engine. They push the plane through the air.
Follow the numbers in the pictures to see how three different jet engines work.

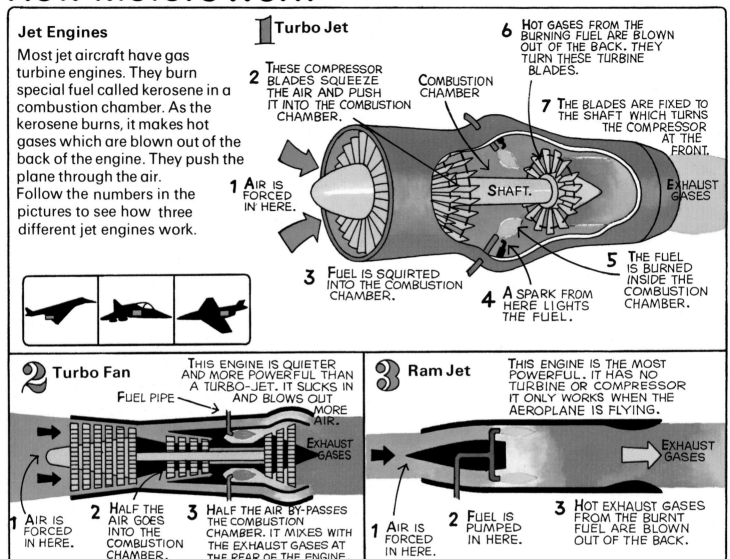

1 Turbo Jet

2 THESE COMPRESSOR BLADES SQUEEZE THE AIR AND PUSH IT INTO THE COMBUSTION CHAMBER.

COMBUSTION CHAMBER

6 HOT GASES FROM THE BURNING FUEL ARE BLOWN OUT OF THE BACK. THEY TURN THESE TURBINE BLADES.

7 THE BLADES ARE FIXED TO THE SHAFT WHICH TURNS THE COMPRESSOR AT THE FRONT.

1 AIR IS FORCED IN HERE.

SHAFT.

EXHAUST GASES

3 FUEL IS SQUIRTED INTO THE COMBUSTION CHAMBER.

4 A SPARK FROM HERE LIGHTS THE FUEL.

5 THE FUEL IS BURNED INSIDE THE COMBUSTION CHAMBER.

2 Turbo Fan

THIS ENGINE IS QUIETER AND MORE POWERFUL THAN A TURBO-JET. IT SUCKS IN AND BLOWS OUT MORE AIR.

FUEL PIPE

EXHAUST GASES

1 AIR IS FORCED IN HERE.

2 HALF THE AIR GOES INTO THE COMBUSTION CHAMBER.

3 HALF THE AIR BY-PASSES THE COMBUSTION CHAMBER. IT MIXES WITH THE EXHAUST GASES AT THE REAR OF THE ENGINE.

3 Ram Jet

THIS ENGINE IS THE MOST POWERFUL. IT HAS NO TURBINE OR COMPRESSOR IT ONLY WORKS WHEN THE AEROPLANE IS FLYING.

EXHAUST GASES

1 AIR IS FORCED IN HERE.

2 FUEL IS PUMPED IN HERE.

3 HOT EXHAUST GASES FROM THE BURNT FUEL ARE BLOWN OUT OF THE BACK.

Steam Turbine

These sorts of engines are used to turn ships' propellers and to make electricity in power stations. Rings of turbine blades are fixed to a shaft inside a steam-tight cylinder. Steam from a boiler is blasted against the blades which spin the shaft round very fast. As the steam passes through the cylinder it gets cooler and expands. So each ring of turbine blades is slightly bigger than the one before.

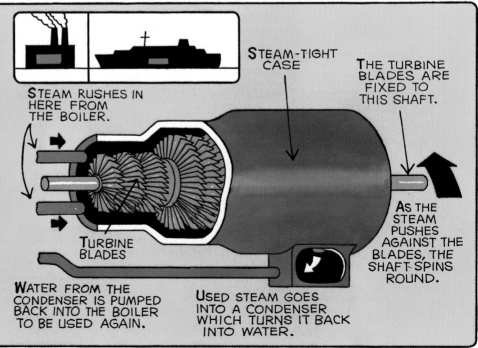

STEAM-TIGHT CASE

THE TURBINE BLADES ARE FIXED TO THIS SHAFT.

STEAM RUSHES IN HERE FROM THE BOILER.

AS THE STEAM PUSHES AGAINST THE BLADES, THE SHAFT SPINS ROUND.

TURBINE BLADES

WATER FROM THE CONDENSER IS PUMPED BACK INTO THE BOILER TO BE USED AGAIN.

USED STEAM GOES INTO A CONDENSER WHICH TURNS IT BACK INTO WATER.

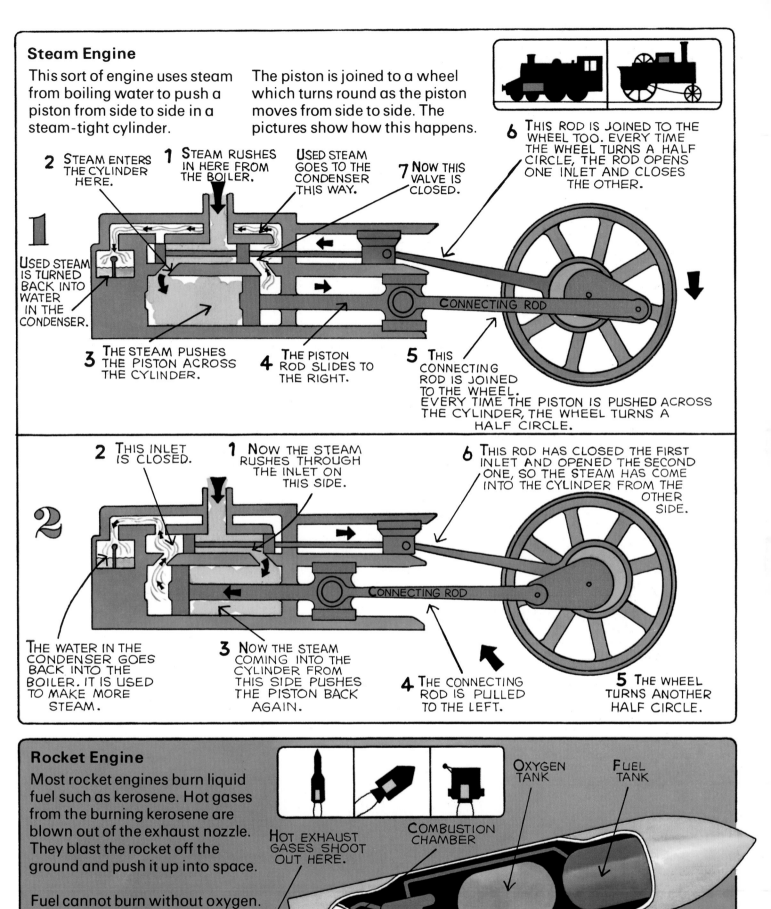

Steam Engine

This sort of engine uses steam from boiling water to push a piston from side to side in a steam-tight cylinder.

The piston is joined to a wheel which turns round as the piston moves from side to side. The pictures show how this happens.

1

2 STEAM ENTERS THE CYLINDER HERE.

1 STEAM RUSHES IN HERE FROM THE BOILER.

USED STEAM GOES TO THE CONDENSER THIS WAY.

7 NOW THIS VALVE IS CLOSED.

6 THIS ROD IS JOINED TO THE WHEEL TOO. EVERY TIME THE WHEEL TURNS A HALF CIRCLE, THE ROD OPENS ONE INLET AND CLOSES THE OTHER.

USED STEAM IS TURNED BACK INTO WATER IN THE CONDENSER.

CONNECTING ROD

3 THE STEAM PUSHES THE PISTON ACROSS THE CYLINDER.

4 THE PISTON ROD SLIDES TO THE RIGHT.

5 THIS CONNECTING ROD IS JOINED TO THE WHEEL. EVERY TIME THE PISTON IS PUSHED ACROSS THE CYLINDER, THE WHEEL TURNS A HALF CIRCLE.

2

2 THIS INLET IS CLOSED.

1 NOW THE STEAM RUSHES THROUGH THE INLET ON THIS SIDE.

6 THIS ROD HAS CLOSED THE FIRST INLET AND OPENED THE SECOND ONE, SO THE STEAM HAS COME INTO THE CYLINDER FROM THE OTHER SIDE.

CONNECTING ROD

THE WATER IN THE CONDENSER GOES BACK INTO THE BOILER. IT IS USED TO MAKE MORE STEAM.

3 NOW THE STEAM COMING INTO THE CYLINDER FROM THIS SIDE PUSHES THE PISTON BACK AGAIN.

4 THE CONNECTING ROD IS PULLED TO THE LEFT.

5 THE WHEEL TURNS ANOTHER HALF CIRCLE.

Rocket Engine

Most rocket engines burn liquid fuel such as kerosene. Hot gases from the burning kerosene are blown out of the exhaust nozzle. They blast the rocket off the ground and push it up into space.

Fuel cannot burn without oxygen. Rockets carry their own supply to mix with the fuel because there is none in space.

OXYGEN TANK

FUEL TANK

HOT EXHAUST GASES SHOOT OUT HERE.

COMBUSTION CHAMBER

THESE PUMPS FEED THE FUEL AND THE OXYGEN INTO THE COMBUSTION CHAMBER.

THE FUEL AND THE OXYGEN BURN FIERCELY.

How Motors Work

Petrol Engine

This sort of engine turns the wheels of most cars round. It has four cylinders. Each one has a piston inside which is joined to the crankshaft.

The pistons are pushed up and down very quickly inside the cylinders. As they move up and down one after the other, they turn the crankshaft round.

Follow the numbers at the bottom of the page to see what happens when the petrol vapour explodes. See how the exhaust gases make the pistons work.

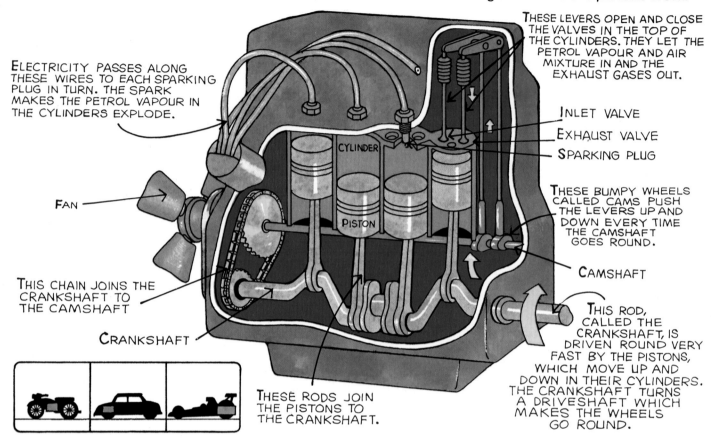

ELECTRICITY PASSES ALONG THESE WIRES TO EACH SPARKING PLUG IN TURN. THE SPARK MAKES THE PETROL VAPOUR IN THE CYLINDERS EXPLODE.

FAN

THIS CHAIN JOINS THE CRANKSHAFT TO THE CAMSHAFT

CRANKSHAFT

CYLINDER

PISTON

THESE LEVERS OPEN AND CLOSE THE VALVES IN THE TOP OF THE CYLINDERS. THEY LET THE PETROL VAPOUR AND AIR MIXTURE IN AND THE EXHAUST GASES OUT.

INLET VALVE

EXHAUST VALVE

SPARKING PLUG

THESE BUMPY WHEELS CALLED CAMS PUSH THE LEVERS UP AND DOWN EVERY TIME THE CAMSHAFT GOES ROUND.

CAMSHAFT

THIS ROD, CALLED THE CRANKSHAFT, IS DRIVEN ROUND VERY FAST BY THE PISTONS, WHICH MOVE UP AND DOWN IN THEIR CYLINDERS. THE CRANKSHAFT TURNS A DRIVESHAFT WHICH MAKES THE WHEELS GO ROUND.

THESE RODS JOIN THE PISTONS TO THE CRANKSHAFT.

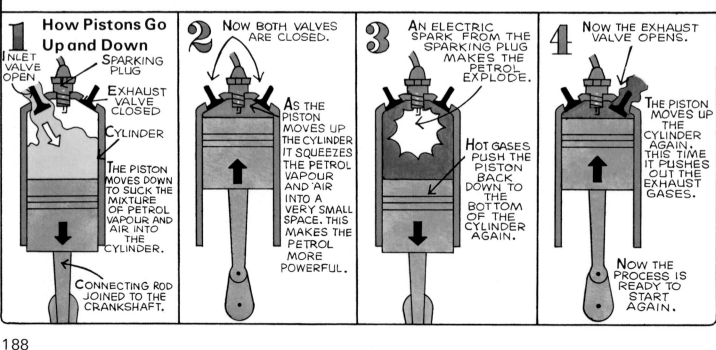

1 **How Pistons Go Up and Down**

INLET VALVE OPEN

SPARKING PLUG

EXHAUST VALVE CLOSED

CYLINDER

THE PISTON MOVES DOWN TO SUCK THE MIXTURE OF PETROL VAPOUR AND AIR INTO THE CYLINDER.

CONNECTING ROD JOINED TO THE CRANKSHAFT.

2 NOW BOTH VALVES ARE CLOSED.

AS THE PISTON MOVES UP THE CYLINDER IT SQUEEZES THE PETROL VAPOUR AND AIR INTO A VERY SMALL SPACE. THIS MAKES THE PETROL MORE POWERFUL.

3 AN ELECTRIC SPARK FROM THE SPARKING PLUG MAKES THE PETROL EXPLODE.

HOT GASES PUSH THE PISTON BACK DOWN TO THE BOTTOM OF THE CYLINDER AGAIN.

4 NOW THE EXHAUST VALVE OPENS.

THE PISTON MOVES UP THE CYLINDER AGAIN. THIS TIME IT PUSHES OUT THE EXHAUST GASES.

NOW THE PROCESS IS READY TO START AGAIN.

Electric Motor

An electric motor has a magnet inside and a piece of iron with wire wound round it, fixed to a shaft. When the motor is turned on, electricity flows through the wires.

The piece of iron becomes an electro-magnet. This spins round as the poles of the outside magnet attract and push away the poles of the electro-magnet.

When the electro-magnet has turned half way round, the electricity flows the other way. This changes the poles. So the shaft goes on turning.

1 ALL MAGNETS HAVE A NORTH AND A SOUTH END. THEY ARE CALLED POLES.

2 WHEN A NORTH POLE AND A SOUTH POLE ARE OPPOSITE, THEY ATTRACT EACH OTHER.

3 WHEN TWO NORTH POLES AND TWO SOUTH POLES ARE OPPOSITE, THEY PUSH AWAY FROM EACH OTHER.

4 A PIECE OF IRON BECOMES A MAGNET WHEN ELECTRICITY PASSES ROUND IT. IT IS CALLED AN ELECTRO-MAGNET.

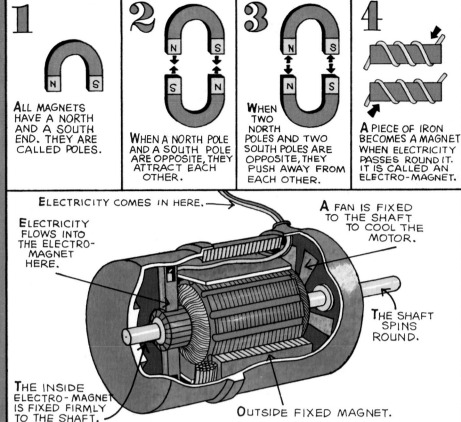

ELECTRICITY COMES IN HERE.

ELECTRICITY FLOWS INTO THE ELECTRO-MAGNET HERE.

A FAN IS FIXED TO THE SHAFT TO COOL THE MOTOR.

THE SHAFT SPINS ROUND.

THE INSIDE ELECTRO-MAGNET IS FIXED FIRMLY TO THE SHAFT.

OUTSIDE FIXED MAGNET.

Diesel Engine

A diesel engine has pistons which go up and down in cylinders just like a petrol engine. But it does not need a spark to make the fuel explode. The fuel used in a diesel engine is a special kind of oil.

As the pistons rise they squeeze the air into such a small space that it becomes very hot. Then a pump shoots a jet of oil into the hot air. This makes the oil burn. Hot gases from the burnt oil push the pistons down the cylinder.

1 FUEL INJECTOR. CYLINDER AIR INLET IS CLOSED. EXHAUST VALVE HOT GAS PUSHES THE PISTON DOWN THE CYLINDER. WHEN THE PISTON PASSES THE EXHAUST VALVE, MOST OF THE GAS IS SUCKED OUT.

2 THE AIR INLET IS OPENED WHEN THE PISTON REACHES THE BOTTOM OF THE CYLINDER. AIR RUSHING IN PUSHES OUT ANY REMAINING GAS.

3 THE PISTON BEGINS TO RISE. IT SQUEEZES THE AIR INSIDE THE CYLINDER. THE AIR INLET IS CLOSED. THE EXHAUST VALVE IS CLOSED.

4 THE PISTON SQUEEZES THE AIR INTO SUCH A SMALL SPACE IT GETS VERY HOT. FUEL IS INJECTED INTO THE CYLINDER. IT EXPLODES WHEN IT MEETS THE HOT AIR. NOW THE PISTON WILL BE PUSHED TO THE BOTTOM OF THE CYLINDER AGAIN.

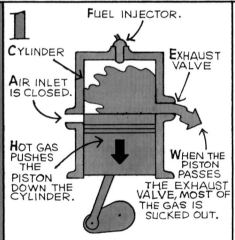
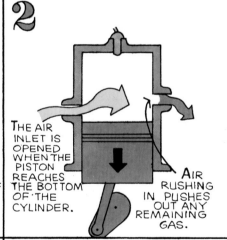
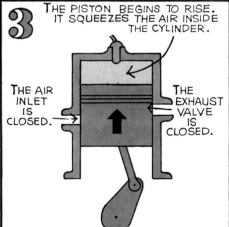
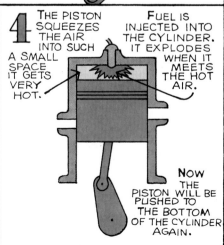

Machines Quiz

You will find the answers to all these questions somewhere in the "How Machines Work" part of this book. When you have done the Quiz, check your answers with the list on page 239.

1. Which part of a space ship do the astronauts leave and return to earth in?
   a) Lunar module?
   b) Nose cone?
   c) Command module?
   d) Service module?

2. The four turbo jet engines in Concorde are fitted:
   a) in the tail?
   b) in the nose?
   c) under the wings?
   d) on the undercarriage?

3. Hovercraft move along on:
   a) the sea.
   b) a cushion of air.
   c) four wheels.
   d) rails.

4. The bottom of a ship is called the:
   a) fin?
   b) keel?
   c) propeller?
   d) rudder?
   e) stern?

5. What does a racing car hold its petrol in?
   a) A tank.
   b) Rubber bags.
   c) A barrel.
   d) It is not run on petrol.

6. A bathyscape is used:
   a) to scrub your back?
   b) on rails?
   c) under the sea?
   d) in space?
   e) in an aeroplane?

7. Match the engine to the machine.
   Engine
   a) gas turbine
   b) petrol
   c) diesel
   d) electric
   Job
   1) refrigerator
   2) racing car
   3) Concorde
   4) passenger liner

8. Lifeboats, fire engines, passenger liners, tractors and cranes are all worked by:
   a) electric engines?
   b) gas turbines?
   c) diesel engines?
   d) steam engines?

9. Which of these machines are used for building motorways?
   a) tunneller.
   b) hydrofoil.
   c) grader.
   d) scraper.
   e) bulldozer.
   f) combine harvester.
   g) roller.
   h) bucket dredger.
   i) excavator.

10. Race track mechanics change all four tyres on a racing car in:
    a) 5 minutes.
    b) 15 minutes.
    c) 30 seconds.
    d) 5 seconds.

11. Which of these things can a tank *not* do?
    a) Cross rivers.
    b) Make a smokescreen.
    c) Lay a bridge.
    d) Cross difficult ground.
    e) Hover above the ground.

12. Match the plane to its job.
    Plane
    1) Hercules transport.
    2) Reconnaissance plane.
    3) Fighter.
    Job
    a) Takes photographs of the ground.
    b) Carries troops and heavy weapons.
    c) Attacks enemy planes in the air.

13. Small propellers on a ship, which are used to push it sideways, are called:
    a) bow thrusters.
    b) rudders.
    c) liners.
    d) funnels.
    e) dredgers.

14. Rocket engines carry a supply of oxygen:
    a) to cool the hot gases in the combustion chamber.
    b) because there is no oxygen in space and fuel cannot burn without it.
    c) to blow out of the exhaust and blast the rocket off the ground.

15. A ram jet works only when:
    a) an aeroplane takes off from the ground.
    b) when its turbine blades are turned by hot gases.
    c) when an aeroplane is already flying.

16. Racing cars have wings on the front:
    a) to help them go faster.
    b) to blow air on to the brakes and keep them cool during a race.
    c) to keep the front tyres on the track.

Picture Index

The numbers show you the pages where you can find all these different machines.

Aeroplanes and Spacecraft

 148

 171

 148

 149

 150, 151

 155

 148-149

Ships and Submarines

 156-157

 171

 157

 156

 152-153

 162-163

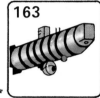 163

Machines on Wheels

 160-161

 158

 161

 158

 159

 158-159

 161

Fighting Machines

 164, 165

 165

 169

 168, 169

 168

 166

 154

Working Machines

 174, 175

 172

 176, 177

 178, 179

 171

 184

 170

 162

 184

 177

 174, 175

 172, 173

 185

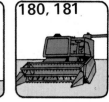 170

 185

 182, 183

 180, 181

 176

 173

 174

 180, 181

191

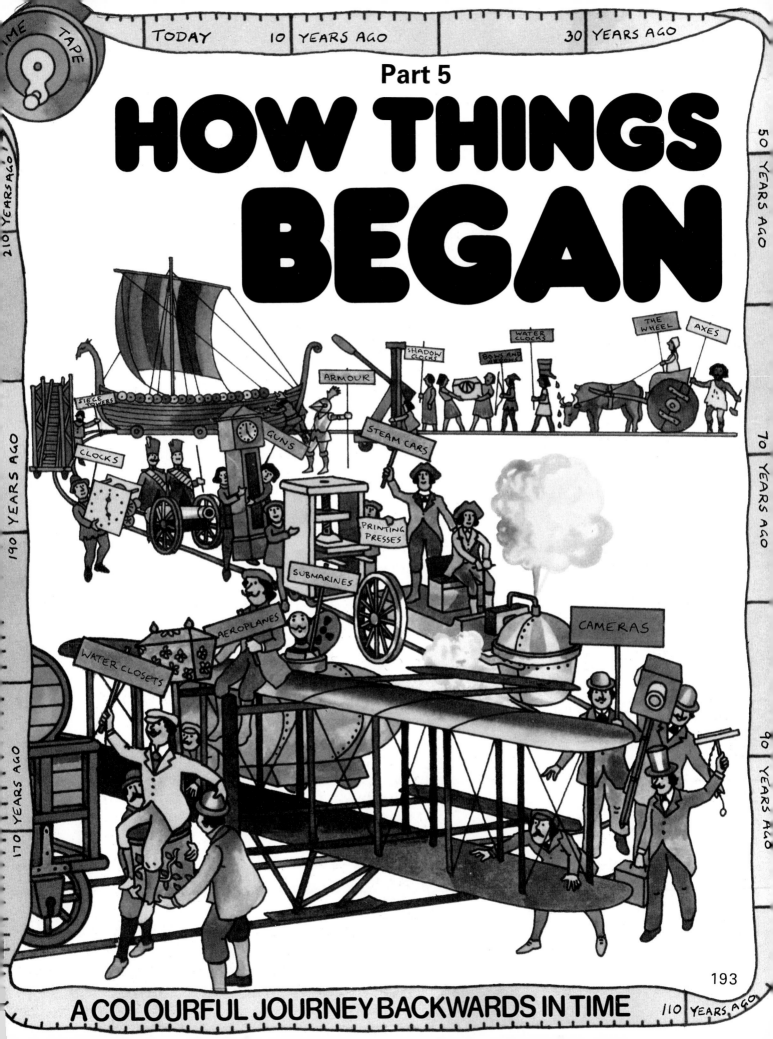

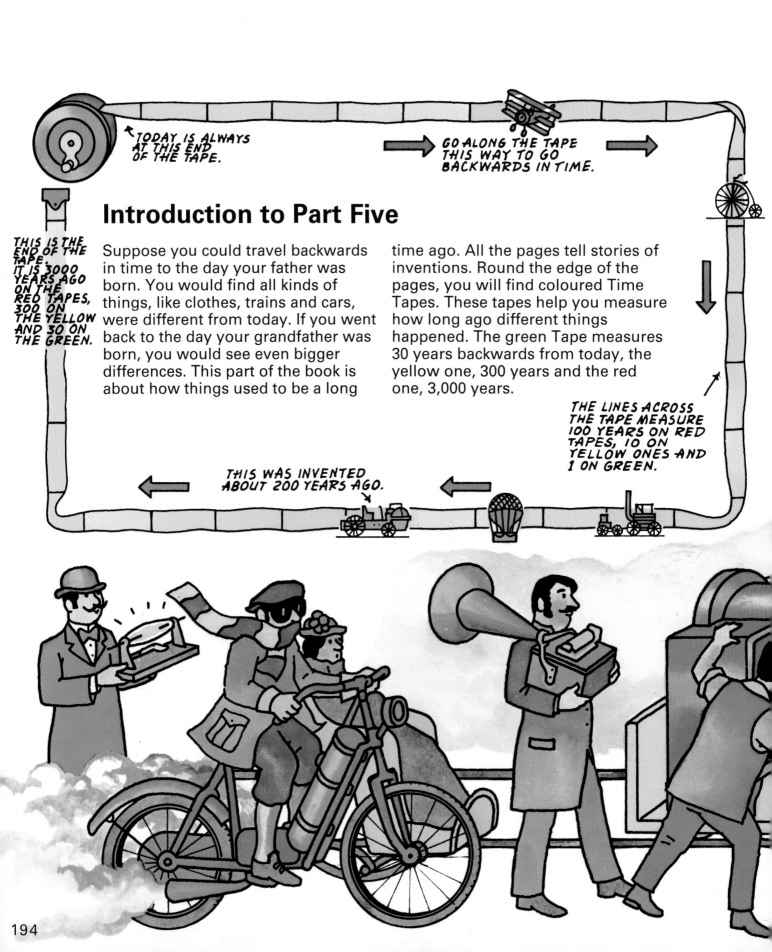

TODAY IS ALWAYS AT THIS END OF THE TAPE.

GO ALONG THE TAPE THIS WAY TO GO BACKWARDS IN TIME.

THIS IS THE END OF THE TAPE. IT IS 3000 YEARS AGO ON THE RED TAPES, 300 ON THE YELLOW AND 30 ON THE GREEN.

Introduction to Part Five

Suppose you could travel backwards in time to the day your father was born. You would find all kinds of things, like clothes, trains and cars, were different from today. If you went back to the day your grandfather was born, you would see even bigger differences. This part of the book is about how things used to be a long

time ago. All the pages tell stories of inventions. Round the edge of the pages, you will find coloured Time Tapes. These tapes help you measure how long ago different things happened. The green Tape measures 30 years backwards from today, the yellow one, 300 years and the red one, 3,000 years.

THE LINES ACROSS THE TAPE MEASURE 100 YEARS ON RED TAPES, 10 ON YELLOW ONES AND 1 ON GREEN.

THIS WAS INVENTED ABOUT 200 YEARS AGO.

Written by Mary Jean McNeil

Illustrated by Colin King
Designed by John Jamieson

Educational Adviser: Frank Blackwell

Contents of Part Five

1973—SKYLAB
AMERICAN SPACE
STATION

1902

Space Race

TSIOLKOVSKII
WORKS OUT
SPEED FOR
ROCKET

30 YEARS AGO

A Russian teacher was the first man to work out that a rocket had to go at 25,000 m.p.h. to leave the earth.

An American, Robert Goddard, made rockets with liquid fuel. They did not go very high.

Step-rockets can go faster and farther than single rockets. The first step-rocket went as high as 244 miles.

The Russians were the first to put a satellite into orbit around the earth. It stayed in space for three months.

The first man in space was also a Russian. He was called Yuri Gagarin.

The Americans launched a two-manned spacecraft. It was called Gemini.

1949
FIRST
STEP
ROCKET—
A MODIFIED
GERMAN
V2

The Russians sent the first rocket all the way to the moon. It crash-landed. It had no people in it.

The first instrument to make a soft landing on the moon was Russian. It was called Luna 9. A special rocket stopped it from crashing.

25 YEARS AGO

2

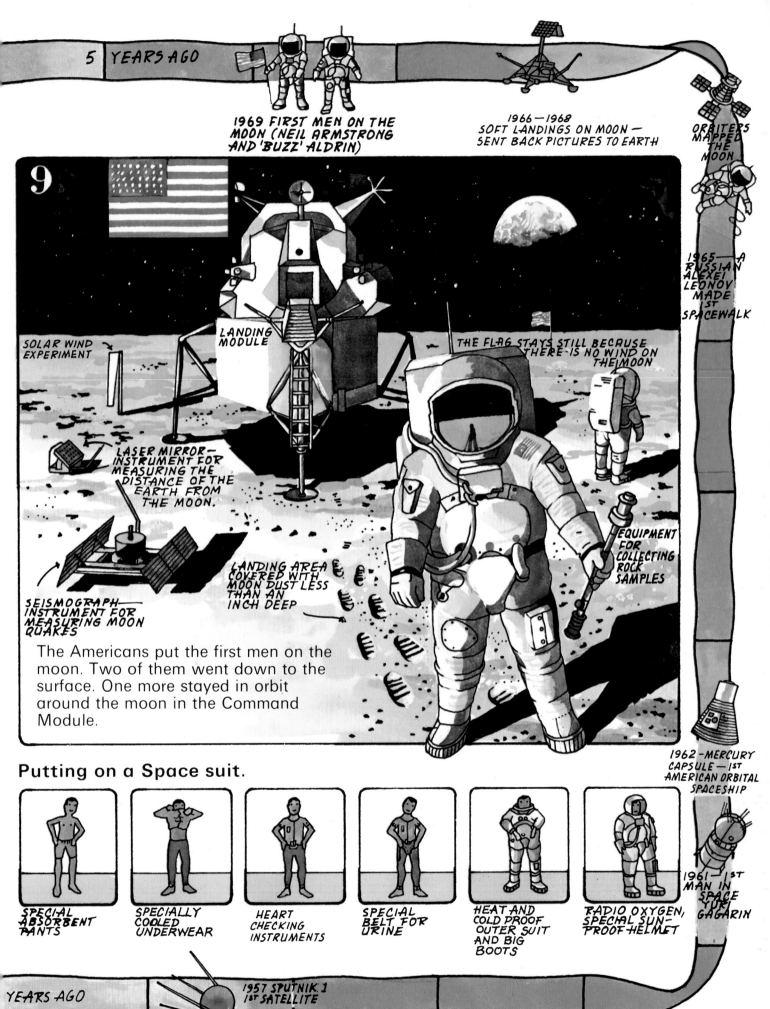

5 YEARS AGO

1969 FIRST MEN ON THE MOON (NEIL ARMSTRONG AND 'BUZZ' ALDRIN)

1966—1968 SOFT LANDINGS ON MOON — SENT BACK PICTURES TO EARTH

ORBITERS MAPPED THE MOON

9

SOLAR WIND EXPERIMENT

LANDING MODULE

THE FLAG STAYS STILL BECAUSE THERE IS NO WIND ON THE MOON

1965 — A RUSSIAN ALEXEI LEONOV MADE 1ST SPACEWALK

LASER MIRROR — INSTRUMENT FOR MEASURING THE DISTANCE OF THE EARTH FROM THE MOON.

SEISMOGRAPH — INSTRUMENT FOR MEASURING MOON QUAKES

LANDING AREA COVERED WITH MOON DUST LESS THAN AN INCH DEEP

EQUIPMENT FOR COLLECTING ROCK SAMPLES

The Americans put the first men on the moon. Two of them went down to the surface. One more stayed in orbit around the moon in the Command Module.

Putting on a Space suit.

SPECIAL ABSORBENT PANTS

SPECIALLY COOLED UNDERWEAR

HEART CHECKING INSTRUMENTS

SPECIAL BELT FOR URINE

HEAT AND COLD PROOF OUTER SUIT AND BIG BOOTS

RADIO OXYGEN, SPECIAL SUN-PROOF HELMET

1962 — MERCURY CAPSULE — 1ST AMERICAN ORBITAL SPACESHIP

1961 — 1ST MAN IN SPACE YURI GAGARIN

YEARS AGO

1957 SPUTNIK 1 1ST SATELLITE

COLOUR
CARTOON
FILMS

Moving Pictures

300 YEARS AGO

The first cameras took photographs very slowly. These pictures were taken, seconds after each other, with three different cameras. When joined they looked like a film.

Cameras became faster at taking photos. This film was about a fire. It was made when engines were pulled by horses. It had no sound or colour and was very short.

Then two men made a camera which was light enough to carry about. It took photos on rolls of film. People made news films.

These men are working the arms and head of a giant creature. It was used in one of the first French science fiction films.

This was one of the first Hollywood epic films. It was about ancient Babylon and lasted for three-and-a-half hours. Hundreds of people acted in it.

This is a scene from a film about a brave hero who saves the heroine just in time. The stories of early films were very simple and usually had happy endings.

1930
BAIRD'S TELEVISION—
1ST TELEVISION SET
SOLD IN BRITAIN

COMEDY
FILM
STARS

1895,
LUMIÈRE BROTHER'S
CAMERA WITH ROLLS
OF FILM

1892–3
EDISON/DICKSON
KINETOSCOPE—
1ST PUBLIC
SHOWING

100 YEARS AGO

1877
MUYBRIDGE'S
GALLOPING
HORSE—
1ST ACTION
PICTURES

These are the Keystone Kops. They were in lots of the first comedy films. The film was speeded up to make them seem to move faster.

The first cinemas often used to pay somebody to play the piano during a film. The music became exciting when the film did.

One problem with the first talking pictures, was where to put the microphone. Actors found microphones difficult to use at first

© Walt Disney Productions

Then people started to make coloured films. Some of the first ones were Mickey Mouse cartoons made by Walt Disney.

The first television sets had a tiny flickering picture. You had to be very close to the screen to see it. Only one person could watch.

This cameraman is working the first electronic camera. It took much better pictures than mechanical cameras.

The picture gets better
The first television pictures were very patchy. Now they are made of so many tiny lines that they look completely clear.

YEARS AGO

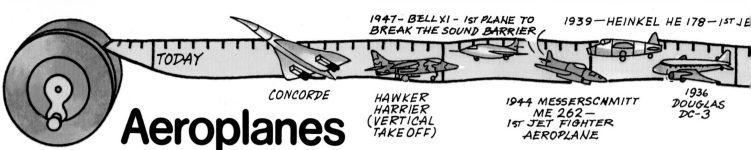

1947 — BELL X1 — 1ST PLANE TO BREAK THE SOUND BARRIER

1939 — HEINKEL HE 178 — 1ST JE

TODAY

CONCORDE

HAWKER HARRIER (VERTICAL TAKE OFF)

1944 MESSERSCHMITT ME 262 — 1ST JET FIGHTER AEROPLANE

1936 DOUGLAS DC-3

Aeroplanes

300 YEARS AGO

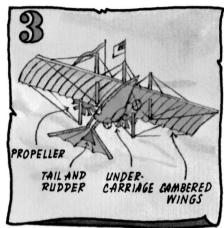

PROPELLER

TAIL AND RUDDER

UNDER-CARRIAGE

CAMBERED WINGS

At first men tried to fly like birds. But people are too heavy. They are not strong enough to flap big wings.

The first plane that flew with a person in it, had fixed wings. A boy flew a short way in it.

This was an early plan for a plane with a steam engine. But it could not have worked. Steam engines are much too heavy.

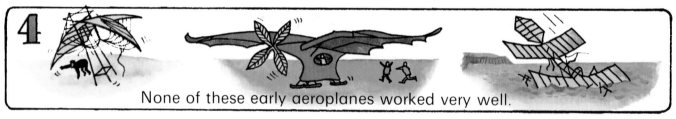

None of these early aeroplanes worked very well.

This glider often flew quite well. But the pilot had to swing his legs to control it. This was very difficult and dangerous.

The first plane to fly properly had a light petrol engine in it. The pilot could bend the wings to control it.

The first proper powered flights were made in America. This aeroplane was one of the first European aeroplanes to fly.

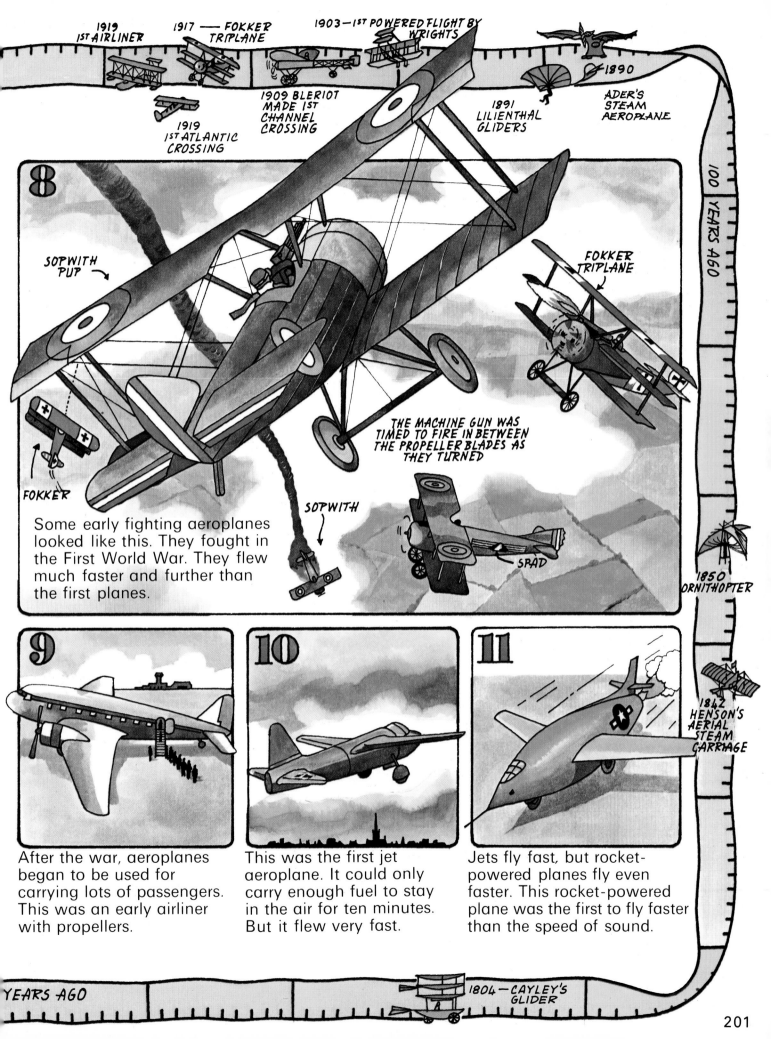

1919
1ST AIRLINER

1917 — FOKKER TRIPLANE

1903—1ST POWERED FLIGHT BY WRIGHTS

1890

1909 BLERIOT MADE 1ST CHANNEL CROSSING

1919 1ST ATLANTIC CROSSING

1891 LILIENTHAL GLIDERS

ADER'S STEAM AEROPLANE

100 YEARS AGO

8

SOPWITH PUP

FOKKER TRIPLANE

THE MACHINE GUN WAS TIMED TO FIRE IN BETWEEN THE PROPELLER BLADES AS THEY TURNED

FOKKER

SOPWITH

SPAD

Some early fighting aeroplanes looked like this. They fought in the First World War. They flew much faster and further than the first planes.

1850 ORNITHOPTER

9

After the war, aeroplanes began to be used for carrying lots of passengers. This was an early airliner with propellers.

10

This was the first jet aeroplane. It could only carry enough fuel to stay in the air for ten minutes. But it flew very fast.

11

Jets fly fast, but rocket-powered planes fly even faster. This rocket-powered plane was the first to fly faster than the speed of sound.

1842 HENSON'S AERIAL STEAM CARRIAGE

YEARS AGO

1804—CAYLEY'S GLIDER

Cars

TODAY

1964 BLUEBIRD-PROTEUS
1ST CAR TO GO OVER
403 m.p.h.

1950
AMERICAN CAR-
CHEVROLET

1943
VOLKSWAGEN

1938
RAILTON
WENT OVER
350 m.p.h.

300 YEARS AGO

1 A long time ago, there were no cars. The gig was probably the fastest thing on wheels. It could go at about 11 m.p.h. until the horses became tired.

2 The first carriage to move on its own had a steam engine. It could only go at 3 m.p.h. The steering-handle was so stiff, only a strong man could turn it.

3 This steam bus could go at 12 m.p.h. But it needed an awful lot of water. It could only go a short way before it had to stop for some more.

4 This was the first car with a petrol engine. The engine was behind the seat. Petrol engines are lighter than steam engines. But this car could only go at 9 m.p.h. It could not go up hill at all.

A STEERING HANDLE → TURNED THE FRONT WHEEL.

THE WHEELS HAD HARD OR METAL EDGES. THIS CAR WAS BUMPY TO RIDE IN.

THERE WERE ALMOST NO REALLY SMOOTH ROADS IN THOSE DAYS. THE BEST ROADS USUALLY HAD COBBLE STONES ON THEM.

1769 NICHOLAS CUGNOT - STEAM CARRIAGE

1927
SUNBEAM
1ST CAR TO GO
OVER 203 M.P.H.

1915 FORD

1908
1ST MODEL T
FORD

1904 DARRACQ
1ST CAR TO GO
OVER 104 M.P.H.

1898
1ST RENAULT

1891 PANHARD-
LEVASSOR. 1ST
CAR WITH GEARS

1886 DAIMLER
1ST 4-WHEELED
CAR

1885
KARL BENZ
1ST CAR

1873.
AMÉDÉE
BOLLÉE
STEAM
BUS

5 **3**

This was a safer car because it had four wheels. But it was still very slow. It could only go at 10 m.p.h.

6

This car was much faster because it had 3 gears for different speeds. It could go at 18 m.p.h. in top gear.

7

People quickly learnt how to make really fast cars with enormous engines. This old racing car could go at 104 m.p.h.

8

As cars got faster, policemen had to stop people driving at dangerous speeds. In 1904, you were not allowed to drive faster than 20 m.p.h.

9

The first cars were very expensive. Then Ford cars were made. They were the first cars lots of people could afford to buy.

Motoring Long Ago

YOU HAD TO TURN A STIFF HANDLE TO START. THIS COULD BE DANGEROUS.

THE WATER IN THE RADIATOR OFTEN BOILED OVER.

IF YOU WENT TOO FAST FOR TOO LONG, THE ENGINE SOMETIMES BLEW UP.

MOST ROADS WERE DREADFULLY DUSTY.

CARS HAD TO BE TALL ENOUGH FOR LADIES WITH BIG HATS.

YOU GOT PETROL FROM CHEMISTS AND IRONMONGERS. BLACKSMITHS USUALLY DID REPAIRS.

1831
STEAM
COACH

200 YEARS AGO

1803 RICHARD TREVITHICK 1ST STEAM COACH

Bicycles

300 YEARS AGO

The first bicycle was a sort of hobby-horse on wheels. It had no pedals so you had to push it forward like a scooter. It was impossible to steer.

You could steer this bicycle by turning the handle-bars. But you still had to push it along with your feet.

This was one of the first bicycles with pedals. Pedalling was very hard work. The pedals went backwards and forwards and drove the back wheel.

The next bicycle had pedals that went round. It was so much better that lots of people bought bicycles. These men even went to a

bicycle-riding school to learn how to ride properly. But the bicycles were so uncomfortable to sit on they were called bone shakers.

Then people discovered that bicycles with very big front wheels went faster. These were called penny farthings. It was easy to fall off them.

GETTING ON AT FIRST

WHEN YOU GET BETTER

GOING DOWN HILL

GETTING OFF

ANOTHER WAY TO GET OFF

AND ANOTHER WAY

20

1917–TRIUMPH
USED IN THE
FIRST WORLD
WAR

1911
INDIAN

1898
DE DION BOUTON
MOTOR TRICYCLE

1891
PETROL-ENGINED
MOTOR BIKE

SAFETY
BICYCLE

1870
PENNY FARTHING

1858—1ST
MOTORCYCLE

1861
BONESHAKER

One man rode all the way
round the world on a
penny farthing. He kept it in
a tent at night.

Some of the first tricycles
were for two people.

This was one of the first
motorcycle side-cars.

This old tricycle had a
small wheel at the back.

Some people did not like
the first cyclists. They set
traps for them.

6

This was the first bicycle
which was safe and fast.
The pedals drove the back
wheel by a chain.

1 Motorcycles

The first motorcycle was a
boneshaker driven by a
tiny steam engine. It had
iron tyres and no brakes.

2

This was one of the first
motorcycles with a petrol
engine. It managed to go at
24 m.p.h.

1839
MACMILLAN'S
CYCLE—1ST
BICYCLE WITH
PEDALS

YEARS AGO

1791
DE SIVRAC'S
BICYCLE—
1ST BICYCLE

1817
KARL VON DRAIS
BICYCLE—1ST ONE
WITH HANDLEBARS

Cameras and Photographs

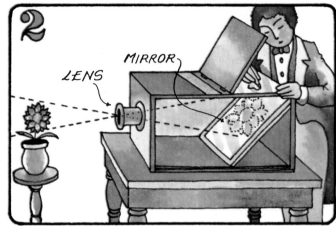

Before there were cameras, only a few people had enough money to have their portraits painted. There were even fewer people who could paint.

People who were not very good at painting could trace a view with a camera obscura. They traced a reflection of the view from the top bit of glass.

This was the first camera which took photos on paper. You could make several copies of each picture.

Later there was another kind of camera. Its photographs were not made on paper, but on metal. You only got one copy of each picture.

It took a long time to take a photograph. People had to sit still all this time. They had clamps round their heads to stop them moving.

Early photographers had to take a lot of things with them. This was because they wet the glass photo-plate before they could take a picture. As people

thought up new ways to take photographs, the photographer's load became lighter. All he needed fitted into a suitcase.

20

1889
DETECTIVE
CAMERA

1889
KODAK
1ST ROLL FILM
CAMERA

1885
PHOTOGRAPHIC
GUN

100 YEARS AGO

6

Kodak cameras were the first to have rolls of film inside. This made taking pictures much easier. You just pressed a button and wound the film on.

1861
1ST ATTEMPTS
AT COLOUR
PHOTOGRAPHY

1851
WET PLATE
PHOTOS

You needed very bright light to take a picture indoors. Photographers made a flash by burning magnesium.

Some cameras looked very odd. This one was called a Photographic Gun.

1840
DAGUERREOTYPE
PHOTOS

1835
FOX TALBOT
1ST CAMERA

This man is taking a picture with a hidden detective camera under his waistcoat.

Often the photographer's flash went wrong and covered everybody with soot.

1825
1ST PHOTO

CAMERA OBSCURA

Trains

CANADIAN TURBOTRAIN

TODAY

1960 ELECTRIC TRAIN

1956 SKYWAY MONORAIL

STANDARD 9— LAST STEAM LOCOMOTIVE BUILT FOR BRITISH RAILWAYS

300 YEARS AGO

1

2

Rails were invented before railway engines. Horses often pulled wagons up hill and followed behind on the way down.

This was one of the first railway engines. It had a steam engine. But it was very slow and took a very long time to get up steam.

COKE MADE LESS SMOKE THAN COAL.

3

A BARREL WITH SPARE WATER

MAN STOKING FIRE WITH COKE

STEAM PUSHED THIS PUMP UP AND DOWN. THE PUMP MADE THE WHEELS GO ROUND

ROCKET

Stephenson's Rocket was a much faster railway engine. It was the first train to go faster than 35 m.p.h.

It was one of the first engines with springs. Without springs, it could have been shaken apart at speed. It had a new sort of

boiler, which heated water up much more quickly. This meant that the engine did not take long to start.

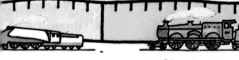

.1935
STREAMLINED
LOCOMOTIVE

1923 - A GREAT
WESTERN CASTLE
CLASS LOCOMOTIVE

SUSPENSION
RAILWAY

1ST CLASS
CARRIAGE

1879
WERNER VON
SIEMEN'S
ELECTRIC
TRAIN

Some trains made much more smoke. This American train made so much smoke and so many sparks the passengers' clothes caught fire.

Building railways through Indian territory in America could be dangerous. The Indians tried to stop the railwaymen.

1869—UNION
PACIFIC RAILWAY OPENED

2ND CLASS
CARRIAGES

1865
1ST SLEEPING
CAR

1863—1ST
UNDERGROUND

At first, second class railway carriages were open, with holes in the floor to let rain run out. First class passengers were more comfortable.

These men are building the first underground. They dug up whole streets, laid the track and made the tunnels. Then they put the streets back on top again.

The first trains in the London underground had steam engines and open carriages. People got very dirty when they travelled.

Railway lines had to be almost level, because it was difficult for trains to go up and down hills. So the men who built the railways made cuttings and tunnels in hills. They made viaducts and bridges over valleys and rivers.

1831
DE WITT
CLINTON

1830—TOM
THUMB 1ST
AMERICAN
TRAIN

1829
STEPHENSON'S
ROCKET

Making the Track Level

YEARS AGO

1808 - CATCH-ME-
WHO-CAN

1825-LOCOMOTION No1
1ST STEAM PASSENGER
TRAIN

1813 - PUFFING
BILLY

1929 — GRAF ZEPPELIN LZ·127
PASSENGER AIRSHIP
MADE FLIGHT AROUND THE WORL

Balloons

These animals were the first air passengers. They flew for eight minutes in a hot air balloon that was as high as a three-storey house.

The first human balloonists could control their balloon a bit. They made it go up by making the fire burn fiercely and down by dampening it.

Another balloon was the hydrogen gas balloon. It went higher if it had a lot of gas in it. This is how people filled it with gas.

People used balloons for lots of different things. These men went up in this balloon to see what the enemy was doing. They put messages in bags and

lowered them down ropes to the soldiers below. Lots of men held the ropes to keep the balloon steady and stop it from blowing away.

Balloons only go where the wind blows them. Airships are balloons with engines. This one could turn corners and fly against the wind.

Sometimes balloons were blown miles off course. These men had to walk for days after landing in ice and snow.

300 YEARS AGO

200

1915 — ZEPPELIN L3
1ST ATTACKING AIRSHIP
ON ACTIVE SERVICE

1910 —
ZEPPELIN
LZ7
DEUTSCHLAND

1898 —
KITE
BALLOON

1897 —
1ST METAL
AIRSHIP

1885 —
1ST ELECTRIC
AIRSHIP

1898 —
1ST STEERABLE
AIRSHIP
SANTOS-DUMONT

100 YEARS AGO

4

When this balloon landed, some people thought it was a strange monster and tried to kill it. They had only seen birds in the air before.

Sometimes balloons went too high by mistake. It is terribly cold and difficult to breathe at great heights.

1863 —
A VERY BIG
BALLOON
CALLED
LE GÉANT

1861 —
INTREPID —
1ST AMERICAN
BALLOON

1852 —
HENRI GIFFARD
MAKES 1ST
BALLOON
WITH AN
ENGINE

For a time, huge airships were used to carry passengers long distances. People stopped using them after several crashes.

Landing a balloon in a high wind is very difficult. This one dragged its enormous basket along the ground for half an hour.

1783 —
1ST HOT AIR
BALLOON —
MONTGOLFIER

1783 —
1ST HYDROGEN
BALLOON

1794 —
1ST WAR
BALLOON

1797 — 1ST
PARACHUTE —
ANDRÉ
GARNERIN

1805 — 1ST
FEMALE
AERONAUT

1811 — 1ST AIRMAIL
SERVICE —
J. P. COLDING

Message Machines

Before message-sending machines were invented, people sent signals with drums, smoke, fires, huge horns, church bells and flashing mirrors.

This was one of the first message machines. It was called the Semaphore. The arms made a special sign for each letter. Semaphore stations were on the top of hills. They took a message and then sent it on to the next station, letter by letter. Messages travelled 90 times faster than men on horseback could carry them.

The Shutter Telegraph was another kind of message machine. You worked it by opening and shutting one of the shutters.

One of the first electric telegraph machines sent electric currents along wires. The current made needles point to different letters.

Samuel Morse invented a code for telegraph messages. The sender tapped out different sets of dots and dashes for each letter. At the other end of the wire, a decoder turned the dots and dashes back into letters and words.

1ST WIRELESS PROGRAMMES

1901 – 1ST TRANSATLANTIC WIRELESS SIGNAL

1894 — 1ST SEMI-AUTOMATIC SWITCHBOARD

1878 – 1ST SWITCHBOARD

1876 – 1ST TELEPHONE—INVENTED BY ALEXANDER BELL

1866 – 1ST SUCCESSFUL UNDERWATER TRANSATLANTIC CABLE

1846 — TELEGRAPH THAT PRINTS LETTERS INVENTED

1843 — MORSE CODE TELEGRAPH

1844 — ELECTRIC TELEGRAPH

6

The telephone turned the sound of a voice into electric currents. It turned the currents back into voice sounds at the other end of the line.

7

HELLO—NUMBER PLEASE

SORRY CALLER, I CAN'T HEAR YOU

CAN YOU REPEAT THAT NUMBER

HOLD ON, I HAVE A CALL FOR YOU

HELLO

Girls at telephone switchboards joined different lines together by hand. You always had to ask the operator for the number you wanted. Once automatic switchboards were invented, you could dial your number without the help of an operator.

8

The wireless worked without any wires. It sends radio waves through space from one wireless set to another. This ship has sent a wireless message to the lighthouse to call for help.

9

Nowadays space satellites help send radio, television and telephone messages further and more clearly.

1793—SEMAPHORE

1795 — SHUTTER TELEGRAPH

Lighting

Indoor Lights

Before electric lights and switches, people lit their homes with candles and oil lamps. These did not give off much light.

People could not leave a candle to burn on its own. They had to cut the wick off every half an hour to stop it smelling nasty.

Then somebody invented a new kind of oil lamp which was much brighter. People did not need to get up all the time to trim its wick.

The first gas lights were just holes in iron pipes. The pipes came into each room from outside.

Later gas pipes were led into specially made lamps.

Gas lighting was even brighter than electric lighting when gas lamps had something called a mantle fixed on to them.

The first electric lamp looked a bit like a glass banana with a thread inside it. This thread became so hot when electricity went through it that it shone.

SHELL LAMP

SAUCER LAMP

ROMAN LAMPS

CANDLES

1500 SNUFFERS

300 YEARS AGO

FLINT MILL

200

RAILWAY READING LAMPS

GAS LAMPS

ELECTRIC SAFETY LAMPS

1878— ELECTRIC INDOOR LAMPS

1859— PARAFFIN LAMPS

STAGE LIGHTING

Street Lights

A long time ago, there were no street lamps. It was so dark at night you had to carry a lantern. It was dangerous to be out.

Gas lights made the streets much brighter and safer. This man was a lamp lighter. His job was to go from lamp to lamp turning the gas on and lighting it.

These were the first electric street lamps. They are called arc lamps. Even though they were very bright, gas street lights were used more often.

Lights in Coalmines

It is very dangerous for miners to take candles and oil lamps into mines. Before gas and electric lamps, a machine like this was often their only light.

This was a special sort of oil lamp. The flame in it was covered so that it would be safer than a candle. It was a sort of warning lamp as well.

Then miners carried electric lamps down in the mines. These were much safer.

BETTER CANDLEWICKS

MINER'S OIL SAFETY LAMP

1784 CARCEL OIL LAMP

1792 - EARLY ATTEMPTS AT GAS LIGHTING

1807— 1ST STREET GAS LIGHTING

1841—1ST ELECTRIC CLOCK

POCKET WATCHES

GRAND CLOCK

TODAY

EARLY WATCHES

1656 PENDULUM CLOCK

Telling the Time

3000 YEARS AGO

SUNDIAL SHADOW CLOCK

SHADOW CLOCK

WATER CLOCK

1 A long time ago, there were no mechanical clocks. These people are watching a shadow move round a stone to tell them the hour. Maybe this was the first sundial.

2 They might have used another sort of shadow clock, like this one.

3 They might have had a water clock, like this. As water dripped out of it, the level went down from one mark to the next, showing the time.

4 Then people made sundials out of blocks of stone. This one had a metal rod sticking out of it, called a gnomon. The gnomon cast a shadow on an hour mark.

5 Later, people used candles to tell the time. They marked each hour on the wax and the candle burnt slowly down from one hour mark to the next.

6 People used sand glasses too. Sailors hung them on their ships. When the ship heeled over, the sand glass always stayed upright.

This is how the first alarm clock may have worked.

300 B.C. ROMAN SUNDIAL

200

1000 YEARS AGO

CANDLE CLOCK

This man's job was to wind up the weights of this old turret clock. It was hard work, because the weights often reached the ground.

The first clocks were not very accurate. People had to check their clocks against sundials.

At first mechanical clocks had no hands. Then some of them had just one, to point out the hour. Some clocks were calendars too. Others had puppet figures.

This man was very proud of his clock. He decided to have his portrait painted with the clock in the picture as well.

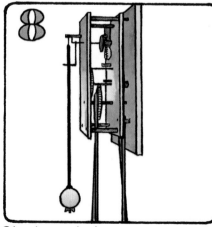

Clocks only became accurate when pendulum clocks were invented. The pendulum swung to and fro very regularly. Clocks began to have two hands.

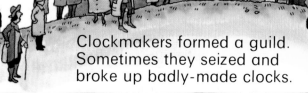

Clockmakers formed a guild. Sometimes they seized and broke up badly-made clocks.

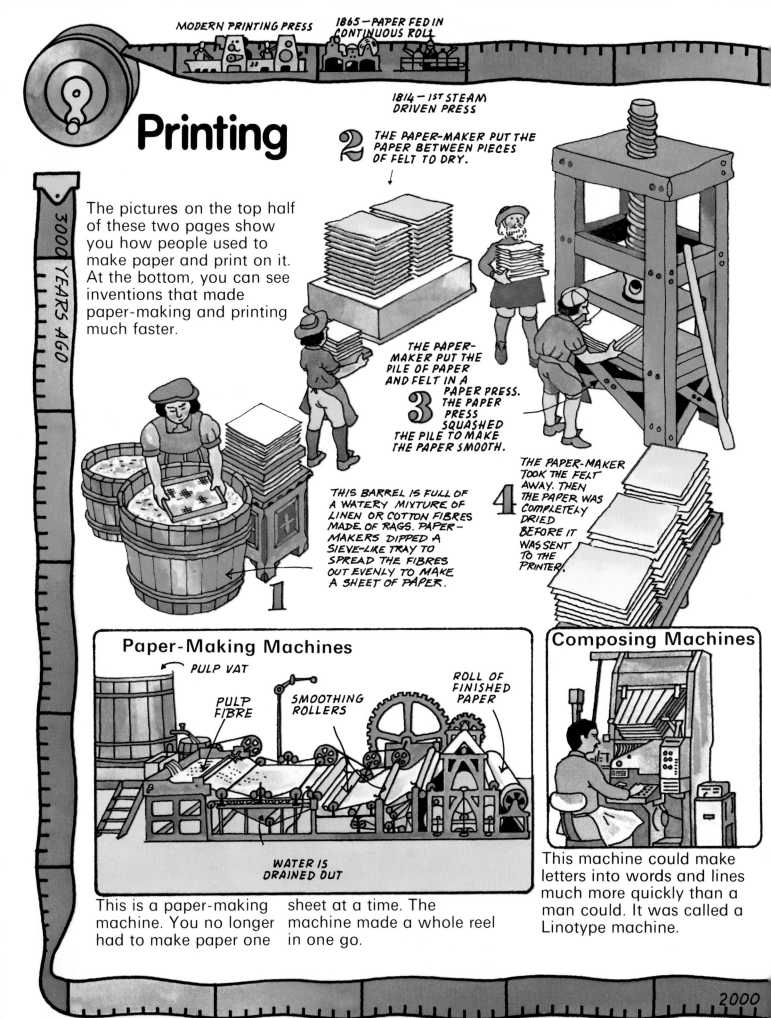

1865 — PAPER FED IN CONTINUOUS ROLL

1814 — 1ST STEAM DRIVEN PRESS

Printing

2 THE PAPER-MAKER PUT THE PAPER BETWEEN PIECES OF FELT TO DRY.

3000 YEARS AGO

The pictures on the top half of these two pages show you how people used to make paper and print on it. At the bottom, you can see inventions that made paper-making and printing much faster.

THE PAPER-MAKER PUT THE PILE OF PAPER AND FELT IN A PAPER PRESS.
3 THE PAPER PRESS SQUASHED THE PILE TO MAKE THE PAPER SMOOTH.

THIS BARREL IS FULL OF A WATERY MIXTURE OF LINEN OR COTTON FIBRES MADE OF RAGS. PAPER-MAKERS DIPPED A SIEVE-LIKE TRAY TO SPREAD THE FIBRES OUT EVENLY TO MAKE A SHEET OF PAPER.

1

4 THE PAPER-MAKER TOOK THE FELT AWAY. THEN THE PAPER WAS COMPLETELY DRIED BEFORE IT WAS SENT TO THE PRINTER.

Paper-Making Machines

← PULP VAT

PULP FIBRE

SMOOTHING ROLLERS

ROLL OF FINISHED PAPER

WATER IS DRAINED OUT

This is a paper-making machine. You no longer had to make paper one sheet at a time. The machine made a whole reel in one go.

Composing Machines

This machine could make letters into words and lines much more quickly than a man could. It was called a Linotype machine.

2000

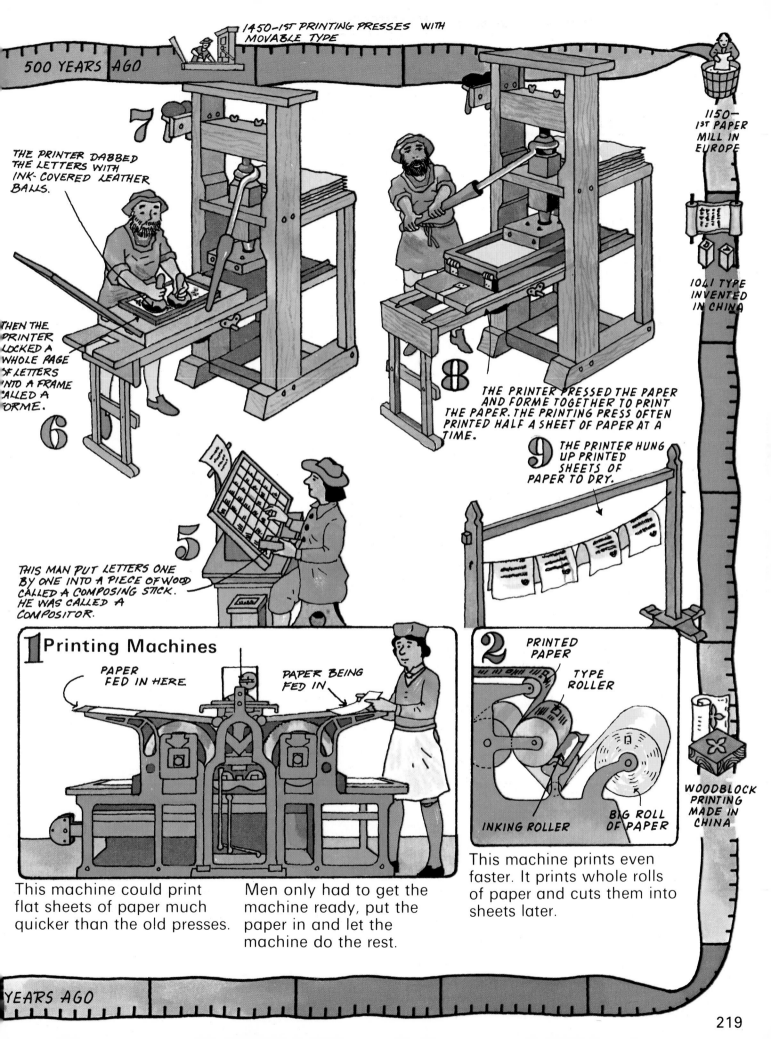

500 YEARS AGO

1150 — 1ST PAPER MILL IN EUROPE

1041 TYPE INVENTED IN CHINA

WOODBLOCK PRINTING MADE IN CHINA

7

THE PRINTER DABBED THE LETTERS WITH INK-COVERED LEATHER BALLS.

THEN THE PRINTER LOCKED A WHOLE PAGE OF LETTERS INTO A FRAME CALLED A FORME.

6

8 THE PRINTER PRESSED THE PAPER AND FORME TOGETHER TO PRINT THE PAPER. THE PRINTING PRESS OFTEN PRINTED HALF A SHEET OF PAPER AT A TIME.

9 THE PRINTER HUNG UP PRINTED SHEETS OF PAPER TO DRY.

5

THIS MAN PUT LETTERS ONE BY ONE INTO A PIECE OF WOOD CALLED A COMPOSING STICK. HE WAS CALLED A COMPOSITOR.

1 Printing Machines

PAPER FED IN HERE

PAPER BEING FED IN

This machine could print flat sheets of paper much quicker than the old presses.

Men only had to get the machine ready, put the paper in and let the machine do the rest.

2 PRINTED PAPER

TYPE ROLLER

INKING ROLLER

BIG ROLL OF PAPER

This machine prints even faster. It prints whole rolls of paper and cuts them into sheets later.

YEARS AGO

SUNKEN BATH

1889—1ST WASHDOWN LAVATORY

MODERN LAVATORY

RAIN BATH SHOWER

FRENCH BATH CALLED DEMI-BAIN

1778—BRAHAMA LAVATORY

BATH SPA

CLOSED STOOL

Keeping Clean

3000 YEARS AGO

1ST BATHS

500 B.C. ROMAN BATHS

1 Baths

A long time ago in Rome and Crete, people built marvellous baths. Some of them even had hot and cold running water. This huge bath was public. Everybody could use it.

2

This bath had to be filled with hot water by hand. It took 30 gallons to fill. The people in it ate meals at the same time as they had their baths.

3

This place had special water. People went bathing there when they felt unwell.

As it took such a long time to fill a bath tub, they did not have baths at home very often.

4

But some people were frightened of getting wet because they had taken so few baths. This lady screamed and struggled when she had her first shower

200

1596 —
HARINGTON'S
LAVATORY

1090 —
MEDIEVAL
BATH

1000 YEARS AGO

5

After thousands of years, running water began to be used in homes again. This bath had a shower and hot and cold water at the turn of a tap.

1 Lavatories

Towns were very smelly and unhealthy places before there were flushing lavatories. People used to empty their slops into the street below.

2

If you were rich, you might have used something like this. When you had finished, you just closed the lid and somebody else emptied it for you.

3

This was one of the first lavatories. You turned the brown knob to flush everything into a pit below. But somebody still had to empty the pit later.

4

Thousands of people bought this lavatory. If you pulled the handle up, two flaps opened. One let the water in and the other let it drain away.

5

This was one of the first lavatories which you flushed by pulling the chain. It made a terrible noise as water streamed from the cistern above.

Money

TODAY

1793
1ST AMERICAN
COINS MADE

1661
1ST PAPER MONEY
IN EUROPE
(SWEDEN)

TOOLS

CHUNKS OF
SILVER
USED AS
MONEY

JEWELLERY
USED AS
MONEY

BRONZE
BAR
SHAPED
LIKE AN
OX-HIDE

690 B.C.
1ST COIN
(LYDIA)

550 B.C.
1ST GOLD
AND
SILVER
COINS

1

A long time ago, there were no shops. If you needed an axe, you would probably have had to make it yourself. Then, if you made many axes, you could swop one for something else you needed. This is called barter.

Barter did not always work. The man swopped his axe for the apples he needed. But, the other man still had many apples. If nobody needed them, they would go bad and he would never be able to swop them for other things.

2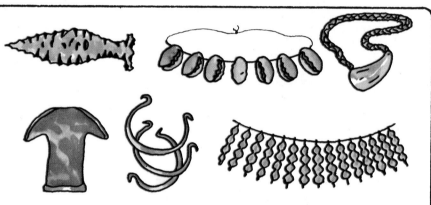

People started to use as money all sorts of things which would not go bad. They used such things as flint spear heads, axe heads, cowrie shells, whales' teeth, metal bracelets and gold necklaces.

3

Then people began to make things to be used only as money. Some of the first metal money that we know about looked like cow skins. Perhaps each bit was worth a cow.

4

Then people started making coins. They were much easier to carry. Coins often had pictures of gods and kings on them to make them seem important.

GREEK TETRADRACHM
THOUGHT TO BE THE
MOST BEAUTIFUL COIN
IN THE WORLD

300 B.C. ROMAN
COIN WITH A
COW ON IT

2000 YEAR

222

500 YEARS AGO

1ST BANKS
(ITALY)

1300 — MINT AT TOWER
OF LONDON OPENED. MADE
COINS FOR CENTURIES.

1000 YEARS AGO

Making Coins

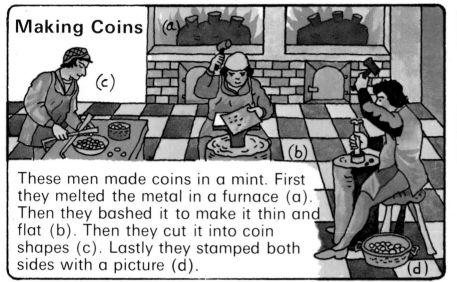

These men made coins in a mint. First they melted the metal in a furnace (a). Then they bashed it to make it thin and flat (b). Then they cut it into coin shapes (c). Lastly they stamped both sides with a picture (d).

Banking

Before there were banks, people had to look after their money themselves. This man hid his money in the safest place that he could find.

If this did not work, he had to find somewhere else to put his money. He probably put it in the safest place in town, which was the goldsmith's shop.

Lots of people started taking their money to the goldsmith's shop. The goldsmith locked it away safely. These shops became the first banks.

The goldsmith wrote the amount of money he had been given on a piece of paper. He gave the paper to the owner of the money. This became a bank note.

650
1ST PAPER
MONEY
(CHINA)

Catching out a Crook

This crook chipped bits of metal off the edge of coins and nobody knew. But when people made coins with tiny dents around the edge, he had to stop. It was easy to see if a coin was chipped.

The crook tried forging bank notes. But the pattern on the note was very complicated and difficult for him to copy. It was quite easy to spot that the note was not real.

AGO

1ST COINS TO SHOW
AN EVENT- THE
ASSASSINATION OF
CAESAR

350 — 1ST COINS
MINTED IN
CONSTANTINOPLE

GUIDED MISSILE 1945 'A' BOMB BREECH LOADING RIFLE EARLY BAYONET FIELD ARTILLERY

Weapons

CLUBS

STONES

SHARPENED STONES

AXES

WOODEN JAVELINS

SWORDS

DAGGERS

JAVELIN WITH METAL HEAD

BOWS AND ARROWS

A long time ago, people probably fought with their fists or with clubs and stones. You can still see some of their simple weapons in museums.

Then men learnt to sharpen bits of flintstone to make spears, axes and knives. They also used slings and flint-tipped arrows.

2 A SOLDIER WITH A SLING WOULD SWING IT ROUND HIS HEAD VERY FAST. THEN HE WOULD LET ONE STRAP GO AND A LEAD PELLET WOULD SHOOT AWAY AT GREAT SPEED.

ROMAN SOLDIERS FOUGHT IN GROUPS CALLED LEGIONS. EACH LEGION HAD A STANDARD.

SHIELD MADE OF LAYERS OF WOOD.

THE JAVELIN TOOK A LONG TIME TO LEARN HOW TO THROW AND YOU HAD TO BE VERY STRONG. EACH SOLDIER HAD TWO.

METAL HELMET

ARMOUR MADE OF STRIPS OF METAL JOINED TOGETHER.

LEATHER TUNIC

For thousands of years, soldiers fought mainly with metal spears, swords and arrow tips. They had shields and armour to protect them.

One of the most powerful bows ever made was the English long bow. Only very strong, well-trained soldiers could use it. It could shoot arrows 150 metres.

The cross bow was a very powerful bow too. It could be used by soldiers who had no special training.

To re-load a cross bow you had to wind it up with handles. This made the cross bow slower to shoot than the long bow.

3000 YEARS AGO 2000

224

SLING

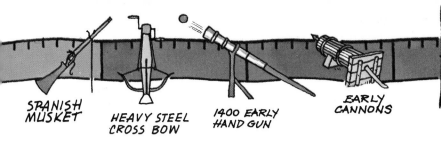

SPANISH MUSKET

HEAVY STEEL CROSS BOW

1400 EARLY HAND GUN

EARLY CANNONS

LONG BOW

CROSS BOW

1000 YEARS AGO

4 CROSS BOWMEN

FOOT SOLDIERS CARRIED PIKES.

THIS KNIGHT'S SHIELD WAS PAINTED WITH HIS COLOURS SO THAT THE SOLDIERS WOULD KNOW WHO HE WAS.

A SHIELD TO PROTECT THE BOWMAN AS HE RE-LOADS.

BROAD SWORD

MACE

LONG BOWMEN

ARROW 1 METRE LONG

BATTERING RAM

The first cannons fired stone and metal balls with gunpowder explosions.

The Chinese had known about gunpowder for hundreds of years. But they did not use it for fighting.

5

Cannons were very heavy. It took a long time to move them from one place to another. They often got stuck in the mud.

6

The first hand-guns were very difficult to fire. You had to load them down the barrel. Then you had to hold them steady while you touched them off.

7

These guns were easier to fire. They had a trigger. But soldiers still loaded them down the barrel. They had pikemen to protect them as they loaded.

8

Guns became more accurate when people cut tiny grooves inside the barrel. These grooves made the bullet spin. This was called rifling.

9
Firing became quicker when guns opened at the breech. Soldiers did not have to push the bullet and powder all the way down the barrel anymore.

10

Then came a new kind of gun. It used cartridges, which contain both bullets and powder. Soldiers could fire many cartridges without having to re-load.

YEARS AGO

TODAY

AMERICAN
CAVALRY
POST

GERMAN
CASTLE

Castles

THORNY
HEDGE

FENCED
VILLAGE

1000 B.C.
VERY
SIMPLE
HILL
FORT

1 RAMPARTS OF EARTH

CHIEF'S HUT

CORN WAS KEPT HERE

CHIEF'S CHARIOT

WAR TRUMPET

THESE MEN OPENED AND SHUT THE GATES

The first castles were probably just villages surrounded by a wooden fence. People usually built them on top of a hill, so that they would be able to see what was going on around them. This Celtic hill-fort had deep ditches and huge ramparts of earth around it. Some of these were over 26 metres high.

2 One of the problems with wooden walls was that if the enemy could get close enough, they could set fire to them.

3 Stone castles with battlements were safer. But attackers could still get in by climbing up the walls on scaling ladders.

4 Even castles with high walls were not safe. Attackers could dig a tunnel under a wall, keep it up with props, set fire to them and make the wall fall down.

226

300 B.C.
HILL FORT

20

CASTLE DEFENDED BY ITS CANNON
AND BUILT AS A PLATFORM

1300 - STRONG, FORTIFIED
MEDIEVAL CASTLE

CRUSADER'S
CASTLE

NORMAN
STONE
CASTLE

NORMAN
WOOD
CASTLE

The weakest part of an outer wall was its corner. This was the easiest place for attackers to knock holes with a battering ram and get in.

Defenders who wanted to attack soldiers right at the base of a castle had to lean right over the parapet. This made them very easy to shoot.

Once the enemy had knocked down the outer wall, the castle had to surrender. This was because all the stores and animals were kept in the courtyard.

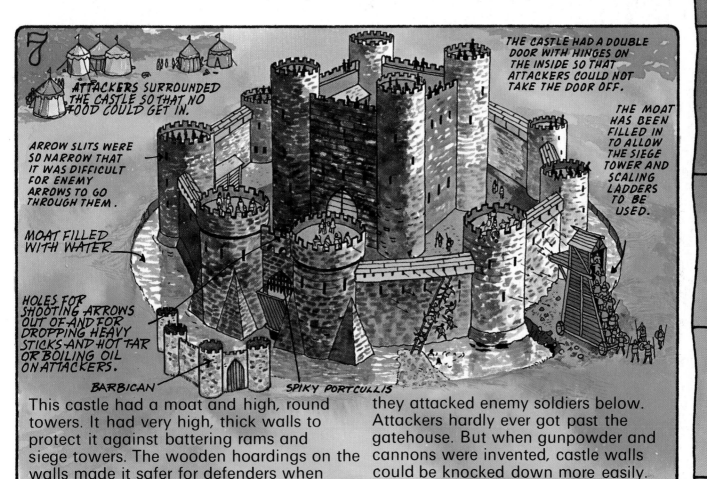

ATTACKERS SURROUNDED THE CASTLE SO THAT NO FOOD COULD GET IN.

ARROW SLITS WERE SO NARROW THAT IT WAS DIFFICULT FOR ENEMY ARROWS TO GO THROUGH THEM.

MOAT FILLED WITH WATER

HOLES FOR SHOOTING ARROWS OUT OF AND FOR DROPPING HEAVY STICKS AND HOT TAR OR BOILING OIL ON ATTACKERS.

BARBICAN

SPIKY PORTCULLIS

THE CASTLE HAD A DOUBLE DOOR WITH HINGES ON THE INSIDE SO THAT ATTACKERS COULD NOT TAKE THE DOOR OFF.

THE MOAT HAS BEEN FILLED IN TO ALLOW THE SIEGE TOWER AND SCALING LADDERS TO BE USED.

This castle had a moat and high, round towers. It had very high, thick walls to protect it against battering rams and siege towers. The wooden hoardings on the walls made it safer for defenders when they attacked enemy soldiers below. Attackers hardly ever got past the gatehouse. But when gunpowder and cannons were invented, castle walls could be knocked down more easily.

YEARS AGO

ROMAN CAMP

LATER CAMP WITH ROUND TOWERS AND WALLS

227

1899 – 1ST SUBMARINE TO GO INTO OPEN WATER

MAN-OF-WAR

1807 – 1ST PADDLE BOAT SERVICE

1959 1ST HOVERCRAFT

1845 1ST CLIPPER

1843 – FIRST SHIP WITH A PROPELLER TO CROSS ATLANTIC

1775 — 1ST SUBMARINE ON ACTIVE SERVICE

Boats and Ships ~ 1

LOG BOAT

1ST RAFT

HOLLOWED OUT LOG BOAT

BLOWN UP ANIMAL SKIN BOAT

4,000 B.C. EGYPTIAN BOAT MADE OF REEDS

2500 B.C. CHINESE JUNK

1500 B.C. WARSHIP WITH RAM

1320 B.C. PHOENICIAN SHIPS SAILED TO AFRICA

The first boat was probably just a log. Logs do not make very good boats, because they roll over easily. Somebody must have tied a few logs together to make something too wide to tip up. This was the first raft.

Then men learnt to hollow logs out with axes and fire to make canoes. Other men blew up animal skins and rode on them.

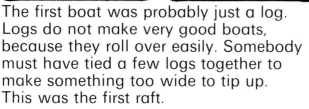

To make warships go faster, builders sometimes made them with two, or even three rows of oars.

The Vikings sailed in cold and stormy seas. Their long, fast ships had high sides to keep the waves out.

The sails were made of leather and often dyed red. Painted shields were hung along the ships' sides.

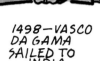

1498—VASCO DA GAMA SAILED TO INDIA

1492—CHRISTOPHER COLUMBUS DISCOVERED AMERICA

SHIPS WITH MORE THAN ONE MAST

1150— 1ST RUDDER

1000 YEARS AGO

800 VIKING SHIP

2

The Ancient Egyptians, who did not have many trees, made boats out of bundles of reeds. They had a sail, so that the wind could blow the boat along.

3

The first warships we know about looked like this. They had lots of men to row them. They had a pointed ram to make holes in enemy ships.

4

Early cargo ships had more room in them than the long and narrow warships. They used their sails more than the warships did.

7

Most early ships were steered by steering oars at the back and at the sides of the ship. The invention of the rudder at the stern made steering much easier.

8

Then people built ships with more than one mast and many more smaller sails. Sailors found it easier to move the smaller, lighter sails. The ships went much faster. They went on great voyages around the world.

1898 — 1ST SUBMARINE TO GO INTO OPEN WATER

MAN-OF-WAR

1807 — 1ST PADDLE BOAT SERVICE

1959 1ST HOVERCRAFT

1845 1ST CLIPPER

1843 — FIRST SHIP WITH A PROPELLER TO CROSS ATLANTIC

1775 — 1ST SUBMARINE ON ACTIVE SERVICE

Boats and Ships ~ 2

LOG BOAT

1ST RAFT

HOLLOWED OUT LOG BOAT

BLOWN UP ANIMAL SKIN BOAT

4,000 B.C. EGYPTIAN BOAT MADE OF REEDS

2500 B.C. CHINESE JUNK

1500 B.C. WARSHIP WITH RAM

1320 B.C. PHOENICIAN SHIPS SAILED TO AFRICA

9

RAT LINES FOR CLIMBING UP TO SAILS

SHARPSHOOTER

POLE TO RAM INTO CANNON

SAILORS TAKING DOWN THEIR HAMMOCKS TO MAKE MORE ROOM FOR FIGHTING

TORCH FOR LIGHTING GUNPOWDER

CANNON BALLS

WATER BUCKET

This is the inside of a fighting ship called a Man-of-War. Cannons were fired through holes in the sides.

10

Some of the fastest sailing ships that were ever made, were called 'clippers'. Each year they raced from China to America and Britain.

Captains who sailed very fast arrived with their cargo of tea still fresh. It could be sold for a high price.

11

The first boats with engines were paddle boats. The engine drove the paddles. This kind of paddle boat was used on the Mississippi.

1000 YEARS AGO

800 VIKING SHIP

12

When propellers were first invented, people could not believe they worked as well as paddles. They held a tug-of-war. The boat with a propeller won.

13

Ship builders discovered that ships could be made out of metal. The first metal ocean liner looked like this. It had a steam engine and masts with sails, in case it ran out of fuel. Metal ships could be built much bigger than wooden ships. They were also cheaper to build.

Making Metal Boats

Metal ships used to be made of ribs and plates riveted together. Today whole sections are built separately and then joined.

An Underwater Boat

One of the first submarines was wooden. There was only room for one man inside it. He had to wind a propeller to make the submarine move forward.

Hovercraft

Hovercraft ride on a cushion of air just above the surface of the sea. They can go up on the beach too.

YEARS AGO

1960 FELT-TIPPED PEN   1944 1ST BALL POINT PEN   1884 1ST FOUNTAIN PEN

Writing

INDIAN ROCK DRAWING

3100 B.C. CUNEIFORM WRITING

3100 B.C. CLAY TABLETS

1500 B.C. EGYPTIAN HIEROGLYPHS

1300 B.C. CHINESE WRITING

1200 B.C. STYLUS ON WAX

1170 B.C. FIRST ALPHABET

1 Pictures and Letters

A long time ago, there was no alphabet. People used pictures to leave messages. This old picture message says 'Path safe for goats, not safe for horse-riders'.

2

This picture tells how a man killed five sheep.

3

Then somebody thought of drawing a picture for each word. Can you read 'Man — killed — sheep — five'?

4

The trouble with this idea is that there are too many words. You had to learn a picture for each one. It was too difficult to remember.

5

SAW   ROW =SORROW
BEE   LEAF =BELIEF

But suppose you make pictures for sounds, and then join them to make words. You do not need so many pictures.

6

The first letters were really sound pictures drawn very quickly and simply.

Here is some of the First Writing

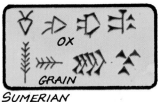

OX
GRAIN

SUMERIAN

1 2 3 4
5 6 7 8

CHINESE

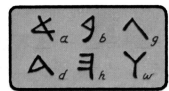

PHOENICIAN

O M S P K
A E L R T

EGYPTIAN

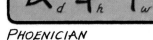

700 B.C. ALPHABET WITH 21 LETTERS

QUILL PENS

100 B.C. ALPHABET WITH 23 LETTERS

200

1000 A.D
ALPHABET WITH
26 LETTERS

1000 YEARS AGO

1 Pens

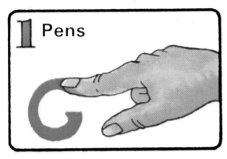

Before there were pens, people used fingers to make lines. They had no ink, so they sometimes used blood.

Then people stamped writing pictures into clay.

Sometimes people cut letters into stone with a hammer and chisel.

Another way was to scratch lines into wax.

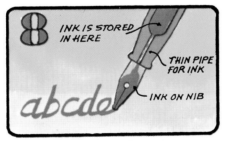

The Chinese used to paint letters with a brush and ink.

SAND FOR DRYING INK

Then people learnt to write with pens made from bird's feathers. These were called quill pens.

Goose feather pen

Crow feather pen

Goose feathers were best for writing. Swan and turkey feathers were good too. If you wanted to make thin lines, you had to use a crow feather pen.

INK IS STORED IN HERE

THIN PIPE FOR INK

INK ON NIB

abcde

Then people used pens with steel nibs. Later fountain pens were invented. They are better than dip pens because they have a store of ink.

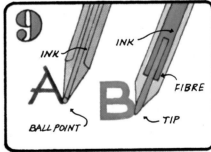

INK   INK

A   B

BALL POINT   FIBRE   TIP

Now there are pens that you do not have to fill up at all, like ball point pens and felt-tipped pens.

Pencils
The first pencils were just chunks of graphite.

Then people wrapped the graphite in string.

Then they covered it with wood.

TYRES
FILLED
WITH
AIR

1819 - ROADS SMOOTHER-
COVERED WITH TAR AND
TINY STONES

COACH WITH
LEATHER STRAPS
FOR SPRINGS

Wheels for Carrying and Travelling

3500 B.C.
1ST
POTTER'S
WHEEL

In the beginning, there were no carriages or carts. Travellers walked or rode on an animal, carrying their luggage themselves. Sometimes travellers pulled their luggage along on a branch. Sometimes they put it on a sort of sledge.

3500 B.C.
1ST WHEEL

2000 B.C.
WHEEL
WITH
SPOKES

Sometimes it was easier to push really heavy things along on rollers, like this.

Then people learnt to make wheels. The wheels were very heavy, because they were made of solid wood. They could not have turned very fast.

Wheels became much lighter when people made them with spokes and rims.

POTTER'S
WHEEL
WITH
PEDAL

Travelling was quicker on good roads. The Romans built miles and miles of roads. The roads often had paving stones on them.

Travelling became smoother when people thought of making springs. The first springs were leather straps.

Then came the rubber tyre filled with air. Roads became smoother too, when people started to cover them with tar and many tiny stones.

3000 YEARS AGO

234

85 B.C. —
1ST WATER WHEEL

POST
WINDMILL

VERY BAD,
BUMPY
ROADS IN
EUROPE

1000 YEARS AGO

Wheels for Making Pots

Before the potters' wheel was invented, it was difficult to make round pots. People made pots by shaping lumps of clay.

Then somebody put a wheel on its side and put clay on it. All the potter had to do was turn the wheel. He could make round pots more easily.

It became even easier when the potter did not have to turn the wheel with his hands. He just pressed a pedal with his foot and the wheel turned.

Wheels for Grinding

WHEEL TURNS
THIS WAY

WATER GOES
THIS WAY

THE WINDMILL
CAN TURN TO
FACE THE
WIND

Grinding grain was a very long, tiring job. People or animals had to spend long hours turning the top mill stone round to grind the grain underneath.

Then somebody tried to make water do the work instead. He made a water wheel turn and this moved the grind stone round.

Then somebody tried using wind instead of water. The wind made the sails of a windmill turn like a giant wheel and the mill stones turned around inside.

2000 YEARS AGO

ROMAN ROADS

Invent your Way to the Moon

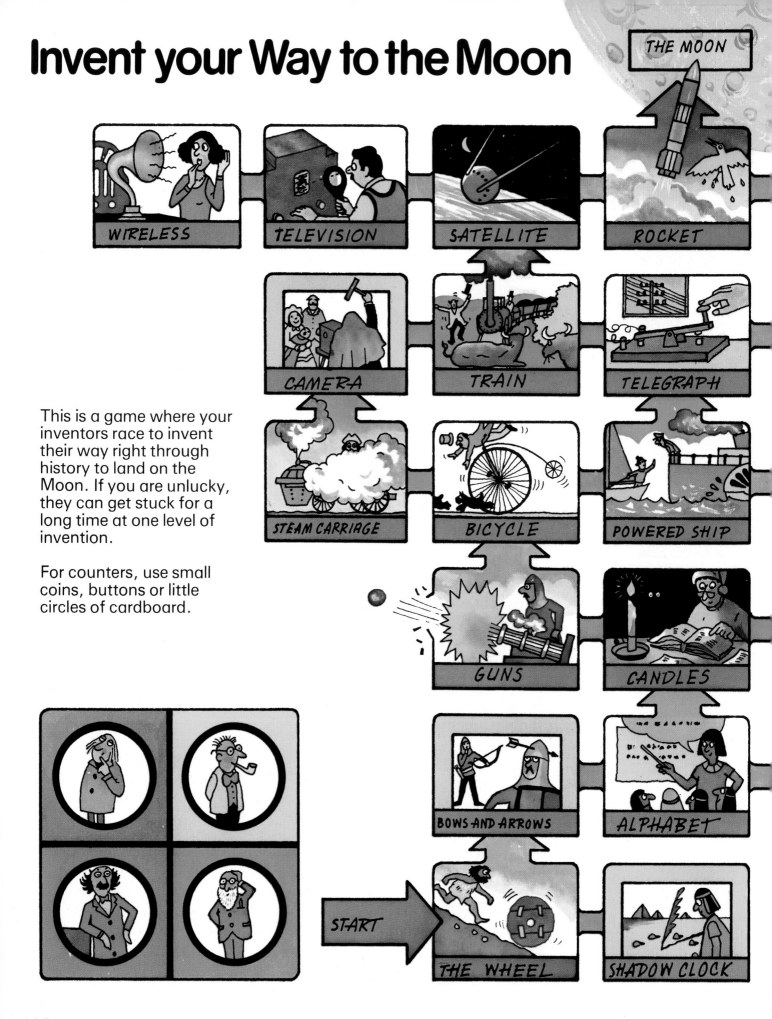

This is a game where your inventors race to invent their way right through history to land on the Moon. If you are unlucky, they can get stuck for a long time at one level of invention.

For counters, use small coins, buttons or little circles of cardboard.

THE MOON

WIRELESS

TELEVISION

SATELLITE

ROCKET

CAMERA

TRAIN

TELEGRAPH

STEAM CARRIAGE

BICYCLE

POWERED SHIP

GUNS

CANDLES

BOWS AND ARROWS

ALPHABET

START

THE WHEEL

SHADOW CLOCK

CINEMA

AIRCRAFT

SUBMARINE

HOVERCRAFT

CAR

GAS LIGHTING

TELEPHONE

BALLOON

WRISTWATCH

PRINTING

PAPER

MONEY

BOATS

This is a race to the Moon for 2 players. Each player has 2 counters. Each counter stands for an inventor. The first player to get both his inventors to the Moon wins.

Throw the dice to see how many boxes you can move. Take it in turns to throw the dice. Each turn, you must move one of your inventors sideways along the row he is on in either direction. If an inventor reaches the end of his row, he must turn round and come back along the row until he has moved the full number on the dice. If an inventor ends his turn on a box with an arrow, he moves straight up to the box above.

If an inventor lands on the same box as any other inventor, the first one there, whichever side he is on, must move down a row to the box with a yellow frame. If the yellow-framed box has an inventor on it, that inventor too moves down a row to another box with a yellow frame.

Inventors can pass through boxes with other inventors on them. When an inventor lands on the Rocket Box, the player must throw a 6 to get lift-off to land on the Moon. An inventor already on the Rocket Box does not have to move unless another inventor lands on it. Then the first one moves down a row to a yellow-framed box.

Picture Index

The numbers show you the pages where you can find the things in the pictures.

ANSWERS

Answers to the Bird Quiz on page 47

1. d
2. a,c,f,i,j
3. a-2   d-1
   b-4   e-3
   c-5
4. c
5. c
6. c
7. 1-a   3-b
   2-d   4-c
8. 1-e   4-d
   2-b   5-a
   3-c
9. c
10. b
11. c,d
12. b,c
13. a,b,f,g,i
14. 1-e   4-c
    2-a   5-d
    3-b

Answers to the Animal Quiz on page 95

1. a-Opossum
   b-African Elephant
   c-Elephant
   d-Chimpanzee, Brown Bear, Bush-baby, Red Fox, Panda, Opossum, Baboon, Spider Monkey
   e-Opossum
2. d
3. b
4. c
5. d
6. d
7. a-Leopard, Cheetah, Jaguar
   b-Tiger
   c-Lion
8. a-Lion
   b-all of them
   c-Leopard
   d-man
9. c
10. b
11. a,b
12. b,c

Answers to the Bodies Quiz on page 143

1. b
2. c
3. 1-b
   2-c
   3-a
   4-d
   5-e
4. d
5. c
6. c
7. a
8. b
9. a,d
10. d
11. c
12. d
13. c
14. c
15. b
16. d

Answers to the Machines Quiz on page 190

1. b
2. c
3. b
4. b
5. b
6. c
7. a-3
   b-2
   c-4
   d-1
8. c
9. c,d,e,g,i
10. c
11. e
12. 1-b
    2-a
    3-c
13. a
14. b
15. c
16. c

INDEX